The Beginnings of Writing

The Beginnings of Writing

THIRD EDITION

CHARLES TEMPLE
Hobart and William Smith Colleges

RUTH NATHAN
Oakland University

FRANCES TEMPLE
Children's Hours School

NANCY A. BURRIS
Texas Lutheran College

ALLYN AND BACON
Boston London Toronto Sydney Tokyo Singapore

Editor-in-Chief, Education: *Nancy Forsyth*
Production Administrator: *Annette Joseph*
Production Coordinator: *Susan Freese*
Editorial-Production Service: *Kailyard Associates*
Manufacturing Buyer: *Louise Richardson*
Cover Administrator: *Linda K. Dickinson*
Cover Designer: *Suzanne Harbison*

Copyright © 1993, 1988, 1982 by Allyn and Bacon
A Division of Simon & Schuster, Inc.
160 Gould Street
Needham Heights, Massachusetts 02194

Library of Congress Cataloging-in-Publication Data

The Beginnings of writing / Charles Temple ... [et al.].—3rd ed.
      p.   cm.
  Includes bibliographical references and index.
  ISBN 0-205-14518-3
    1. English language—Composition and exercises. 2. Children—
Writing.   I. Temple, Charles A.
LB1576.B424 1992   92–14836
372.6'23—dc20   CIP

Printed in the United States of America

10 9 8 7 6 5 4 3 2   97 96 95 94 93

Acknowledgments:

Figure 1–1, p. 2, is reprinted by permission from *Word*, Vol. 27 (1971).
Figure 2–15, p. 30, is from William Longyear, *Type and Lettering*, 4th ed. Copyright © 1966 by Watson-Guptill Publications. Reprinted by permission.
Figure 6–1, p. 101, by permission of J. Richard Gentry Ph.D.
Figure 11–22, p. 235, is reprinted by permission of Donald M. Murray, Professor of English Emeritus, University of New Hampshire.
p. 252, excerpt from Fielding Dawson's letter reprinted by permission.
p. 254, excerpt from *The Polar Express*. Copyright © 1985 by Chris Van Allsburg. Reprinted by permission of Houghton Mifflin Co.

This book is dedicated to the memory of Edmund H. Henderson, late Director of the McGuffey Reading Center at the University of Virginia. Without his insight as a researcher and his spirited encouragement as a teacher, this book—and a wonderful banquet of good things besides— would never have come to be.

BRIEF CONTENTS

CONTENTS

PREFACE

Ten years have passed since we published the first edition of *The Beginnings of Writing*. This new edition goes out to a language-teaching profession that has dramatically changed. The process approach to teaching writing is by now, if not universally practiced, at least familiar to teachers throughout the English-speaking world. Language-experience, the whole-language approach, and the study of children's emergent literacy—these allied movements have generated a deeper appreciation of children's discovery processes in the tasks of learning to read and write and a greater understanding of the constructive role teachers play in children's literacy development.

More and more teachers are persuaded by the wisdom of teaching reading and writing together. Research shows unequivocally that early writing helps children develop concepts about written language they need in order to read, and reading makes children familiar with language structures they need in order to write.

As these movements have matured, teachers have recognized that the techniques of managing whole-language, or process-writing, classrooms cannot be successful without a deep commitment to letting children express themselves in their own voices and an informed appreciation of children's development as literate people. It is here that the first edition of *The Beginnings of Writing* most valuably served the profession. The book was a clear and richly illustrated description of children's writing development from preschool through about fourth grade. Readers of the first edition told us that it helped them to learn much more from their children's writing.

The second edition of *The Beginnings of Writing* added exciting new material to the original work. Frances Temple, who provided much of the inspiration and all of the artwork for the first edition, signed on as an author of the second one. She opened up her classroom at the Children's Hours School, where she teaches the same children for two consecutive years. She has been in a unique position to observe the factors that influence children's writing and reading over the long term and has made connections that visiting researchers inevitably would have missed. She brought to that volume a careful study of the influence of literature on children's writing development. Also included was an observation of first, second, and third graders who used writing in a social studies unit, and we saw how her assignment allowed them to translate content that they had heard, read, and acted out into texts that they wrote.

Another big addition in that volume was the detailed guide to setting up and managing a process approach to teaching writing. Ruth Nathan distilled the best instruction from her successful work as a writing consultant in the Detroit area and wrote a set of procedures that have helped hundreds of teachers carry out the process approach in their own classrooms.

In this third edition, we have refined our presentation to make it more useful for teachers who are setting up and teaching emergent literacy programs. We have kept a strong emphasis on understanding children's early literacy learning because we know that Frank Smith's advice is still sage: "Figure out what children [who are learning to read and write] are trying to do, and help them do it." But we have elaborated on the practical applications of the material, too, to keep pace with the rapid progress teachers have made in carrying out emergent literacy and whole-language programs. For example, the sections on children's early graphics are less experimental now and more teacherly because the need to prepare children for literacy—even in preschools and Head Start programs—is now widely recognized. As we write these words, the newspaper reports that up to half the children entering school are "unready" to learn. Emergent literacy, family literacy: We need to get on with the job.

A great strength of the book has always been the careful treatment of children's spelling development, including invented spelling. With the elimination of basal spelling programs from many classrooms, however, a number of teachers now find themselves having to construct spelling programs entirely on their own. We have tried to address this need in this edition.

Many process-writing programs—including the new commercially published language arts series—now recognize that there are many kinds of and purposes for writing, and children need a balanced range of them. We have revised and reorganized the section on composition to give clearer guidance to teachers who wish to help children write in a variety of modes.

Finally, even though our focus is still primarily on writing, we have added, as a new Epilogue, a spirited discussion on ways to set up a reading-writing classroom.

Acknowledgments

We continue to appreciate the support of Hobart and William Smith Colleges. Margaret Quinlan, now publisher of Peachtree Press, first made the decision to publish this book; and Sue Canavan, now Vice President of Christopher-Gordon Publishers, shepherded the first two editions in her delightful way. Sean Wakely and Nancy Forsyth made it possible for this third edition to go forward. The authors are deeply grateful to all four. We appreciate the caring and skillful copyediting of our old friend, Susan Mesner, of Kailyard Associates, Montpelier, Vermont. It has been a pleasure working with her on three books now.

We are grateful to the children, teachers, and parents who have shared their work and their insights with us. They are too numerous to name here, but we appreciate each one.

Finally, we owe a debt of gratitude to our inhouse "guinea pigs"—Amy, Emily, Julie, Annabrook, Jessie, and Tyler—who as young children taught us much about children's writing. They are all fast approaching adulthood. That should tell you, the reader, if you don't know already: Life goes by too quickly.

CHAPTER 1

A Child Discovers How to Write

At a preschool in Cambridge, Massachusetts, a four-year-old girl had just completed a drawing of a person fishing. At her side was a language researcher who was studying the beginnings of writing in young children. The researcher wondered what would happen if she asked the girl to write about her picture. The girl looked at her quizzically for a moment and then began to write these letters:

YUTS A LADE YET FEHEG AD HE KOT FLEPR

She whispered laboriously to herself as she wrote the letters one at a time. The researcher was elated, and she read the words immediately: "Once a lady went fishing and she caught Flipper."[1] (See Figure 1–1.)

There are at least two mysteries in that story: How was the girl able to write those words? She was too young to have been taught to write, and anyway, nobody would have taught her to write like that. And how was the researcher able to read her words? This second question we can answer quickly. The researcher could read what the girl wrote because the made-up system of spelling she used to write her words was exactly like the invented spelling of many other children that the researcher had observed, and therefore the researcher knew what to expect. The first question, how the girl was able to write those words, will take us much of the rest of this book to answer.

Children can discover how to write if adults surround them with print and encourage them to produce print of their own. Writing, the act of expressing thoughts by means of written symbols, is a mysterious process. No one understands exactly how we learn to do it, but it appears that we learn to write at least as much by discovering how as by being taught. Learning to write is largely an act of discovery. This book is about that act. It is also about another act of discovery, as teachers see revealed in children's early productions outlines of the nature of the writing process, the nature of our written language, and the nature of the process by means of which children learn to write.

If every child went about discovering how to write in his or her own unique way, this book could not have been written, for there would have to

Figure 1–1
Four-year-old
From Carol
Chomsky (used
by permission)

be as many books on young children's writing as there were young children. But research and the experience of teaching and parenting have shown us a remarkable thing: Even when they are not taught about writing, most children make essentially the same discoveries about it, in essentially the same order.

This is truly mysterious, for our writing system and how to use it is a vast and complex matter. That most children should follow the same path in coming to understand it is remarkable, and it is not the result of mere coincidence. Children, it seems, have a unique biological endowment that disposes them to learn to talk.[2] Given the proper circumstances, it is likely that this language-learning facility extends to the learning of written language as well. Children learn to talk by following a very narrow path. Moreover, they learn to talk by exerting an intellectual effort that appears natural, yet has tremendous force.

Learning to talk has been more thoroughly scrutinized and is better understood than learning to write, and the dynamics involved are clearer. Therefore, a brief sketch of how children learn to talk is in order. In many ways, this discussion will continue to inform us throughout the book.

How Children Learn to Talk

Have you ever wondered how children learn to talk? Many people, when asked that question, respond that they do it by imitating. This is at least partially true. Without imitation, we couldn't account for the fact that children in Texas usually learn Texan English, children in Paris usually learn Parisian French, and not vice versa. But imitation as an answer doesn't take us very far. For one thing, children routinely say things they've never heard: "Mommy, come quick—Waldo swallowed a frog!" That is a novel statement for a novel situation. When you think about it, it is inconceivable that children could learn in advance by imitation all of the sentences they will ever have to say.

At this point some would amend their position to say that children don't imitate others sentence by sentence. Instead, they imitate the nouns and verbs and sentence structures of others around them; they can fit their own words into these imitated structures to create novel sentences. But the facts of children's speech do not fit this explanation either. Children produce many sorts of grammatical constructions that they have not heard before. A two-year-old says, "Allgone milk" and "Daddy bye-bye" and for a time, rarely utters sentences of more than two words. A three-year-old says, "I seed two gooses" and "I have small foots"—two particular plural forms that nobody else in the family uses.

At any given point in development, a child's speech more closely resembles the speech of other children at the same stage of development than it does the speech of adults in the child's environment—even if there are not other children around. Any explanation of children's speech that depends on strict imitation cannot stand up to these facts.

What *do* children do as they learn to talk? Children seek from their early days to make sense of the communication around them. As their minds mature, they attempt—through a sort of gradual trial-and-error process—to construct a system of *rules* that will allow them to produce sentences like those they hear others use. "Rules" is used here in a loose sense. They are not consciously saying to themselves, "Hmm . . . whenever I mean more than one, I must put an S on the end of the noun." Yet some sort of unspoken assumption close to this must have been made or else why would the three-year-old say "gooses" and "foots"?

There is much evidence that children's early sentences result from the use of some sort of rules—and not simply from the haphazard imitation of adult sentences.

Imagine that you are in a kitchen with a two-year-old and his mother. The child is seated in his highchair eating. Suddenly he bangs his cup on the highchair tray and says, "Mommy milk, Mommy milk." We assume from the context—his gesture with the cup and so forth—that he means something like, "Mommy, get me some more milk." If we have spent much time around this child, this may seem like one of his typical sentences—typical for one thing in that, for the past few weeks, at least, we have rarely heard him utter sentences with more than two words in them.

On reflection, we may be struck by what a good sentence it is for having only two words! If we had to pick two words to convey the idea in "Mommy, get me some more milk," we could not improve on "Mommy milk." A lot of young children's sentences are like this; that is, they are of a uniform shortness, starting out as one-word sentences. Later, as children mature a bit, they begin to use two-word sentences and then move up to three-word sentences and so on.

Most early sentences are like this sample sentence, too, in that children show a knack for picking the most important words to convey their meanings. "Mommy milk" packs a lot of information; "get more" conveys less. Early sentences use informative words and leave out in-between words such as "and," "to," "with," "should," "have," "will," "the," "very," and the like. We assume that the limits to the number of words children can put in their early sentences have to do with biology and maturity. But the nature of their choice of words and the order they put them in reveals some deliberation, some rules.

Another piece of evidence for the operation of rules in early speech is seen when a child is asked to imitate adult sentences. Normally, young children cannot correctly imitate a sentence that is more complicated than one they could produce on their own. The following exchange between a psychologist and his young daughter illustrates this point:

> *Child:* Want other one spoon, Daddy.
> *Father:* You mean, you want the other spoon.
> *Child:* Yes, I want other one spoon, please Daddy.
> *Father:* Can you say, "The other spoon"?
> *Child:* Other . . . one . . . spoon.
> *Father:* Say, "other."
> *Child:* Other.
> *Father:* "Spoon."
> *Child:* Spoon.
> *Father:* "Other spoon."
> *Child:* Other . . . spoon. Now give me other one spoon?[3]

Similar difficulty was encountered by a researcher who attempted to lead another child away from an incorrect use of a past tense of the verb "hold":

> *Child:* My teacher holded the baby rabbits and we patted them.
> *Adult:* Did you say your teacher held the baby rabbits?
> *Child:* Yes.
> *Adult:* What did you say?
> *Child:* She holded the baby rabbits and we patted them.
> *Adult:* Did you say she held them tightly?
> *Child:* No, she holded them loosely.[4]

This child apparently is not going to say "held" until she changes the rule in her head that produces that form. And language rules, like other habits, take some time to change!

Children do not trade in their immature speech for mature speech all at once. They always go through a sequence of stages of language use, moving from simple to complex. Thus, we hear a child at two years of age ask, "Why you singing?" and we note that all of her questions are of the same form. At two years, four months, we hear her ask, "Why you are singing?" and other questions of this more complex form. Just before the age of three, she arrives at the standard form for the English question, "Why are you singing?"[5]

It is obvious that this child is not learning to talk simply by memorizing sentences or sentence types. Rather, she is formulating her own rules to help her understand sentences she hears around her to produce sentences like them. Once she formulates a rule, she uses it confidently until she begins to notice differences between her sentences and the sentences adults use. Then she will gradually add to and amend her rules so that she is able to produce sentences more like adults'. She doesn't junk her old rules altogether; this would be too disruptive. Feature by feature, she makes her rules more and more like the rules adults use to produce mature sentences.[6]

Remarkably, children usually go through the same *sequence* of rule learning as they mature in speech production. A study by Brown[7] showed that three separate children started using major grammatical features in roughly the same order:

present progressive	I rid*ing*
plural nouns	two skate*s*
linking verbs	I *am* big
articles before nouns	*the* birds
past tense markers	we skat*ed*

Child language researchers are not sure why children tend to acquire language rules in the same order, although one theorist has suggested that it may be because children are born "prewired" to learn language in a certain way.[8]

The uniformity of order surely has nothing to do with what we teach. The language children hear around them cannot be much different from age one to age two, or from age two to age three—though their own language changes dramatically during that time. Whatever the explanation turns out to be, it is bound to be related to language-learning processes going on inside the child.

Not all of children's early speech is different from adult speech. Sometimes we do hear two- and three-year-olds repeating phrases—learned by imitation—that seem more advanced than normal speech for that age. We sometimes hear "Why *dincha* tell me?" at two and a half, but later, oddly enough, the child reverts to a less mature form: "Why *you didn't* tell me?" Eventually he will come to use the correct form: "Why *didn't you* tell me?"

The implication is that some imitated but unassimilated forms may be used for a time as *formulas*—that is, as whole structures that the child hasn't analyzed and for which rules have not been found that will generate them. But as language development advances, the rules invade the formulas; the utterances produced by formula disappear, and they may not be heard again until the rules have been developed to produce them.

If children construct their own rules to use and understand language, how is it that everyone winds up speaking English instead of her or his own private language?

We sometimes do hear of sets of twins who—being raised in isolation from others or in other unusual circumstances—make up a private idiomatic language that makes no sense to anyone but themselves.[9] But that doesn't happen very often. Every year, millions and millions of children learn to speak English (and, in their respective settings, hundreds of other languages) through their own efforts, without being taught. That is the normal pattern of things.

Clearly, when children construct language rules, they are attempting to find rules or patterns that account for the language used by others in their presence. It is as if they were carefully feeling and probing the language to find its joints and seams, its outer shape and its inner workings.

Children's early hunches about the way spoken language works can be wrong, of course. An area of language where this is sometimes seen is in naming things. We have an example in our young friend, Will, who produced voluminous speech throughout his second and third years. Except for a few words, most of Will's speech was unintelligible to his parents or other adults. One of Will's recognizable words was "bupmum," used to refer to his favorite vehicle, the family's Land Rover (a British-made jeep). According to Will's father, "bupmum" was a pretty fair rendering of the sound made by the exhaust popping out of the Rover's rusted tailpipe. When the family sold it and bought a Volkswagen, Will reflected the change in his name for the new car: "mummum" (a smoother-sounding name for a better-running engine). Later, he used "mummum" to refer to all cars and trucks. Still later, an element of the name showed up in his name for motorboat: "boatmum." At four, Will was speaking standard English. But in those early years, it seemed to those who knew him that he was seeking names for things in the sounds that emanated from them—a perfectly sensible strategy, really, but not one around which English is organized.

So far in this discussion of children's language learning, we have emphasized the child's own efforts to make sense of and construct rules for the language she hears around her. But what do the adults contribute? Have they only to keep up a patter of talk, from which the child can abstract rules of grammar? Such may have been the drift of earlier descriptions of language acquisition, but now it is widely recognized that adults—parents or primary caregivers—are much more actively involved in children's language learning.

First of all, adults do provide the raw material of language from which children construct their own ideas of the way language works. In those fortunately rare cases in which children have been kept isolated from human contact, the children have been found not to have developed language—to no one's surprise. But secondly, it seems clear that when adults are speaking to children, they modify their speech considerably, into a form of speech that is sometimes called "motherese": they use fewer words per utterance and simpler syntax; they speak more slowly and in a higher range (babies have been shown to prefer high-pitched voices to low-pitched ones); and they exaggerate the stress and intonation of their speech. One researcher has compared all this exaggeration to the way an instructor demonstrates a golf swing. It is as if the mother were saying, "Here, pay attention to upness and downness and stress and words—these are the important things."[10]

But there's more. Most parents in English-speaking countries read to their children. The practice of reading to children has long been believed to help those children learn to read. However, recent assessments of its benefits are more specific. Some argue that reading to children leads them to associate pleasure with written language and enables them to formulate schemata for stories and other forms of written discourse. Other researchers go further and suggest that children who are read to *learn a written form of language from the very beginning.* They learn that language can be elaborated to explain things that are not in the context of the speech. This *decontextualized language* is just the sort of language that is used in reading and writing.[11]

So the picture that emerges from more recent studies of language learning shows that (1) parents are actively involved in their children's language learning, that they tend to direct a form of language toward their children that is easier to learn from than the speech they use with older people; and (2) written language—complete with the word choices and structures of stories, and the use of language to create a world of understanding on its own, a world removed from the context in which it is read—is often part of children's language experience from the very beginning.

How Children Learn to Write

How do children learn to write, then? Our analogy to children's learning to talk, or children's *language acquisition,* has so far suggested two things. First, children have a powerful capacity to discover how language works, a capacity that surely applies to written language as well. Second, parents and other older people make special efforts to model a kind of language with children that is more easily learned than the language they use with other adults. This sort of simplified modeling—or *scaffolding,* as it has been called—is a significant factor in the acquisition of written language, as well as speech.

Figure 1–2
"Parking
Ticket"
Rob
Kindergarten

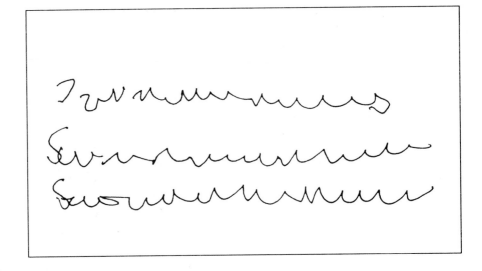

But there is a third source of learning that we haven't mentioned yet: other children. Children influence and learn from each other to a degree that is gaining more appreciation all the time. Let us give an example.

If making scribbles is Rob's way of writing, he'll scribble consistently and enthusiastically every time he has occasion to write, as, say, when he is writing his classmate's tricycle a parking ticket in a kindergarten play area (Figure 1–2), or writing a caption underneath the big blob of orange he has just painted on his paper. But imagine that at sharing time Michelle holds up the big orange blob that *she* has just painted. She's written a caption under hers, too. But her caption consists not of scribbles but of individual squiggles that resemble letters (Figure 1–3).

"What are those?" asks Rob, meaning the individual squiggles.

"Those are letters, 'cause this is writing," answers Michelle.

Before long, squiggles begin to show up in Rob's writing, though he may continue to use scribbling when "he is writing a lot," as he puts it.

Let us highlight, then, some conclusions about children's learning to write that flow from the preceding discussion.

Children learn to write by means of discovery—by actively venturing their own strategies for writing. With any encouragement at all, most children will not hesitate to produce things that they call "writing," even if they have not been taught to spell words or even how to form letters. It is important therefore that teachers offer children opportunities and encouragement to engage in writing activities, especially informal ones, early on—even before regular reading, handwriting, and spelling instruction is begun.

Children "write" by using certain strategies for writing. Often, these strategies don't look much like adult writing. But when a child "writes," at any

Figure 1–3
"Sun"?
Michelle
Kindergarten

given time she is trying out certain unspoken rules or patterns that she believes will produce written language. She may draw a picture or embellish it
with letters; she may spell words almost by abbreviating them; she may
match names of alphabet letters with sounds she hears in words; she may
write a story by naming a character and then saying something about him.
All of these acts reveal a strategy, an underlying idea—for now, at least—
about how writing works.

Children move developmentally from strategy to strategy as they grow in expe-
rience and sophistication as writers. The younger the child, the more possible it

is to plot that child's progress along a known continuum of development in writing. Knowing "where a child is" makes it possible to offer her or him appropriate help and encouragement as a writer. Thus, it is important for teachers to know the developmental benchmarks in learning to write and what is appropriate teaching for each level. This book will describe both.

Children don't discover writing strategies in a vacuum; they need plenty of meaningful examples of writing. The typical inner-city street corner has a lot more print—and a lot more people reading—than many preschool and kindergarten classrooms. If children are going to get curious enough about print to go to the trouble to figure out how it works, they must see lots of print around them, and many people making use of it. Progressive preschool and kindergarten teachers are beginning to work print into the classroom in ingenious ways—not just in reading to children and posting labels on things, but by setting up activity centers where children pretend to read and write naturally, as part of their play. We will discuss ways to do this in later chapters.

Children learn from each other as they try to figure out how to write. As noted psychologist Jean Piaget pointed out, it is often easier to learn something new from someone who is only slightly ahead of us. For a child just starting out, it is easier to learn about invented spelling from someone who is actively sounding out words than from someone who already can spell virtually everything by heart. And it is easier to learn a new strategy for writing a story from someone who is talking excitedly about a new technique she has just discovered than it is from reading a professional author who dazzles us in a dozen ways at once. Children need opportunities to share their writing and talk about how they write. In this book, we will discuss strategies for managing this sharing.

When children are learning about writing and learning to write, discovery learning "works"; moreover, it is good for children. When process-writing approaches and the practice of invented spelling were widely introduced in schools a dozen years ago, many teachers worried that children, if permitted to write words and letters incorrectly, would surely "overlearn" or memorize these incorrect forms and be sidetracked from normal progress toward learning the correct forms. It was much better, many teachers thought, not to allow children to do any writing until they had been explicitly taught the correct ways to make letters, spell words, craft sentences, and arrange them on the page.

This, progressive teachers protested, was likely to be a very long wait. Besides, if children learning to talk were similarly made to hold off speaking until they could speak correctly, they would never learn to speak at all.

Learning to talk, then, offered an encouraging parallel case that could be applied to learning to write. Since all children quite naturally use incorrect forms of speech (such as "all-gone milk" or "I got two foots"), which they readily discard as their ability to use language matures, wouldn't children do the same with writing strategies if they were allowed to use immature forms of writing? Teaching experience and formal research results offer resounding proof that this hunch is correct. Children who are encouraged to write early using pretend writing and invented spelling learn to write more words correctly than children who are taught conventionally.[12]

Two living and breathing examples of this hunch are Annabrook and Jessica, two children whose inventive writings as preschoolers were collected for the first edition of this book (and also appear in this edition) and who were both winning spelling bees by fourth grade. By late elementary school they were avid readers and skillful writers and were singled out repeatedly for writing honors throughout elementary and high school. Both left high school with advanced placement credit in English, high verbal SATs, and scholarships to very competitive colleges.

But children do not need to come from highly literate families to benefit from early writing. One careful study[13] showed that being encouraged to use invented writing led to even greater gains in children who came to school less verbally advanced.

Not only are the fears about inventive writing unfounded, but the benefits are clear. Two benefits deserve special mention.

First, children who are encouraged to write early and often, not surprisingly, write more text—more imaginative and interesting text—than children who spend their early years copying letters and short phrases off the board.

But there is another benefit that may surprise you. Children who are encouraged to write early and inventively perform better in reading, especially in word recognition, than children who do not have this practice.[14] Why this is so relates to the alphabetic nature of our English writing system, a topic we will explore shortly. The finding is extremely important, though, since early writing seems to exercise a core of abilities where written and spoken language intersect. This core of abilities, or the lack of them, is increasingly being pointed to as the source of later reading failure of the kind called dyslexia.

So the answer to the question of whether discovery learning of writing is good for children turns out to be a resounding yes!

But is discovery learning enough? Given opportunity and encouragement, will children learn to write—to form legible letters, to spell correctly, and to compose texts effectively—without formal instruction? This question evades a categorical answer.

It helps to ask, first, what is meant by instruction. Formal instruction traditionally includes a commercial spelling program with workbooks containing a whole range of activities—everything from memorizing spelling words to exercises in alphabetizing to working crossword puzzles. The activities are designed as much for management concerns—they have to occupy the children more or less productively for fifteen to twenty minutes a day, five days a week—as for pedagogical ones.

Traditional instruction also includes language textbooks that teach children the names of the parts of speech, stress errors to avoid, and, perhaps, show the form of a friendly letter.

It is easy to see that neither the traditional language program nor much of the traditional spelling program is necessary for a child to learn to write. In fact, much of both has been shown to be a waste of time; and now that teachers have begun encouraging children to write and read and share, they increasingly resent workbook and skills-based programs that tie up so much of the children's time to no obvious real purpose.

But is it true that *no* direct instruction in handwriting, spelling, or mechanics of language is needed by children learning to write? There is frustratingly little research evidence on this question.

On the issue of handwriting, research has always shown that

- some systematic instruction can help children write legibly;
- what matters most is that children be encouraged to write legibly, not stick slavishly to some form or other; and
- many children need refresher lessons in legible writing even past third grade, when formal spelling instruction usually stops.[15]

But we know of no research that spells out *how much* handwriting instruction children need—especially not research conducted in recent years, when children have begun writing sooner and have written more than at any time in memory. Most primary grade teachers we know still give children some amount of formal handwriting instruction. Many are finding more and more informal and situational ways to help children with their handwriting. (We will share several of these in the next section.)

As a related issue, those working with high-risk children often report having children enter first grade without knowing how to form any letters of the alphabet. Obviously, the benefits of invented spelling will not accrue to these children until they learn to make some letters and begin to associate some sounds with them. Direct instruction in forming letters seems well advised for these children. (We will demonstrate techniques for this instruction in coming chapters.)

When it comes to spelling, the situation is more confused. Some sources[16] have argued that children can learn to spell by writing and revising what they write, without ever memorizing lists of correct spellings. They put forward only anecdotal support for this position, but it has been widely accepted—perhaps too widely.

In an era of declining resources, many school districts have not needed much encouragement to stop purchasing spelling instructional materials, leaving teachers to teach spelling however they see fit. The abrupt change from having spelling instruction completely covered by published materials to having it left completely up to the teacher has surely resulted in a significant decrease in formal spelling instruction in many classrooms. Is this a good thing or not?

As far as we know, there is no systematic research that offers convincing evidence one way or the other. Anecdotal and informal research sometimes suggests that children's knowledge of correct spellings has declined in proportion to the decline in the amount of systematic spelling instruction they receive. But are children making more errors because they are writing more and being more adventurous in the words they attempt to write? Or do they really know less about correct spelling? *Could* they learn more correct spellings without jeopardizing their enthusiasm for writing?

We believe that many children could benefit from systematic spelling and word study—much scaled down from what used to be the norm. We further believe that this study should be tied where possible to the words they are using and the topics they are studying and that it should reinforce common spelling patterns. Moreover, children should write, write, write and read, read, read.

What's to Learn about Writing?

What *is* writing, anyway? Boiled down to essentials, *writing is a way of making marks that call to mind the ideas you had when you wrote.*

Now this definition has a lot of slack in it, to be sure. Some would want to tighten it up so that it excluded drawings. But leaving the definition as open as this means we can give children writing periods and sharing time, even in kindergarten. Although some children will draw pictures, others will scribble, and still others will tease out the spellings of words, all will be able to "read" their ideas to their classmates at sharing time. And as our example of Michelle and Rob demonstrated, as children see what other children have produced, and as their own concepts of what writing is evolve, their marks will gradually gain sophistication.

Others would insist that writing should be *conventional:* that it should employ readily identifiable symbols so that other people can pick up a piece of your writing and know what it says. This is certainly true. Nonetheless, to write conventionally requires that the writer be *outwardly directed*—that she be aware, first, of other people's points of view, of other people's need to know; and second, of conventions of writing that are "out there," too.

Everything we know about child development reminds us that children's perspectives are self-centered, or *egocentric*, at first. Only gradually and through much social experience do they gain awareness of others' points of view and of conventions outside of themselves. It stands to reason, then, that precisely the kind of social experience young writers need is to write things however they can, share them with others, and come face-to-face with their audience's lack of understanding. Then they will be motivated to write in more and more communicative, and hence conventional, ways, especially when they are surrounded by models of more successful communication by professional authors and even by other children. But they must start where they are.

To learn to write, a young person must master three sets of conventions. The first has to do with what writing looks like and how it works. That is, how do written marks communicate ideas? On this level, children learn that adult writing consists of strings of conventional symbols called *letters*, which are loosely related to spoken words—by the sounds of those words, by the smallest units of the sounds of those words.

On a more complicated level, children must learn that certain conventions govern the patterns of letters that can represent words. This is the whole issue of *spelling*.

On a still more complicated level, writers must learn that there are patterns around which ideas can be organized, that give the writing a certain form, which is put to a certain purpose. Whether the purpose is to vent feelings, to persuade, to inform, to recount, or to delight, certain conventions of *composition* must be learned if a writer is to have real success in communicating ideas to readers.

These three aspects of writing will occupy us for the remainder of this book.

Conclusion

The 1960s and 1970s saw exciting breakthroughs in research in children's language acquisition. It was established that children learned the complexities of oral language through discovery learning, by formulating trial rules of language and revising them in stages until they reached mature speech. In short order, we discovered that many of these same principles held true for children's development of writing as well. Children largely discovered how to write by venturing their own ideas of how the writing system might work and revising these in stages as they approached mature writing.

In the eighties, our understanding of children's language acquisition was revised somewhat as we recognized the importance of adults modeling writing for children and of social learning, in which children learn about writing from each other. These social-oriented theories soon led to new ways of looking at children's processes of learning to write.

The recognition of the role of discovery learning in children's learning to write raised the question of whether they needed to be explicitly taught about writing. Our reading of the research on this issue suggests that to some extent, explicit instruction in spelling and handwriting is necessary, at least with some children.

What's to be discovered about writing? Three things: (1) what writing looks like, or how to make marks that look like letters; (2) how letters work, or how to spell; and (3) how writing organizes and communicates ideas, the area of composition.

ENDNOTES

1. Carol Chomsky, "Invented Spelling in the Open Classroom," *Word 27* (1971): 499–518.
2. Noam Chomsky, *Language and Mind,* enlarged ed. (New York: Harcourt Brace Jovanovich, 1972).
3. Martin Braine, "The Acquisition of Language in Infant and Child," in C. E. Reed, ed., *The Learning of Language* (New York: Appleton-Century-Crofts, 1971). Quoted in Jean Aitchison, *The Articulate Mammal* (London: Hutchinson, 1973), p. 74.
4. Courtney Cazden, *Child Language and Education* (New York: Holt, Rinehart & Winston, 1972). Quoted in Aitchison, p. 72.
5. Aitchison.
6. Jill DeVilliers and Peter DeVilliers, *Language Acquisition* (Cambridge: Harvard University Press, 1979).
7. Roger Brown, *A First Language* (Cambridge: M.I.T. Press, 1973).
8. Chomsky.
9. Catherine Gorney, "'Gibberish' Language of Identical Twins Still Baffles the Experts," *The Houston Chronicle,* 29 July 1979, sec. 10, p. 4.
10. Daniel Stern, *The First Relationship: Infant and Mother* (Cambridge: Harvard University Press, 1977).
11. David Olson, "'See! Jumping!' Some Oral Antecedents of Literacy," in Hillel Goelman, Antoinette Oberg, and Frank Smith, eds., *Awakening to Literacy* (Portsmouth, NH: Heinemann, 1984).
12. Linda Clarke, "Invented Versus Traditional Spelling in First Graders' Writings," *Research in the Teaching of English, 22* (Fall 1987): 281–309.
13. Clarke.
14. See Clarke, "Invented Versus Traditional Spelling in First Graders' Writings"; Linnea Ehri, "Does Learning to Spell Help Beginners Learn to Read Words?" *Reading Research Quarterly, 22,* 1 (Fall 1987): 47–65; Darrell Morris, Laura Nelson, and Janet Perney, "Exploring the Concept of 'Spelling Instructional Level' Through Analysis of Error Types," *Elementary School Journal, 87* (1986): 181–200.
15. Charles Temple, "Understanding and Teaching Handwriting and Spelling," in Charles Temple and Jean Gillet, *Language Arts: Learning Processes and Teaching Practices,* 2nd ed. (New York: HarperCollins, 1989).
16. See, for example, Wendy Bean and Christine Bouffler, *Spell by Writing* (Portsmouth, NH: Heinemann, 1987).

PART ONE

The Beginnings of Writing

When does writing begin? Is it when the child composes a readable message to serve some communicative purpose? Is it when the child uses letters to spell words with some approximate degree of accuracy? Or is it when the child makes some wiggly lines on paper and pretends that she is writing?

It is clear that much writing development unfolds in children well before they spell or compose.

The earliest tasks in learning to write concern making marks that look like writing—whether they be long wiggles that fill a page the way writing does or smaller shapes that resemble letters. Thanks to the work of Eleanor Gibson, Emilia Ferreiro, and Marie Clay, we can list and describe the concepts and principles children must master in order to make marks that look like writing. We turn to these matters in the next two chapters.

CHAPTER 2

The Precursors
of Writing

A four-year-old was bent over a piece of paper, deeply engrossed in the act of making the marks shown in Figure 2–1, when her older sister, a first grader, entered the room.

"Jessie, what are you doing?" asked the sister.

"I'm writing," she replied.

"No, you're not."

"Yes, I am."

"You can't be. I don't see any letters!"

Jessie's sister is certainly a realist, a clear-sighted spotter of naked emperors. But we rather agree with Jessie. Her marks do contain many of the rudiments of writing. Our purpose in this chapter and the succeeding one will be to demonstrate the growth of writing—starting with youngsters who "write" as Jessie does and continuing until we see children begin to spell.

Consider the samples in Figures 2–2 and 2–3. How is it possible to examine samples like these and find elements of writing in them? Real writing is composed of combinations of discrete symbols that stand in some socially agreed upon relation to language.[1] These scribbles do not meet this definition by any stretch of the imagination. Indeed, as Jessie's sister pointed out, they don't even have letters in them.

Figure 2–1
Jessie
Age 4
Early writing

Figure 2–2
Kindergartner
The child called
this writing

Figure 2–3
Kindergartner
This, too, was
called writing

Early Writing and a Theory of Perception

People who know how to read and write, even newcomers to this endeavor like Jessie's sister, think of writing as something composed of letters and words. Learning to write, it would seem, is nothing other than learning to make letters and to combine them into words. But studies of writing development carried out against a theory of perceptual learning have suggested that young children learn to write through a process that is really quite the opposite. Rather than learning to write by mastering first the parts (letters) and then building up to the whole (written lines), it appears that children attend first to the whole and only much later to the parts. But what is there to be attended to in the whole of written language if not words and letters?

Let us now explore the process of perceptual learning for a bit to establish a background for an answer to this question. (Our discussion will draw mostly from Eleanor Gibson.[2]) Imagine a newborn baby just home from the hospital, lying in a crib in his nursery. What does he see? At first his eyes are closed in sleep much of the time, and for several months he cannot focus on objects more than a foot or two away from his face. But from the time he opens his eyes he is bombarded by sensations: light, shadow, and dark; objects that loom into view and withdraw; and objects that do not move.

What does he hear? There is the constant sound of his own breathing, the sound of voices—some loud and distinct (voices of people close by) and some less loud and echoing (voices of people further away). He may hear sounds of traffic outside, lawnmowers, birds chirping, and dogs barking. The child is surrounded by a "blooming, buzzing, bustling confusion" of sights, sounds, and feelings.

At first we may imagine that the sensations are all undifferentiated—that is, the baby has no way to distinguish one sight, sound, or feeling from another. But soon he must begin to do some basic sorting. Things that move can be distinguished from things that are static. Human voices can be separated from other nonhuman noises, such as passing motorcycles, ringing telephones, and barking dogs.

These first gross distinctions can be taken further. Things that move can be sorted into parts of the baby himself, and other things that move. Or they can be sorted into things that move on their own accord, and other things that move (people and animals versus balls and mobiles). Sounds can be further distinguished as voices that are close by versus voices that are far away, a woman's voice versus a child's, and so on.

This process of sorting and classifying is the child's way of finding out about the world and getting some control over it. The process continues throughout childhood and adult life, though it never again reaches the intensity of the child's first years.

When the child begins to use words to stand for things, we begin to get a clearer idea of how this sorting process works. Take the case of Annabrook, for example. The first word uttered by this little girl was "dog." During that phase of language development when all of her sentences consisted of a single word, she delighted in pointing to the family beagle and sagely pronouncing him, "dog." But the beagle was not the only animal to qualify for that label. Goats, sheep, cats, and even an occasional cow (she lived on a farm) were all pronounced "dog." During this period it happened that Annabrook was taken to a circus. She and her family had taken their seats and were arranging themselves when a large elephant appeared at the back of the circus tent and swayed into the center ring. "Dog!" cried Annabrook, and in fear and amazement she clapped her hand over her eyes.

It seems that what Annabrook had been doing was lumping together several objects in the world into the category that she labeled "dog." She did the lumping on the basis of features these objects had in common. "Dogs" apparently were four-legged, self-propelled living things. Chickens, having two legs, were never called "dog." Annabrook must have been aware that there are differences in the appearance of dogs, sheep, goats, cats, and certainly cows. For the time being, she chose to ignore the differences and group them together because of the features they did have in common. When she saw the elephant, however, she seemed to realize at once that her category for "dog" must be amended to take size into account. In other words, she found it necessary to add another *distinctive feature,* size, to the set of features that defined "dog."

Distinctive features are central to an understanding of perceptual learning. They are the necessary set of features or attributes that we use to define a category of things. For Annabrook, "four-legged," "living," and "self-propelled" appeared to be the distinctive features that made up her category "dog." Distinctive features are acquired with experience. In general, the more experience we have in the world, the more distinctive features we add to our categories. Then two things happen: Membership in a particular category becomes reserved to fewer varieties of objects, while at the same time we set up new categories to include those items that were not adequately described by our earlier categories.

To summarize our points about perceptual learning:

1. Our environment presents us with an abundant potential of sensory data all of the time. The task of perceptual learning is to carve out classes of objects and events from the undifferentiated confusion around us—classes of things that somehow act or can be acted upon in the same way.
2. The differentiation of things in the environment usually starts with gross categories defined by gross distinctions and then proceeds to finer categories defined by finer distinctions.
3. We assign things to categories on the basis of distinctive features that the things share. In doing this, we initially ignore some differences. However, if the differences become important enough, we will create a new category and assign some things to the new category that will not fit the old.

How Children Perceive Writing

If the perception of things in the environment starts with gross distinctions and moves progressively to finer ones, it stands to reason that letters—being the fine elements of writing—would be the last elements to be differentiated. The theory of perceptual learning would lead us to believe that children should first discover gross differences between writing and other similar things. When children first become aware of writing as a separate thing, they must have some rough set of distinctive features to help them decide when something is writing and when it is not. As they gain experience, they should become aware of finer and finer distinctive features that separate writing from other kinds of graphic displays, and the smaller components of writing, such as letters, from each other.

When children make marks on a page and say "I just wrote . . ." or "This says . . ." we have an opportunity to study the marks and see just what distinctive features constitute that child's idea of what writing is at that moment. From Eleanor Gibson's perceptual learning theory we have come to expect that younger children's notions of writing will be based upon global features of print, and only gradually be concerned with the formation of identifiable letters. Marie Clay's studies show that Gibson was right. Clay outlined a set of features, or graphic principles, that is common in young children's early writing, before they can reliably produce the letters of the alphabet.

In the following pages we will describe the *recurring principle,* the discovery that writing uses the same shapes again and again; the *generative principle,* the discovery that writing consists of a limited number of signs in varied combinations; the *sign concept,* the idea that print stands for something besides itself; and the *flexibility principle,* the idea that there is a limited number of written signs and a limit to the number of ways we can make them. Finally, we will describe a number of principles related to the way print is arranged on a page, *page-arrangement principles.* All of these principles must be learned by children before it can be said they write. And many of them may be seen emerging in children's scribbles before anyone notices that they are trying to produce writing.

The Recurring Principle

Study the picture and the handwriting sample in Figure 2–4. On a very general level, what makes the writing look different from the picture? You may notice several differences. The writing is arranged in rows across the page, while the picture makes more use of two-dimensional space. If you squint your eyes and look at the writing and the picture, the individual letters lose their identity. Now you may notice that the writing seems to be composed of

Figure 2–4
Picture and
words for the
same idea

There was a house. It had a chimney with smoke coming out, and two flowers in the yard. There was a bird and a cloud in the sky.

Figure 2–5
Carlene
Age 4
Recurring
principle

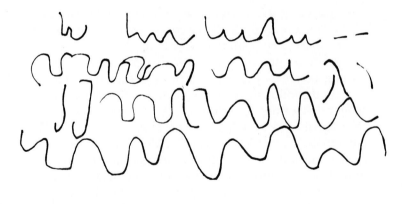

Figure 2–6
Matt
Kindergarten
Recurring
principle

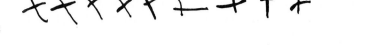

loops and tall sticks repeated over and over again. Children's early attempts to imitate writing often have this characteristic repetition of loops and sticks or circles.

Clay applied the label *recurring principle* to the idea that writing consists of the same moves repeated over and over again. She noted that children derive a great deal of satisfaction from filling whole lines or pages by repeating the same moves over and over.

The displays in Figures 2–5 and 2–6 were produced by children who said they were writing. Note how each gives evidence of the recurring principle.

The Generative Principle

It is possible to fill an entire page with repetitions of the same basic mark. That is what the child in Figure 2–7 has done. But as we saw in the previous chapter, children learn early on that the same character repeated over and over again is not writing. To be called writing, there must be variety in the arrangement of marks.

Figure 2–7
Three-year-old
Filling a line
with the same
form

Figure 2–8
Tammy
Kindergarten
Generative
principle

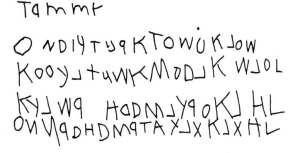

Figure 2–9
Four-year-old
Generative
principle

It *is* possible to create writing with just a few characters, *but they must be repeated in different combinations.* Every book written in English simply combines and recombines twenty-six letter symbols. The writer in Figure 2–8 uses considerably fewer, but it is clear that she has discovered the same principle around which English writing is organized: A limitless amount of writing can be generated by using a small set of letters, provided they are combined in different ways. This is what Clay calls the *generative principle* (see Figure 2–9).

The generative principle may be employed with words, too. In Figure 2–10, note how Wes has recombined a small repertoire of words to make a list of sentences covering a whole page.

The Sign Concept

All of the items in Figure 2–11 could be called *graphic displays*, but only some of them could be called *signs.* Illustration l) is a picture, not a sign. Illustration 2) is a design, such as might decorate the hem of a skirt; it is not a sign either. Illustration 3) *might* be a sign to someone who reads Chinese (the author made it up). Illustration 4) contains three signs—the graphic configurations for the letters a, b, and c, respectively. Illustration 5) contains the three signs c, a, and t; collectively these make up the sign "cat," the English word for a small feline animal.

What is a sign? A sign is a display that stands for something else. In writing, signs are arbitrary—that is, there is no reason why a particular

Figure 2–10
Wes
Grade 1
Generative
principle
applied to
sentences

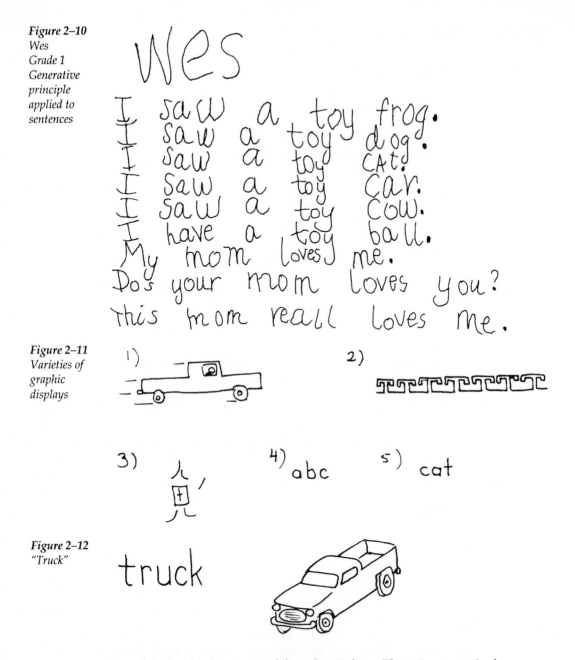

Wes

I saw a toy frog.
I saw a toy dog.
I saw a toy cat.
I saw a toy car.
I saw a toy cow.
I have a toy ball.
My mom loves me.
Dos your mom loves you?
This mom reall loves me.

Figure 2–11
Varieties of
graphic
displays

1)

2)

3)

4) abc

5) cat

Figure 2–12
"Truck"

truck

graphic display *has* to stand for what it does. There is no particular reason why a sideways hook should stand for the letter C. Generations of readers and writers of English have simply agreed that it does. This is what separates *writing* from *pictures:* Writing represents something arbitrarily, while drawing does not.[3] The relation between the graphic display in Figure 2–12 and the idea "truck" is *not* arbitrary. The graphic display shares many features

Figure 2–13
Shawn
Age 4
About his father

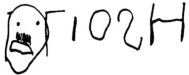

(wheels, back and front, steering wheel, window, etc.) with the object it represents. But the written word *truck* has none of these things in common with the object "truck." The written word can represent the object only because the community of literate English speakers agrees that the word stands for the thing, and the letters stand for the word.

At some point in their development as writers, all children must come to understand that writing uses graphic displays to stand for something else. This understanding is called the *sign concept.* Children understand the sign concept when they intend, even in play, to have the things they put on paper stand for words, ideas, or messages.

The sign concept seems to be present when children make marks that begin to look like writing. Note the evidence of the sign concept in the piece by Shawn, a four-year-old (see Figure 2–13). We need some background information to interpret Shawn's markings. His father is a football coach at Stroman High School. Stroman High School students often wear sweatshirts emblazoned with a Teutonic letter S. The H in this passage probably stands not for the letter but for a goalpost. The face at the left-hand end of the figure has a mustache, just like Shawn's father. Thus, we can interpret this display to say something about the fact that Shawn's father is connected with football at Stroman High School.

Shawn's signs are not arbitrary. Perhaps he is showing us that it is natural for a beginning writer to think of concrete relations between signs and the things they stand for. Emilia Ferreiro has argued that this is the case.[4] (Her ideas will be discussed in Chapter 3.)

Most beginning writers are willing to *pretend* that the marks they wrote stand for something—leaving the relation between the marks and the things they stand for up to the reader's imagination. Note the grocery list written up by Susan, at her mother's suggestion (see Figure 2–14). After she had written down her marks for each item, her mother went back and asked her what each one was. To the left of each mark is written her answer.

Where does the sign concept come from? Children who grow up in homes where literacy is practiced have many indications that writing stands for things. Children whose parents read to them hear a certain story come from a certain book with certain pictures and print. And although for a time they may believe that the story is somehow contained in the pictures, it eventually dawns on them that the print is the source of the story.[5] Perhaps they notice that a variety of spoken comments may be induced by a picture,

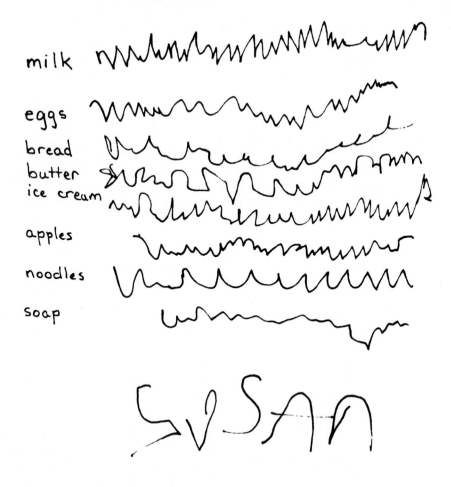

whereas an exact story line is stimulated by print. Recognition of the sign potential of the print is certainly made easier when parents occasionally run their finger along with the print as they read.

Even if children are not read to, there are other indications available to them of the sign potential of print. Logos on popular restaurants, such as McDonald's, Burger King, and the like, are quickly picked up by children. A three-year-old at home who is shown a McDonald's hamburger wrapper may easily say, "McDonald's!" No wonder businesses so jealously protect their logos from use by competitors!

The Flexibility Principle

In our discussion of the sign concept we noted that signs stand for things on the basis of social agreement. Hence, the figure D stands for the letter D, and the figure P stands for the letter P. We know this because it is taught in school and used consistently in any society where English is read and written. It follows that signs must be used *carefully*. In writing there is a limited set of agreed upon signs. To write English, we *have* to use the agreed upon signs and no others. On the present author's typewriter there are fifty-two of these: abcdefghijklmnopqrstuvwxyz, ABCDEFGHIJKLMNOPQRSTUVWXYZ. Some scripts add *a* and *g* to total fifty-four. If we use any other figures than these as signs for letters, we must not assume that others will know what we mean by them.

On the other hand, we know that letters are made up of combinations of a limited number of features. All of the letters we use are made up of lines that are horizontal, vertical, and diagonal; of loops that face left or right, up or down, or that are closed; and dots. These nine shapes account for all fifty-four of the letter forms in English. We can say that writing English letters is a matter of writing correct or allowable combinations of those ten basic shapes.

Once children begin to experiment with writing, a period of months or years may go by before they know all of the letter forms. During that time, they may be constantly surprised that letters they know can be varied to produce new letters. For example, the letter d may be turned upside down to make a letter p, or flipped around to make a letter b. If we add two horizontal bars to the letter L, we get E; if we take the lower bar off E, we get F. Children can discover ways to make letters they didn't previously know how to make. But in the process, they are likely to invent letters that do not exist.

Clay has referred to this whole problem as the *flexibility principle.* The flexibility principle might be stated as follows: By varying letter forms that we know, we can produce letters that we didn't know how to make. But we must be careful, because not all of the letter forms we produce in this way are acceptable as signs. There is one more aspect of the flexibility principle that is of great importance to beginning writers. That is the fact that the same letter form may be written many different ways. Depending on the reading matter a child picks up, he may see quite a variety of printed forms for the same letters (see Figure 2–15).

Observe in Figure 2–16 how Carlene, a four-year-old, came upon the flexibility principle. Which of her figures are allowable letters? Which are unallowable variations? Which ones are allowable forms that she might have invented? That is, has she produced some allowable letters by accident?

Jessie's figures all appear to be allowable letter forms (see Figure 2–17). But what might have influenced her to put the loops on her letters? The embellishments Jessie puts on her letters may be her attempt to imitate the serifs on standard type that she sees in books.

When young children explore the flexibility principle, this should be considered a positive sign.[6] In this way children gain active control over the features or principles of print. It is only speculation, but it seems likely that children who explore the flexibility principle will be better able to respond

Figure 2–15
Some variations
of print style

ABCDEFGHIJKLMNOPQRSTUVWXYZ&
abcdefghijklmnopqrstuvwxyz $1234567890
PLAYBILL · 24-36-48-72 FOUNDRY

ABCDEFGHIJKLMNOPQRSTUVWXYZ& $123
POST TITLE MEDIUM · 6S-6L-8S-8L-10S-10L-12-14S-14L-18-24S-24L-30-42-48 FOUNDRY

ABCDEFGHIJK
LMNOPQRSTUV
WXYZ   123456
PROFIL · 18-20-24-30-36-48-60 FOUNDRY

ABCDEFGHIJKLMNOPQRSTUVWXYZ
abcdefghijklmnopqrstuvwxyz   &$1234567890
QUILLSCRIPT THOMPSON · 14-18-24-30-36-48 FOUNDRY

ABCDEFGHIJKLMNOPQRSTUVWXYZ&
abcdefghijklmnopqrstuvwxyz $1234567890
RADIANT MEDIUM · 12-14-18 (Single Character) LUDLOW

ABCDEFGHIJKLMNOPQRSTUVWXYZ&
abcdefghijklmnopqrstuvwxyz $1234567890
RADIANT BOLD · 14-18-24-30 (Single Character) LUDLOW

ABCDEFGHIJKLMNOPQRSTUVWXYZ&
abcdefghijklmnopqrstuvwxyz $12345678
RADIANT HEAVY · 14-18 (Single Character) LUDLOW

ABCDEFGHIJKLMNOPQRSTUVWXYZ&   abcdefghijklmnopqrstuvwxyz   1234567890
REGNUM · 24-36-48 FOUNDRY

ABCDEFGHIJKLMNOPQRSTUVW
XYZ&   abcdefghijklmnopqrstuvwxyz $1233567890
RESPIGHI · 24-30-36 FOUNDRY

Figure 2–16
Carlene
Age 4
Flexibility principle

Figure 2–17
Jessie
Age 4
Flexibility principle

appropriately to varieties of print type encountered in their reading than children who memorize letter configurations one at a time. This is because practice with the flexibility principle helps children attend to the defining features of letters, to consider what features constitute a letter and what features make it something else.

Linear Principles and Principles of Page Arrangement

Perhaps one of the hardest things for young children to grasp in approaching early writing is the fact that the direction in which written characters face is so important. Psychologists of perception have taught us to marvel that a child can look at a chair from the top, from the bottom, and from any side and know that what she is looking at is still a chair.[7] The information available to the child's eyes changes markedly as she moves from one perspective to another vis-à-vis the chair. Still, the child learns to ignore the difference imposed by changes in perspective and attend to the features of the chair that do not change from one perspective to the next—the fact that it has four legs, a horizontal platform, and a vertical back (see Figure 2–18).

When the child begins to write, the rules change. Now the visual differences brought on by shifts in perspective change the very identity of the object! The same combination of circle and stick can be the letter b, p, d, or q, depending on its arrangement in space. Writing is one of very few areas of our experience where identity changes with direction. The orientation of letters

Figure 2–18
A chair is still a
chair,
regardless of
perspective

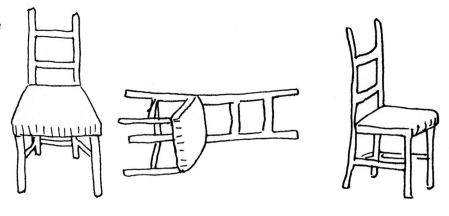

Figure 2–19
Jessie (left)
Age 5
Letter direction
problems

Figure 2–20
Will (right)
Age 4
Started with
"W" and went
both ways

gives children problems for months and even years after they begin to write (see Figures 2–19 and 2–20).

Directionality is also an important issue with regard to the arrangement of print on a page. When we write in English, we start on the left-hand side of the page at the top, proceed straight across to the right side, return to the left, drop down one line, and proceed to the right again. This fairly complicated

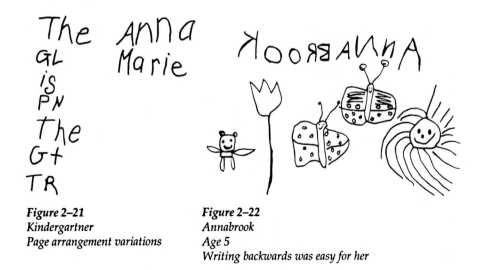

Figure 2–21
Kindergartner
Page arrangement variations

Figure 2–22
Annabrook
Age 5
Writing backwards was easy for her

directional pattern is arbitrary, and it does not extend to all writing systems. Hebrew readers read across from right to left. Chinese readers read top to bottom and right to left. Ancient Greeks used to read from left to right on the first line, then right to left on the second line, then left to right on the third line. Our English pattern of left to right and top to bottom is one set of choices selected arbitrarily from many possibilities.

Clay found in a study that directional problems were common in the five- and six-year-olds she studied in New Zealand. Most of her five-year-olds and many of her six-year-olds had not yet settled on the left-right-top-bottom pattern. Her subjects read from right to left, from bottom to top, or from the middle of the line out to either end.[8] She also noted that children continue to have directional difficulty in writing well after this issue is settled in reading.

If children draw a picture first and then write, the direction in which they arrange their print is often a matter of the best use of the space available on the page. The child in Figure 2–21, for instance, glued a picture onto her page first, and then wrote the text in the vertically extended space that was left over.

Young children's habits of directionality are remarkably fluid. Adults cannot easily write their names backwards, but many beginning writers appear able to do this with little trouble (see Figure 2–22).

During the time when their notions of directionality have not yet been cast solidly in favor of left to right, top to bottom, we should avoid exercises with writing that violate this principle. Note, for example, what happened to the kindergartner in Figure 2–23 when she was given a commercially printed worksheet to complete. The worksheet asked that she fill in the letters of the

Figure 2–23
Shelley
Kindergarten
The "A" and
"Z" were
already printed

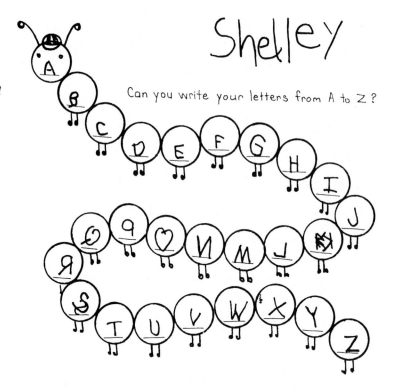

alphabet in their proper order in the cells of the snake (or is it a tapeworm?). But since the snake meandered from left to right, then from right to left, then from left to right again, the girl took her cue from the snake's orientation and wrote those letters backwards that were to fill the blanks running from right to left. Then she straightened out and pointed them correctly when the snake ran from left to right again. This was a thoughtful response to a confusing exercise. Children deserve materials that are more sensitive to the real problems of learning to write than this sheet was.

When children violate directional principles in writing, part of the reason must be their tendency to focus on one letter or word at a time—they do not appear to give much forethought to the question of how the whole page is to be arranged (see Figure 2–24). It is therefore a good idea for the teacher to give them some guidance. Here are some suggestions for an exercise where they are drawing a picture first and then writing about it:

- Fold the papers so as to leave a crease separating the top of the page from the bottom. Then instruct the child to draw their picture on the top (or the bottom) and do their writing on the bottom (or the top).
- Put a green arrow on the left-hand side of the page, pointing to the right, to remind the children where to begin and which way to arrange their writing.

Figure 2–24
Karan
Grade 2
Page
arrangement
problems

Spaces between Words

In Chapter 7 of this book, in which we discuss early spelling behavior, we raise the question of whether or not beginning readers and writers know what a word is. One reason that the question comes up is that so many beginning writers give no indication of what their word units are. Or when they do, they sometimes do so incorrectly (see Figure 2–25). Our writing system routinely indicates word boundaries by leaving spaces between the word units in print. Beginning writers quite often fail to leave these spaces.

Nevertheless, a child's failure to leave spaces between words should not be taken too quickly to indicate that he doesn't know that the words exist as separate units. It happens that leaving spaces is a highly abstract procedure for children to manage. The present writer remembers his difficulty some years ago when reading an introductory book on architecture. The book called attention to the use of positive and negative space in building design. Positive space is what you put in; negative space is what you leave out. At the time, negative space seemed a very difficult concept to understand. The space left between words is negative space, and the concept probably causes difficulty for children, also. Many children appear to prefer inserting periods between

Figure 2–25
Lisa
Grade 1
Word spacing
problems

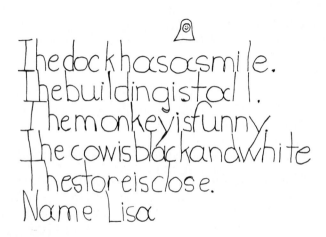

Figure 2–26
Stella
Grade 1
Indicating
word spacing
with periods

words rather than leaving spaces. It seems that they prefer to manipulate positive rather than negative space (see Figure 2–26).

Conclusion

The graphic principles we saw in this chapter were first identified by Marie
Clay. We have seen these principles show up again and again in children's
early writing; indeed, we had little trouble collecting samples from children
we know that demonstrated Clay's features.

To repeat them, the features were the *recurring principle,* the idea that a
simple move may be repeated over and over again and strung across a page
to look like writing; the *generative principle,* that a few marks can be made to
look like writing if they are written over and over again in varied order; the
flexibility principle, that in exploring the limits to how much we can vary a
character without changing its identity, we may sometimes accidentally produce characters we didn't know how to make before; the *sign concept,* that
marks on the page might *mean* something, somehow; and *linear and page arrangement principles,* that writing goes across the page left to right and from
top to bottom.

ENDNOTES

1. Marie Clay, *What Did I Write?* (Portsmouth, NH: Heinemann, 1976).
2. Eleanor Gibson and Harry Levin, *Psychology of Reading* (Cambridge: M.I.T. Press, 1975).
3. Gibson and Levin.
4. Emilia Ferreiro and Ana Teberosky, *Literacy before Schooling* (Portsmouth, NH: Heinemann, 1983).
5. Marie Clay, *Reading: The Patterning of Complex Behavior,* 2d ed. (Portsmouth, NH: Heinemann, 1980).
6. Clay, *What Did I Write?*
7. Jerome Bruner, "On Perceptual Readiness," in Jeremy Anglin, ed., *Beyond the Information Given* (New York: Norton, 1976).
8. Clay, *What Did I Write?*

CHAPTER 3

What Children Do with Early Graphics

In the previous two chapters we observed that children learn about writing not by acquiring letters one after another but by first becoming sensitive to the principles that generate written language. Before children use a selection of letters with any stability, we see first a slow revelation of certain graphic principles in the children's scribbles—principles such as *directionality, flexibility, generativity*, and *recurrence*. With repeated writing practice children produce marks that more and more closely resemble the writing they see in the print around them. This learning proceeds not letter by letter but feature by feature. But *why* do children go through this learning process in the first place? What are children trying to do when they make scribble after scribble, only gradually producing letter forms that look like those of adults?

They are most likely doing two things. First, they may be almost purely imitating adult writing, trying to do the activity of writing they have seen adults doing, and better yet, trying to produce writing that resembles adult writing. They may even "read" imitated writing by telling a story while they point at their marks. But they are not yet intending any particular relation between the marks on the page and the things they mean; they are producing marks that may *look* like writing, but they are not yet concerned with having them *work* like writing. The second thing children may try to do with marks, then, is to make them work like writing: to make them represent meaning. How do they do that?

A prior question is, How do *we* do that? That is, how does our adult writing system *work*?

How Writing Systems Are Organized

When you and I write, we employ letters of the alphabet to represent words. The letters represent parts of words—the individual sounds that make them up. But this is not the only way we *could* write if we chose to use letters in a different way. There are other approaches to writing—to the representing of words with symbols—that have been used by different peoples. There is no reason to believe English-speaking children are genetically programmed to use symbols for the sound components of words. So we should consider some different ways to write in order to clarify the alternatives that are open to a child when she decides to represent a spoken message with written symbols.

Symbols for Ideas: Ideographic Writing

One approach to writing is to let each symbol stand for an idea, in the manner that a road sign conveys the idea to motorists that a winding road lies ahead.

Chinese writing is a modern system based on the principle of using a single symbol to represent an idea. In ancient times the symbols were pictures of the things they represented. Through constant usage the symbols came to look less like pictures, and the meanings became abstracted from the original concrete things that the symbols stood for.

The ancient drawing 火 used to stand for "fire," by representing its jumping, dancing quality. The modern character for fire has changed to 火. By abstraction, two fires, 炎 means "brilliant." The ancient drawing for "sunrise" depicted the sun between the branches and the roots of a tree: 東. Gradually the symbol was changed to 東, and the meaning was extended to include the direction "east," since that is where the sun is seen to rise.[1]

As a result of the abstraction of both symbol and meaning, modern Chinese writing has evolved as an elaborate and versatile system capable of representing approximately the same range of ideas that English writing can. The pictorial basis of Chinese writing gives it one advantage that alphabetic writing systems do not have: Chinese writing can be read and understood by people who speak dialectical versions of Chinese, which can differ greatly from one another so that speakers of some different dialects cannot understand each other.

> Both a Peking man and a Cantonese will understand 日 means day, and 月 means moon. But a Peking man will pronounce the words r and ywe, while the Cantonese will pronounce yat and ut. . . . If the Peking man reads to the Canton man, the Canton man will not understand one word. If each man reads a text for himself, he can understand it, completely.[2]

This is so because the Chinese symbol is independent of the *sound* of the word and represents directly the *idea* that is conveyed by the spoken word. Because the symbols represent ideas and not spoken words, they have come to be called *ideographs*, which means, simply, "idea writing." We use a few of them in our own writing system: $, ¢, &; the number symbols 1, 2, 3, 4, etc.; and the mathematical operation signs X, —, and +. Note that these symbols are found in languages other than English and are paired with different words: 1, 2, 3 can stand for one, two, three in English; *uno, dos, tres* in Spanish; *eins, zwei, drei* in German; and *moja, mbili, tatu* in Swahili.

Writing words with a single symbol, then, is a perfectly workable approach to writing.

Children and Ideographic Writing.   Children who are first working on the *sign concept* (see Chapter 2) are producing something that could be called ideographic writing. Note the use of the Valentine shape in five-year-old Jessie's sample (Figure 3–1).

At age four, Annabrook used her mother's initial (F) and her father's (C) to symbolize her parents standing beside her as she appeared as a bride—or is that a dazzling princess? (See Figure 3–2.)

Symbols for Syllables: Syllabic Writing

A few thousand years ago, an Egyptian scribe thought up a joke that eventually revolutionized writing. His language had a hieroglyph ➡️→ that stood for the Egyptian word for "arrow," called *ti.* There was another Egyptian word, also called *ti,* that meant "life," an idea not easily represented by a picture. The scribe's joke was to represent *ti,* meaning "life," with the hieroglyph ➡️→ which stood for "arrow."[3] With that pun he invented the phonetic principle—the principle that relates symbols with words on the basis of *sound.*

For an illustration of the sort of writing that resulted, consider *rebus*—the picture writing found in many young children's prereading books. We

Figure 3–1
Jessie
Age 5
A somewhat ideographic message

Figure 3–2
Annabrook
Age 4
A more clearly ideographic message

write ⬙ 4 for "before" and intend that the reader ignore the honey-gathering insect and the numerical quantity of "four" and think only of the sounds of their respective names. This is a phonetic use of hieroglyphics.

With this first use of the phonetic principle, the scribe may have been using symbols to spell whole words, but it is more likely that he was using them to spell syllables. After the invention of the phonetic principle, Egyptian hieroglyphics spelled syllables of words. That writing system has been obsolete for centuries; but the system of syllabic writing lives on in modern Japanese.

The spoken language of Japanese makes use of forty-six different syllables. Combinations of those forty-six syllables make up every word in the language. A Japanese writing system, called *kana,* provides a symbol for each of the forty-six syllables. The syllable *ro* is written ⌷ ; the syllable *ku* is written ⁊ . The word for "green," *roku,* may thus be written ⌷⁊. If we know that ⁊ represents the syllables *tsu,* then we can write the word *kutsu* "to bend" ⁊⁊. Note that the syllable symbols ⁊ , ⌷ , and ⁊ mean nothing in themselves. They gain significance only by representing the sounds of the syllables of Japanese words.

There are few syllabic writing systems besides Japanese in active use nowadays, but in ancient times these systems were widespread. Just as ideographic writing systems mostly gave way to syllabic systems, the latter mostly evolved into alphabetic writing systems or disappeared altogether.

Children and Syllabic Writing.   Do our young spellers in English attempt to produce syllabic writing? Sometimes we see writings that have words represented at the level of the syllable. In one kindergartner's sentence (Figure 3–3), the number 2 and the letter T in DELTKO represent syllables.

The next sample is another kindergartner's response to the question "If you could go anywhere in town for lunch, where would you go?" (See Figure 3–4.) The B and Z in Bonanza also serve as syllables.

Both of these samples differ from true syllabic writing because they have other symbols in them that represent units smaller than syllables. Few children seem to spell consistently at the level of the syllable—though, as we shall see, they occasionally do represent syllables with single consonants, a practice that standard English spelling does not allow.

Figure 3–3
Melanie
Kindergarten
Syllabic use of
"2" and "T"

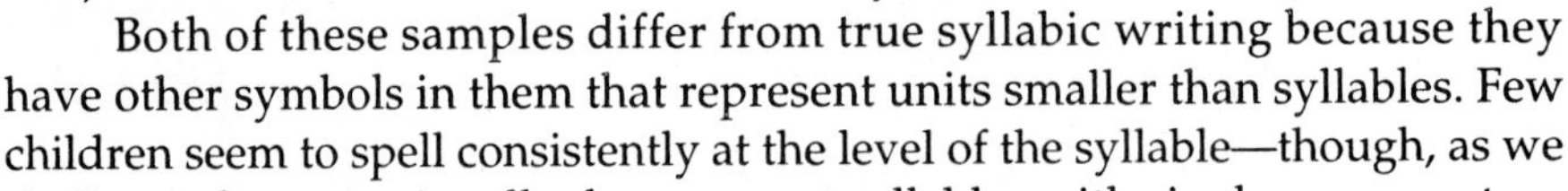

LSNT WE WNT ⌐ DELTKO

(Last night we went to Del Taco.)

Figure 3–4
Annabrook
Kindergarten
Syllabic use of
"B" and "Z"

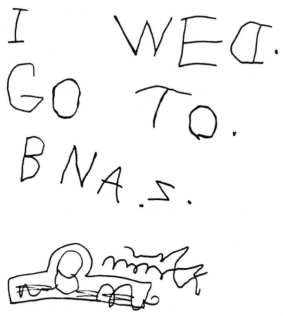

(I would go to Bonanza.)

Symbols for Small Units of Sound: Alphabetic Writing

The use of the alphabet as we know it was a Greek invention. Five thousand years ago, the Greeks discovered that the syllabaries in circulation at the time did not fit their language. For example, the word *anthropos*, meaning "man," was rendered a-to-ro-po-se by an early syllabary. "The crown," *ton choron*, was written to-ne-ko-ro-ne. It wouldn't do. What was plainly needed was a writing system that would let the scribes choose what combinations of consonants and vowels they wanted.

So they made some changes in the syllabaries. Instead of representing a whole syllable (a vowel plus a consonant), the new Greek symbols would represent either a consonant or a vowel but not both. Thus the alphabet and the alphabetic principle were born.[4]

It may be that some children who seek to understand how English writing works reject the syllabic approach for the same reasons the Greeks did. English *could* be spelled syllabically, if the names of the letters of the alphabet could be associated with syllables in words—but it wouldn't work very well.

English is better suited to the alphabet than it is either to ideographs or to syllables. It has too many words for an ideographic system. A large dictionary has more than 130,000 entries; if we used ideographs, we would have to learn to look up that many! English is not suited to any syllabary either, because—unlike Japanese—the syllable patterns in English are many and varied and would require a large number of characters to represent them. The twenty-six letters of the alphabet can, in some combination, represent all of the sounds contained in all 130,000 plus words in a large English dictionary. No other writing system offers such economy.

The match between our alphabet and the sounds of our words is far from perfect, however. English has forty-four sounds but only twenty-six letters. A few of the letters, moreover, are redundant: K and C can represent the same sounds, as can S and C, and Y and I. Some letters represent many different sounds, and some sounds may be spelled with many different letters. All of these features have consequences for learning to write in English.

That is enough about writing systems. To review, we have briefly described three major types: (1) the ideographic system, which uses symbols to represent whole words or ideas; (2) the syllabic system, which uses symbols to represent syllables; and (3) the alphabetic system, which uses symbols to represent individual speech sounds, or *phonemes,* as linguists call them. All three systems are in use today.

The Evolution of Children's Writing Strategies

A noted Argentine researcher, Emilia Ferreiro,[5] studied the evolution of writing strategies of Spanish-speaking children in Mexico and Argentina. While she found a similar course of development to one just described—going from *ideographic* to *syllabic* to *alphabetic* writing—her observations were different enough from ours to bear repeating. In order to understand Ferreiro's ideas, let us begin with an illustration.

In the English language that we adults read and write, we may say that written figures represent letters that combine into representations of words, which stand for real or imaginary things. We may illustrate this series of relationships by means of the diagram in Figure 3–5.

Some children who are new to writing hypothesize relations between writing and language that are different from the relations described in Figure 3–5. Emilia Ferreiro worked with some four- and five-year-old children in Argentina who had some exotic notions about how writing represents language. One little boy named Javier said "cat" could be written $O \mid A$, while "kittens" could be written $O A \mid O A \mid O A \mid$. Ferreiro concluded that he had the following hypotheses about the relation between writing and the things represented by writing:

1. Written words for similar things should *look* similar, even though the spoken words for those objects may not *sound* the same.
2. When characters refer to more than one object, the child uses *more* characters to represent them.

Figure 3–5
The way writing represents language for fluent readers

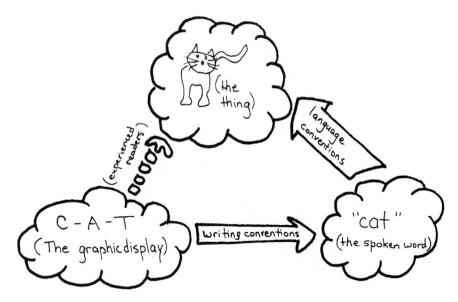

Ferreiro found many children who thought there might be a concrete relation between written marks and the things they stood for. She suggested that there may be a developmental continuum that would have children looking first for concrete relations between graphic characters and the things they stood for *without reference to sound.*

At a later stage, the relation between graphics and language became based on sound. Specifically, the children put the same number of letters in a graphic display as the number of syllables in the spoken word for which the graphic display stood. Thus, "chicken" was written ⌠ ⁄ and "fencepost" ⌡ ⌐ . There is no relation between the graphic characters and the individual speech sounds in either word. Letters are used as syllable counters only in this sort of writing.

In terms of the diagram in Figure 3–5, Ferreiro's finding was that children

- look first for a concrete relation between *A* and *C* (see Figure 3–6).
- and only later for a *sound* relation between *A* and *B* (see Figure 3–7).

Writing Your Own Name

The first pieces of writing most children produce are their own names. In kindergarten the child's coat bin is marked with his own name. In first grade his name is printed neatly on tagboard and taped to his desk. When he draws a picture, his kindergarten or preschool teacher prints his name on the paper. In writing the child's name so often, the teacher may be motivated as much by management concerns as instructional ones. For the child, though, the re-

Figure 3–6
Concrete rela-
tionship of
letters to
language

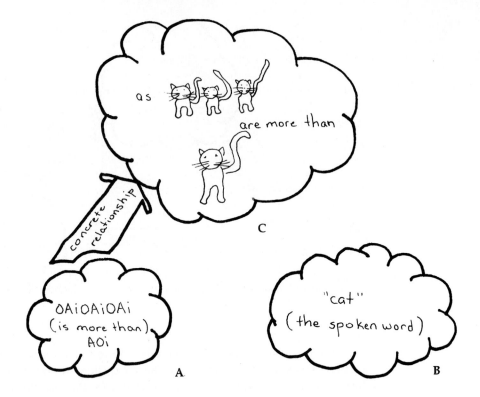

Figure 3–7
Sound relation-
ship of letters to
language

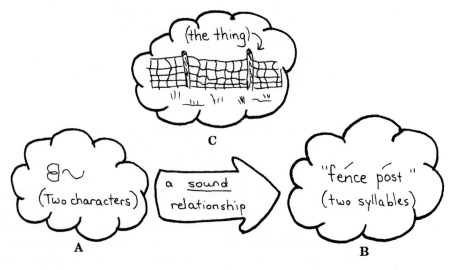

sult is that his own name is the meaningful printed array that he sees most often in his surroundings. It is certainly the message most children first attempt to write.

Writing their own names may teach children several lessons at once. Ferreiro notes that the child's own name provides the first real challenge to his early hypotheses about the relation of writing to language. The child who thinks the *size* of the graphic display should be related to the size of the referent must wonder as he looks at name labels why Ted is the biggest boy in the class, while he, Anthony, is among the smallest. In a similar vein, the child who relates the number of characters in a graphic display to the number of syllables in the word for which it stands will wonder why "Ma-ry" has four letters while "Keith" has five.

The children's early hypotheses cannot explain the spelling of their own and their classmates' names. So they look for new hypotheses. As we shall see in Part Two of this book, children's thinking about spelling will go through many interesting changes before they learn to spell correctly.

Learning to write one's own name carries with it another advantage for the learner. The name becomes a repertory of known letters. That is, letters that one gains in the course of learning to write one's own name can be recombined to form other words. Note in Figure 3–8 how Annabrook, age six, used many of the letters in her name to write two additional words. This, of course, is exactly what Marie Clay described as the generative principle, whereby children use a limited set of letters in varying combination to fill whole pages with print.

The child's own name as a repertory of known letters also pays off in a more abstract sense. As we noted in our discussion of Clay's flexibility principle, a beginning writer can start with a standard letter and embellish it until it becomes another letter. Thus, the letter L with a few more horizontal lines becomes Ŀ, E, Ɛ, and F, two of which are standard letters. Knowing how to write his own name may give a child a fairly good variety of letter forms, a point of departure for coming up with still other letter forms by means of the flexibility principle.

Figure 3–8
Annabrook
Grade 1

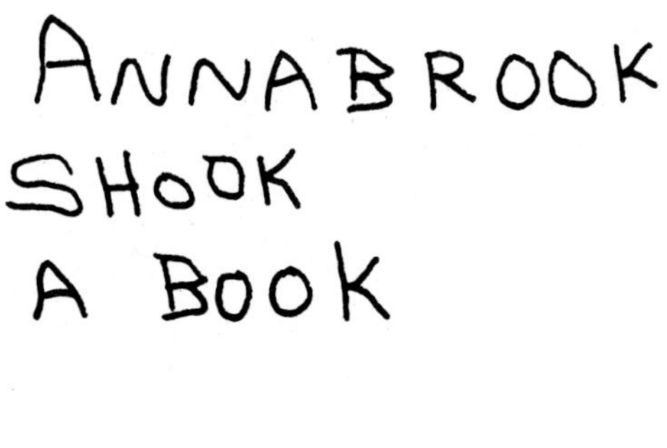

ANNABROOK
SHOOK
A BOOK

Strategies for Early Writing

Clay points to three common processes children use to begin writing words and longer messages—*tracing, copying,* and *generating.*[6] It is not claimed that children will always employ each of these processes in the order used here. However, tracing does seem to be the easiest of the three, with copying being the next most difficult, and generating being the most difficult process. Some children trace, then generate. Others copy, then generate.

Many children trace spontaneously, without being instructed to. Carlene, age four, traced first, then copied. Her sample gives an indication of the relative difficulty of the two tasks (Figure 3–9).

Note in Figure 3–10, however, that she was generating letterlike graphics at the same time she produced Figure 3–9. Her generated products are more abundant than those she either traced or copied, but they are not limited to standard letters. This conforms to a finding of Clay's, namely, that copying may be a shortcut to accuracy, but most children prefer to generate letter forms on their own over copying. Her subjects stayed at the task much longer when they were generating rather than copying.

Which strategy is best? Ultimately, we want children to be able to write letters on their own without having to rely on a model of correctly formed letters to copy. On the other hand, they must eventually learn to produce standard letter forms, not just invented ones. Generating letters is the process children should aim for, but they should pay attention to the details of standard letters. In our schools, many children need to be encouraged to take risks—to rely on their own devices and generate writing even if it's "wrong." Nevertheless, there are a few children who are less mindful than they should be of the ultimately conservative nature of the writing system; that is, that there *is* a right way to make each letter. Teachers can safely encourage children to generate, knowing that they will copy anyway. With an occasional child it may be necessary to encourage copying. In our opinion, copying is probably encouraged far more often than need be.

Figure 3–9
Carlene
Age 4

Figure 3–10
Carlene
Age 4

Children's own names are usually the first objects of print to be traced, copied, and eventually generated. But after performing these feats with their names, children do not hesitate to carry them out with other words, known or unknown.

The Inventory Principle

Clay noted that "until I observed five year olds closely I had no idea that they took stock of their own learning systematically."[7] She was referring to what she called the *inventory principle*—the widespread tendency of beginning writers to make ordered lists of letters or words they can write. Next to writing their own names, *listed inventories* are the most common objects of children's first writing efforts.

Jessica's first compositions consisted of inventories of letters she could write. These were the sole content of her writing for some months. Another first-grade child offered inventories when her teacher asked the whole class to write something about a picture. She did not feel free to compose on that topic, apparently, so she listed her known words instead (see Figure 3–11).

Figure 3–11
Linda
Grade 1

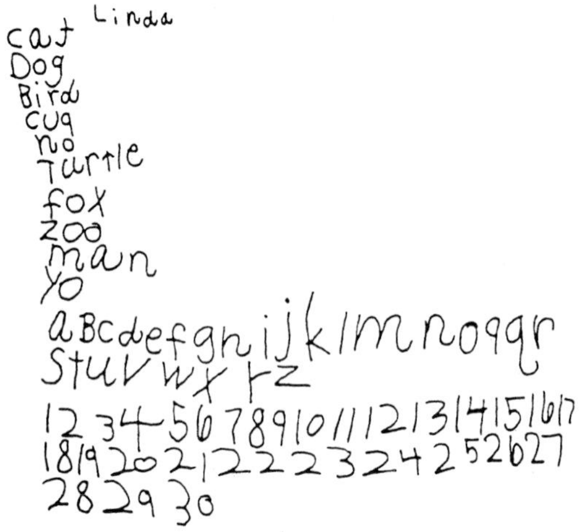

cat   Linda
Dog
Bird
cug
no
Turtle
fox
zoo
man
yo
aBcdefghijklmnoqqr
StuvwxYz
1 2 3 4 5 6 7 8 9 10 11 12 13 14 15 16 17
18 19 20 21 22 23 24 25 26 27
28 29 30

Encouraging Children to Make Print

As we said at the beginning of this book, a child who knows that language can be written down has made a discovery that must come before she can make any other advances in writing and reading. Such a child can think about the medium of her thoughts and messages and not just their contents; she knows that language is a thing. David Olson believes that this discovery comes early to children whose parents read to them from infancy.[8] Indeed, such children's initial learning about language may include a budding consciousness that the medium can be reflected on, recorded, and read. For these children, opportunities to explore and produce print in preschool and kindergarten will be a natural extension of what they already know.

But what about the other children? Although we may associate very early writing experiences with preschools and kindergartens that serve the middle class, such activities can provide experiences in literacy that are at least as essential to children from families that are poor and overworked, or unstable or neglectful or dominated by television or lacking in books and people to read them. Maria Montessori was the first to advocate giving children early experiences with writing before they began to read. Although her program is now fashionable with the well-heeled in North America, she developed it for the deprived children of Rome. And Marie Clay's study of five-year-olds' conceptions of written language, the subject of the previous chapter, was motivated by a need to learn about and help children who came from the diverse ethnic populations— some without traditions of literacy—that are served by the schools in New Zealand.

No, early writing is for the have-nots as much as for the haves. If we do not already, we should begin to conceive of preschools and kindergartens as places where all children—especially high-risk children—can gain rich exposure to the medium of print, by being read to and by having opportunities to produce print themselves. High-risk children can then be spared the often impossible task of learning what print is all about at the same time the first-grade program is trying to teach them to read.

The kind of encouragement children can profit by is of three types:

1. Having plenty of models of print at children's height around the classroom;
2. Having materials that the children can write upon, and utensils with which to write; and
3. Asking an occasional question, or setting up an occasional challenge, that will lead the child to emulate print.

Providing Models of Writing.   Probably the best way to encourage children to explore writing—both the act of writing and the writing that is produced—is to have plenty of models around for children to imitate. The obvious starting point for showing children models of print is to read to them. Reading to children on at least a daily basis is a necessary nutrient for their growing literacy. This is true for many reasons, one of which is that the children gain, by being read to, a notion that print is somehow a means to a desirable end—a good story. When reading to children, it is a good idea occasionally to point to the words as you read.

Marie Clay has found that many children entering school do not realize that in a storybook it is the print and not the pictures that provides the words that mother or father reads. Using a book that has both a picture and an array of print on a page, she tests this understanding by instructing the child, "Put your finger where I should read." She observes to see whether he puts his finger on the print or on the picture.[9]

There are static models of print, too. Obviously we label the child's desk and coathook; but labels on other things around the classroom are good sources of print: "clock," "coats," "flag," "paper," "crayons," and so forth. If the child draws a picture that the teacher wants to tape to the wall, it is useful to put the child's name on the picture. (For older children, the teacher can ask the child to "name" and describe the picture, writing the caption on the picture for him, too.) Things that belong to the child can be labeled, also. A crayon box with masking tape can be labeled, "Jimmy's Crayons."

Print makes messages. Print is arranged in horizontal displays. Print is made up of discrete graphic units, some of which are repeated, but never more than two right next to each other. All of these concepts can be brought home to children from meaningful print that is displayed in their surroundings.

Another sort of modeling that is valuable to children who may wish to explore writing is to have someone else write in their presence. Is writing a worthwhile activity? If it is, then adults should be seen doing it. Is writing a regular and important part of human communication? If it is, then adults should be seen doing it. For many adults, writing is a source of pleasure, an

Figure 3–12
Jessie
Age 4

opportunity to reflect and think clearly. It is sometimes an occasion of frustra-
tion and hard work. Do children get a chance to see teachers and other adults
approaching writing seriously? The ones who do are likely to be eager to get
started becoming writers, too.

One of the authors was writing a children's book one year, at a time
when her daughters were four and six years old. Every day the author would
go into her bedroom and sit down before the big drafting table. There, for one
or two hours, she would write and draw, throw away, and rewrite and re-
draw. Occasionally, the rest of the family got a glimpse of what she had produced. The children were captivated by the mystery of the quiet room where
mother would go and create, and enthralled by the fragments of story and
flashes of colorful pictures mother would share with them when she came
out.

Soon the four-year-old had taken to stealing quietly away to her bedroom, too. She would stay sometimes for twenty or thirty minutes at a
stretch, after which she would bring out writings for the rest of the family to
read (see Figure 3–12). Fourteen years have passed, and the girl's writing has
picked up rules of spelling and composition, style, and originality; she has
never really stopped writing since the day she decided to imitate her mother.

Teachers should take every opportunity to write important messages to
others in the school and explain to the children what they are doing: "Look,
I'm writing a note to the lunchroom to let them know our class will be going
on a field trip during lunchtime tomorrow. See? I'm starting it out, 'Dear Mrs.

Washington . . .' See the letter 'D'? Now who will deliver the letter for me when I'm through?"

The central message teachers put across to children when they write in front of them is that writing is important—it is a worthy use of time. But there must be other messages as well. All of the *dynamic* principles of writing must be observed in process to be understood. If writing proceeds from left to right, then children must see someone doing it to comprehend this point. If writing can record a message and convey it to a distant receiver, then children must participate in the drama of remembering absent friends, thinking of messages for them, writing the messages down, sealing them up, and mailing them out.

To whom can young "prewriters" write? Certainly to a classmate who is home with an illness, to a visitor who is coming to the class, to a person in the school who has done the children a special favor or who needs cheering up.

Writing Materials in the Early Childhood Classroom.   What materials are best for children to use when they are first writing? Almost anything will do, the only guiding considerations being (l) the safety of the child, (2) the well-being of your classroom walls and furniture, and (3) cheapness and convenience.

Safety concerns would militate against giving a sharp pencil to a very young child. But very young children do not sustain an interest in writing anyway. By the time children do become interested in writing—say, in their fourth and fifth years—a standard-size pencil is a fine thing for them to write with. We normally hear that children should use the big, fat "primary pencils" first. But children seem to find them unwieldy, and they are disappointed by the faint and indistinct silver trails they leave on paper. Our children prefer a *pencil* pencil, though they like colored marking pens even better.

For safety's sake, it is a good idea to make a rule against children moving around the classroom with pencils in hand, or generally crowding up on each other when they are writing. Writing is inherently a quiet and solitary activity, and writers know it. These rules are more necessary to enforce for the nonwriters in your classroom than the writers; that is, you sometimes have to point out to a child not to leap on the back of another child who is writing.

Practically any sort of paper is good for children to use to explore writing. It is probably best if it is not lined. Dealing with the proper height and staying on a horizontal line are unnecessarily difficult concerns to a child who is simply fooling around with the letter forms. The lines do not seem to help at first and may even be a hindrance. Therefore, there is no reason why parents or preschool teachers should buy paper for children to write on. The back side of practically any paper will do. Old memos from the office are perfect. Even better, perhaps, is computer paper, since the big format seems to invite big ideas. Any university computer center and most businesses have used computer paper around.

Suggestions That Get Children Writing.   In addition to modeling writing and providing writing materials, a teacher can lead children to find challenge and delight in writing by well-considered and timely suggestions. The best of these suggestions seem to be situational. That is, a person who spends time with a child or a group of children will know the things that interest them and can often extend this interest into writing with a good suggestion.

A friend of ours invites her child to write each time she writes herself. When the mother is writing out a grocery list, she hands her daughter a piece of paper and asks her to make out a list of things she wants to buy, too.

Another parent works writing into the children's play. If a child comes to her and complains that her brother is not picking up his shoes from the living room floor, the mother says: "I'll tell you what. You be the policeman and write him a ticket. You can leave the ticket in his shoes."

Of course these writings will be unreadable by a stranger, but in the context of the situation they were written in, they have meaning. And they are fun ways for children to begin to explore writing. This sort of idea works in the classroom as well as at home.

Children like to be invited to slip a note into a letter that their parents are writing to a friend or relative. Contributing a note—whether it is on a separate piece of paper or is written on the bottom of someone else's page—is less responsibility than writing the whole letter, even if it is understood that the child doesn't really know how to write. The child knows that the parent can explain what the child meant to say; but it is an added pleasure to the recipient of the letter to hear directly from the child.

Another suggestion that works in some classrooms is for the teacher to hand the child some paper and some markers and invite her to write something. For many children, that is all they need to get started. But occasionally a child will not write. Perhaps it is reluctance to do something he knows he does not do correctly. After all, a child who has seen models of print around him in books recognizes immediately that what he himself writes on paper looks almost nothing like what he sees in books (which is another reason why the teacher's own writing is a very important model for children who are beginning writers). How do we get such children started? The first advice is for the teacher to write in the child's presence—and then invite the child to try it. But if that doesn't work, the teacher might show the child a page from this book. Show the child another child's bold efforts to make things that look like writing. We've known children to say, "Oh, I can do better than *that!*" and then write up a storm.

More Ideas for Encouraging Early Writing.   In recent years, many preschool teachers have come up with effective ways to work reading and writing into the fabric of the children's day. Dorothy Strickland and Lesley Morrow had a regular column in *The Reading Teacher* in the late 1980s in which they described proven ways to engage children naturally with print. One of the ideas was to organize materials in a play center around a theme that naturally used writing. For example:

- A *neighborhood grocery store center* has shelves of empty cans and boxes of the different food groups (labels intact, of course). There is a cash register with money, a telephone, a pad and pencil for taking down orders, and a map for deciding where to take deliveries.
- A *veterinarian's office* has a waiting room stocked with magazines and children's books and a sign that says NO SMOKING. The receptionist's desk has an appointment book, appointment cards, and a telephone directory. The veterinarian herself has a prescription pad and folders with paper for writing notes about patients.
- A *short-order restaurant* has a menu, signs advertising food, an order pad, a cash register, and money. The chefs have recipes to use during cooking.
- A *newspaper office* has reporters' desks, pads, press passes, maps of the city, a telephone and phone book, and, of course, newspapers.

Activities that grow out of play centers such as those just described[10] will be more engaging if the children have taken field trips to the sites that they simulate and if a teacher or aide goes into the center and encourages play that employs print. In a multitude of ways, reading and writing can be made an integral and enjoyable part of children's school experience.

Conclusion

The earliest stage of writing is a sort of make-believe—children make designs that look like writing but are still a long way from the real thing. Like other kinds of children's play, this make-believe writing is serious business—it is experience from which children learn.

As Ferreiro has shown us, children may be speculating on the ways in which written marks can represent ideas. They also seem to be experimenting to see where writing comes from, whether it is most efficiently produced by tracing, copying, or by generating marks of their own.

Finally, as in many other areas of endeavor, early writers are forming attitudes and behavior patterns. Some approach the task of writing with curiosity, energy, and confidence; others do not approach it at all. Some seek to make their own sense of how the writing system works; other wait to be shown. Some children experiment boldly and make mistakes; other do not experiment for fear of making mistakes. Some of the differences between children are attributable, no doubt, to deep-seated differences in personality. But to a degree, children's daring, initiative, and enthusiasm can be encouraged by parents and teachers. In the case of writing, it is certainly in the best interests of children to give them this encouragement.

ENDNOTES

1. This discussion of Chinese writing and our later discussion of Japanese writing is taken from Diane Wolff, *An Easy Guide to Everyday Chinese* (New York: Harper Colophon Books, 1974).
2. Wolff, p.26.
3. For an in-depth look at syllabic writing systems, which were used extensively in ancient times, see Ignace Gelb, *A Study of Writing* (Chicago: University of Chicago Press, 1963).
4. Gelb.
5. Emilia Ferreiro and Ana Teberosky, *Writing before Schooling* (Portsmouth, NH: Heinemann, 1975).
6. Marie Clay, *What Did I Write?* (Portsmouth, NH: Heinemann, 1975).
7. Clay, p. 31.
8. David Olson, "'See? Jumping!' Some Oral Antecedents of Literacy," in Hillel Goelman, Antoinette Goldberg, and Frank Smith, eds., *Awakening to Literacy* (Portsmouth, NH: Heinemann, 1984).
9. Marie Clay, *Concepts about Print Test* (Portsmouth, NH: Heinemann, 1975).
10. Dorothy Strickland and Lesley Morrow, "Emerging Readers and Writers," *The Reading Teacher*, 43, 2 (Nov. 1989): 178–179.

PART TWO

The Beginnings
of Spelling

A four-year-old produces a string of letterlike forms that looks like writing (see Figure 1). A five-year-old deliberates carefully, inscribes a sparse collection of letters on the page, and claims it says, "Our car broke down" (see Figure 2).

These two presentations differ in more than appearance. The four-year-old is trying to make forms that look like writing, but the five-year-old is trying to make her letters do what writing does.

Writing uses marks to represent words. The marks represent words according to a socially agreed upon set of relationships. In some writing systems like Chinese, the relationship holds between symbols and whole words. In others like Japanese, it holds between symbols and syllables. In alphabetic systems like English, it holds between symbols and individual speech sounds, or *phonemes* as they are called. Anyone who wants to write must know what unit of language written symbols represent.

The would-be writer must also know how the symbols do the representing. In our English language, particularly, weathered old tongue that it is, the relations between symbols and phonemes have become

Figure 1
Jessie
Age 4
These letters represent no sounds

Figure 2
Five-year-old
This says, "Our car broke down."

55

somewhat peculiar—knowable, but peculiar. Beginning writers of English seem to proceed like this: They first discover the unit of language the symbols are to represent (word, syllable, or phoneme); they invent a plausible way for the symbols to represent language units; then they revise their invented spelling in favor of the standard spelling.

CHAPTER 4

Invented Spelling

The Disappointments of English Spelling

Some years ago George Bernard Shaw told of an acquaintance of his named Fish, who did not like the conventional way of writing his name and came up with the spelling GHOTIUGH. This spelling, he argued, found precedent in the spelling of common English words. The letters GH for the sound of *f* in his name was established in the spelling of the word "tou*gh*"; the O for the short sound of *i* is found in "w*o*men"; the TI for *sh* is heard in words like "ini*ti*al," "ter*ti*ary," and "spa*ti*al"; finally, the letters UGH are silent, as in "tho*ugh.*"

This story points out some of the more bizarre relations that seem to obtain between sounds in English words and the letters that represent them. And if each letter in a word is to have a clearly identifiable sound, some disappointment is inevitable. Just look at the spellings of some of the following words: What is the sound of the *i* in "complaint"? Of the *e* in "failure"? Of the second *l* in "spellings"? Of the *a* in "each"? And of the *h* in "paragraph"?

A large portion of the words in English contain letters that do not themselves directly represent sounds. Look, however, at the words in the sentences in Figures 4–1 and 4–2, written by the beginning speller, Annabrook.

Figure 4–1
Annabrook
Grade 1
Invented
spelling

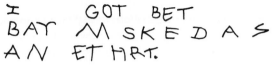

(I got bit by mosquitoes and it hurt.)

Figure 4–2
Annabrook
Grade 1
Invented
spelling

(I am going to Virginia and I have a headache.)

Every one of Annabrook's letters represents a sound. There are no "silent" letters, no extra letters at all.

The early spellings that children produce on their own—we call them invented spellings—observe the same dictum: letters talk. Any letter that a child puts in a word is intended to represent some sound.

Why children select the letters they do to represent sounds presents a problem. Why is Virginia spelled FR JEYE? Why does it begin with the letter F? Why are the last two vowels E's? Why is "bit" spelled BET and not BIT? Why does "it," ET, follow the same pattern? As we shall see in this chapter, there are usually very good reasons why young spellers choose the letters they do to represent sounds. Seen together, these reasons constitute what has been called a system of spelling "logic."[1] Our purpose in this chapter will be to make this logic explicit, so that the reader can understand invented spelling the same way a child does.

Letter-Name Spelling

Recall the sample we saw in Chapter 1: YUTS A LADE YET FEHEG AD HE KOT FLEPR ("Once a lady went fishing and she caught Flipper"). This sample fits the pattern we have just described: Every letter in the sample stands for a sound, and no letters are supplied unnecessarily. Let's try to determine why the child chose the letters she did to represent the sounds in those words.

Notice the spelling YUTS for "once" and YET for "went." Why the letter Y for the sound we normally represent with a letter W? The answer lies in the name by which each letter is known. The letter Y is "wye" and W called "double-yu." Which name sounds more like the beginning sound "once" and "went"?

The child who wrote YUTS A LADE . . . is apparently using a letter to spell a sound if the name of the letter closely resembles the sound. This technique for spelling has been called the *letter-name strategy*. The letter-name strategy accounts for the spellings of almost all the letters in YUTS A LADE YET FEHEG AD HE KOT FLEPR.

Two factors influence the use of the letter-name strategy in determining which letters will represent what sounds in a word. The first factor is the availability (or lack) of a good letter-name-to-sound match. The English alphabet has twenty-six letters, but the English language has forty-four standard sounds, or phonemes. Some of the sounds children wish to spell have ready matches in letter names. For others, no direct letter-name matches exist. In these latter cases, children will select the nearest fit and have good reasons—albeit subconscious ones—for the selections they make.

The second factor involved in the choice of letters for spellings has more to do with the sounds in words themselves. As we noted above, when speech sounds come together in words, some odd things happen to them. Some sounds are changed around, and children perceive changes that we don't and tend to spell what they hear. Some are overshadowed by others and not heard distinctly. Let's consider a range of possible sound and letter combinations and see what happens when children put the letter-name strategy into practice.

Initial Consonants

As Daryl's sample shows (Figure 4–3), initial consonants—consonants that come at the beginning of a word—usually find close matches to letter names. The name "ell" has in it the first sound in the word "live." "Tee" for "Texas " is clear enough, as is "em" for "my." Note that "gee" does not match the initial consonant sound in "Goliad," which begins like "gold." Neither does the letter name "aitch" sound anything like the beginning sound of "house." Daryl has learned that letter G represents the beginning sound of "gold" and that the letter H represents the "huh" sound in the beginning of "house."

The letter N in Daryl's sentence stands for the word "in"—a reasonable procedure since the name of the letter sounds the same as the word.

A sample of Daryl's writing taken a month later shows the initial consonants still being unambiguously represented and his words filled out in other ways, too (see Figure 4–4). In this sample, the G's and the H's are used correctly—not as letter-name matches, but for their representational value.

What sort of problems do beginning consonants present young spellers? Which ones work by letter name and which ones by an arbitrary presentational relationship? Table 4–1 lists all the consonants that have a stable and predictable letter-name match.

Figure 4–3
Daryl
Grade 1
Early invented
spelling

(I live in Goliad, Texas.)

Figure 4–4
Daryl
Grade 1
Later invented
spelling

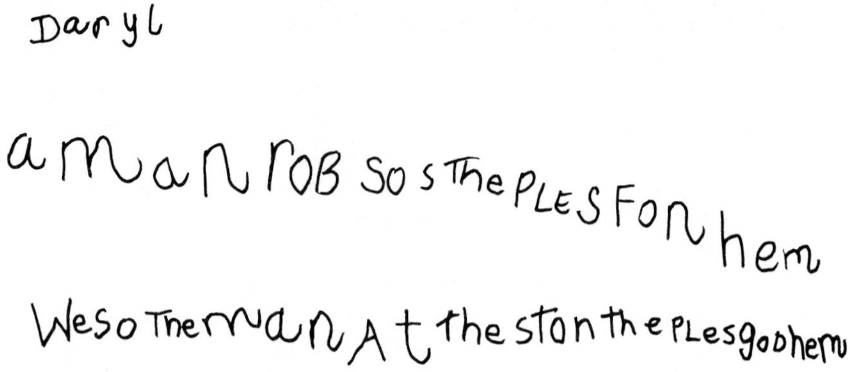

Daryl

a maN roB so s The PLeS FoN hem

Weso TherNuaNA t the sTon the PLesgooheru

(A man robbed shoes. The police found him. We saw the man at the store. The police got him.)

Sound	Letter	Examples
b as in bat	B	BBGON (B B gun) BABE (baby) B (be) BEG (big) BLW (blue)
p as in pat	P	PEC (pick) PAT (pet) PLAG (playing) POGOSTECK (pogo stick) PANS (pants)
f as in fat	F	FEH (fish) FES (friends) FEN (friend) FOWS (flowers) FAS (face) AFTR (after)
v as in very	V	HAV (have) LUV (love) LEV (live) VOT (vote)
m as in man	M	MI (my) HOM (home) MENEKDE (manicotti) GAM (game) MOTR (mother)
n as in note	N	NAM (name) NIS (nice) EN (in) BLON (balloon) NAW (now)
t as in tan	T	TXS (Texas) TIM (time) DOT (don't) WUT (what) SURT (shirt)
d as in Dan	D	DOT (don't) GLEAD (Goliad) DESES (dishes) TODA (today)
s as in sun	S	BICS (bikes) HAS (house) SCIEY (sky) SIK (sick) SUMS (swims)

Table 4–1
Letter-name
matches for
consonants

Sound   *Letter*   *Examples*

Sound	Letter	Examples
k as in kick	K	SIK (sick) WRCK (work) KAT (can't) SKIY (sky) SEK (sick) TAK (take)
j as in joke	J	JOPT (jumped) JEP (jeep)
z as in zoo	Z	PLEZ (please) ZB (zebra)
l as in lay	L	LETL (little) LAS (last) PLES (police) PLANS (planes) BLON (balloon) LAT (let)
r as in ray	R	RETTE (ready) RAD (red) GRAON (ground) STOR (store)

Other consonants, like G and H, do not have a letter-name match with the sounds they normally represent. Nevertheless, they regularly represent one sound, and they appear frequently enough to be learned easily by children. Table 4–2 shows these *representational* consonants.

Spellings like WRRX for "works" and HAWS for "house" are so strange to the eye it is safe to conclude that the children who created them were not imitating anyone else or dimly remembering a standard spelling they had seen somewhere. These are 100 percent original! Yet as far from standard

Table 4–2
Representational consonants

Sound	Letter	Examples
k as in kick	C	CENT (can't) PEC (pick) CUM (come) CLAS (clouds) CADY (candy)
g as in good	G	GUD (good) GAM (game) GLEAD (Goliad) GOWE (going) GIT (get)
h as in hay	H	HOO (who) HED (head) HEM (him) HAS (house) HORS (horse)
w as in way	W	WUT (what) WET (went) WEO (will) WERRE (wearing) WEH (with) WRRX (works)
y as in yes	Y	YALO (yellow) YOR (your) YASEDA (yesterday) YIU (you)

spelling as they are, they do employ the consonants C, G, H, W, and Y to represent their standard sound values. So the children must have learned something about spelling from someone outside of themselves; these relationships cannot be invented.

Another type of consonant representation that children have more difficulty mastering is the spelling of consonant digraphs.

Consonant Digraphs

Anyone who trains as a reading teacher comes across the terms *consonant blend* and *consonant digraph*. After a few years of teaching, though, a person is likely to have forgotten the difference between them. Knowing the difference between a blend and a digraph is probably not necessary to successful reading instruction. But digraphs do present serious challenges to young spellers.

The word "digraph" comes from the Greek, meaning "double writing." It describes a single sound spelled with two letters. The "ph" in "digraph" is a digraph, since the two letters together spell a single sound, which is often represented by the letter F.

The *gr* sound in the word "digraph" is not a digraph but a blend. Blends occur when the letters that represent two or three distinct consonant sounds are pronounced closely together. *Cl* in "closely" is a blend, as is the *bl* in "blend." Blends differ from digraphs in that it is possible to hear each of the sounds that make up a blend, if you pronounce the blend slowly. The same is not true of digraphs. No matter how slowly you pronounce the word "digraph," you will never hear separate sounds for the p and h.

Young spellers seem to perceive correctly that digraphs represent one sound. What they do not know is that digraphs have to be spelled with two letters and not one. So inventive spellers are forced to puzzle out which individual letters are best suited to represent digraphs. Note in Figure 4–5 what one first grader did with the digraphs.

The digraph *th* received three different spellings. "The " was correct, but it is likely that Joey had memorized the spelling of this word as a whole. In "they" he spelled it T, twice. In "each other," IHOVR, he spelled it V; and he used the same spelling for *th* the second time he wrote "the."

Note, too, his spelling of the digraph *ch* in "each other," IHOVR. In both digraphs, *th* and *ch*, Joey's tendency was to represent the single sound with a single letter.

Figure 4–5
Joey
Grade 1
Note spellings
of th

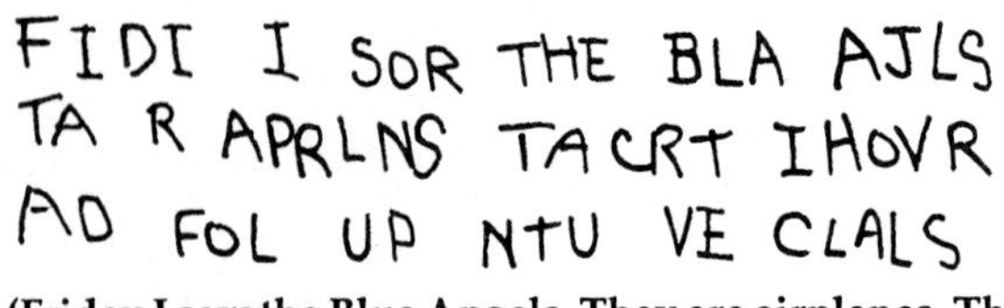

FIDI I SOR THE BLA AJLS
TA R APRLNS TA CRT IHOVR
AO FOL UP NTU VE CLALS

(Friday I saw the Blue Angels. They are airplanes. They crossed each other and flew up into the clouds.)

On what basis did he choose the letters to represent the sounds? Again, the basis seems to be the similarity between the sound to be represented and the name of a letter of the alphabet. The spelling of the H in IHOVR is an interesting example of this. Say to yourself the letter name H ("aitch"). Note the *ch* sound contained in that name. If you sound out the names of all the letters of the alphabet, you will not find another that contains the sound *ch*. Of all the single letters that could spell the digraph ch, the letter H is the best choice.

There is no such clear candidate to represent the digraph *th*. The child made two inventive entries: T and V. In order to understand why those two consonants are good choices to represent the sound of *th*, we must digress for a moment to explore the question of how we make consonant sounds.

How We Make Speech Sounds: A Long but Necessary Digression

To begin, it won't surprise anyone to hear that breath is the substance of speech. But there is more to speech than breathing. We direct our breath through the vocal bands in the throat, and the resulting vibration of these vocal bands makes the sound that we call our voice. Stretching or loosening these bands makes the pitch of our voice go up or down.

Breath and vocal bands, however, still do not give us speech. The activation of those two alone will enable us to (1) cry and (2) ooh and ah. (No wonder these are children's first utterances!) But we still cannot *say* anything without adding something more.

What we add is the *shaping* activity of the tongue, lips, teeth, mouth, and nasal passages. How do all these so-called shapers work together to form speech sounds, like the ones represented by the letters B, Y, A, Z, CH, and so on?

When we breathe through our vocal cords and set them vibrating, and then allow the sound to pass uninterrupted through the mouth and out into the air, we have produced a vowel. Say "ahhhh" and you will see that this is so. All spoken languages employ several vowels. We produce different ones depending on the position of the tongue when the vibrated air passes through the mouth. After saying "ahhh" say "eeeee"; if you pay attention to your tongue, you will see that this is so. We will say more about vowels later.

Consonants are made when we use the shapers in the mouth to interrupt the flow of vibrating air through the mouth. For example, when we say "ahhh," and then open and close the lips repeatedly, we produce a series of *b*'s: "ababababab." If we stop the air flow by repeatedly raising the back of the tongue against the roof of the mouth, we get a series of *g*'s: "gagagag." And if we stop the flow by hitting the tip of the tongue against the fleshy ridge right behind our upper front teeth, we get a series of *d*'s: "adadadad." Try it and see.

Consonants are produced by interrupting the flow of vibrated air through the mouth. But *which* consonant we make depends on three further concerns: (1) the *place* in the mouth where we make the interruption; (2) the *manner* of the activity that produces the interruption; and (3) whether or not the vocal cords are vibrating while the interruption is being made (*voicing*).

The three consonants we just produced, *b, g,* and *d,* were alike in the *manner* in which they were made: All three temporarily stopped the air flow—in linguistic parlance they are therefore called *stops.* They were also alike in that the vocal cords were vibrating as we made them—they are therefore said to be *voiced.* They differed only in the *places* they were made: the *b* on both lips, the *g* between the back of the tongue and the rearward roof of the mouth, and the *d* between the tip of the tongue and the ridge behind the front teeth.

Now let's try some variations. Hold your fingers over your Adam's apple and say "abababab" again. With your fingers still in place, now substitute *p:* "apapapap." Notice the difference? The sound of the letter *p* is like *b* in both *place* and *manner;* it differs only in being *unvoiced*—that is, the vocal chords don't vibrate as it is made. Try alternating "agagagag" with "akakakakak "—*g* and *k* are alike except that *k* is *unvoiced.* The same is true of *d* and *t, z* and *s, ch* and *j,* the *th* in "thin" and *th* in "their." All of these pairs are alike in the *place* and *manner* in which they are made, but different in *voicing.* These facts have consequences for children's spelling.

Try another variation. Say the sound of the letter D—"duh." Notice the spot on the fleshy ridge behind your teeth where your tongue tapped. Now hold your tongue just short of touching that spot and blow air out through the constricted space over your tongue. You should hear a sound like that of the letter S. Now, if instead of blowing out, you say "ahhh" while you raise your tongue to that same spot (raise it until you hear a whistle, but don't let it touch), you should hear a sound like that of Z. You will be saying "ozzzzzz." Two points: First, we have demonstrated that the sounds of *s* and *z* are alike except for voicing. Second, we have demonstrated another manner of making consonants—by restricting the air flow so that we hear a sort of whistling friction.

The name *fricative* is applied to consonants made in this manner. Let's make some others. Say "ozzzzzzzzzzz" again. While you are saying it, slide your tongue forward and down, until it is behind the upper front teeth themselves and almost—but not quite—touching them. You should hear the sound *th* of "then." If you'll leave off saying the "ahh" part and just whistle air through that space, you will hear the other *th* of "thin." The two *th*'s, *then* and *thin,* are voiced and unvoiced fricatives, respectively.

Here's another pair of fricatives. Place your lower lip against your upper teeth in Bugs Bunny fashion. Now say "ahhh" again, and you should hear a *v* sound: "ahhvvvvvv." If you turn off the voicing and just blow air out through the space, you should hear a long *f* sound. The sounds of *f* and *v* are alike in the *place* and *manner* in which they are made, but different in *voicing.*

There are other manners in which consonants are made and other places also. But our brief exploration should enable us to answer an important question: Suppose a child wants to represent a sound in spelling a word, but he cannot find a perfect fit with a letter name. He chooses a near fit—a letter name that is *somewhat* like the sound he wants to represent. In what specific ways can sounds of letters be *like* each other or *unlike* each other?

Our discussion of consonants provides a way of answering. Speech sounds—for instance, sounds of consonants—can be like each other in the *place* and *manner* in which they are made, and perhaps in *voicing*. With these features in mind, let's return to our examination of digraphs.

A Return to Digraphs

Digraphs present a special problem in invented spelling because children don't accept the notion that two letters can represent one sound. So they are forced to search for a single letter whose name sounds most like the sound they wish to spell, a sound that adults represent with a digraph. This sometimes causes them to make some strange looking substitutions.

In Figure 4–5, Joey represented the *th* sound of "then" (the *voiced* sound) five times. He spelled it once correctly in "the," a word he probably had memorized. Twice he spelled it with the letter T, and twice with the letter V. His inconsistency is strange, but his choice of letters makes sense.

Remember that the *th* sound is made by placing the tongue behind the front teeth and vibrating (fricating as linguists would say) forced air between the tongue and the teeth. To make the sound *t*, we touched the tongue to the fleshy ridge just behind the front teeth—a place very close to the place where *th* is made. The sound of *t* stops the air, though, and it is unvoiced. But we can say *t* is quite similar to *th* in the *place* where it was made.

The letter V for the sound of *th* appears to be a stranger choice. But recall that the sound of *v* is made by a frication, just as *th* is, and that it is voiced just as *th* is. These two facts, plus the fact that *v* is made in the forward region of the mouth, make the sound *v* fairly similar to *th* and hence justify the spelling V for the *th* sound.

The sound represented by the digraph *sh* gets various spellings in children's inventions. The spelling S for it, in Figure 4–6, is frequently offered. The letter S seems to be a natural choice, first because it is one of the letters of the digraph *sh* and the child may have remembered seeing it in other words. But the letter S is a good choice, too, because it is identical in *voicing* and *manner* to the sound of *sh* and very near it in the *place* in which it is made. If you make a long hissing stream of S's, then change to make the *shhhh* sound without stopping the air flow, you'll find that your tongue simply moved back a

Figure 4–6
Susie
Grade 1
Note spelling
of "dishes"

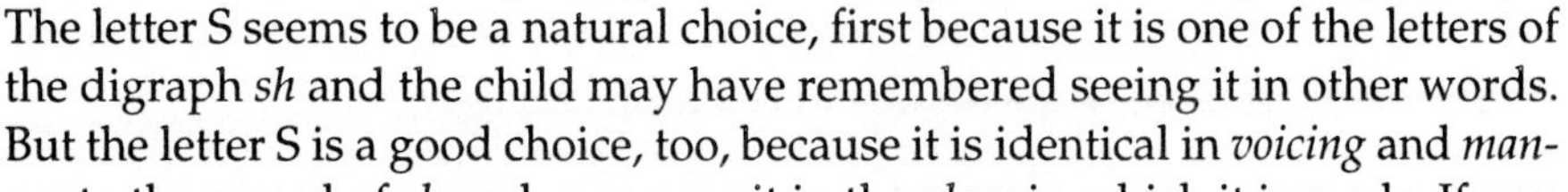

Susie

I got BaBeyulivardsumdesesandaPogoSteck.

(I got Baby Alive and some dishes and a pogo stick.)

	Sound	Letter	Examples
Table 4–3 *Digraph* *consonants*	*ch* as in chip	H	HRP (chirp) IHOVR (each other) TEHR (teacher)
	sh as in ship	H	FIH (fish) FEH (fish) HE (she)
	sh as in ship	S or C	SOS (shoes) COO (show) SES (she's)
	th as in the	T	BATEG (bathing) TA (they) MOTR (mother) GRAMUTR (grandmother)

fraction of an inch along the roof of your mouth while you continued to blow the air through.

When children invent spellings, they virtually always come up with something other than standard spellings for consonant digraphs. Table 4–3 shows some frequently offered inventions for them.

"But," you may ask, "surely children do not deliberately set out to find consonants that are alike in place, manner, and voicing—what five-year-old ever used these terms?"

Let us remind you of our earlier discussion of language development. There we said that children learn to talk by developing a system of language rules that enables them to understand and produce speech. We see evidence, for example, in the three-year-old's statement "I got tiny foots" that the child has formed a *rule* to the effect that plurals are formed by adding the letter S to a noun. We doubt, though, that a three-year-old would give you a definition of the word "noun" or "plural" or even "word." Nevertheless, on some level she knows what a noun is because she only pluralizes nouns—not adjectives, adverbs, or prepositions. We conclude that she knows some things about language on a working level that she can't explain.

The same is true of spelling. If you watch a youngster invent spellings, you will see and hear him exaggerating the production of speech sounds: whistling her S's, stabbing repeatedly at her D's, choo-chooing her H's. On a

Figure 4–7
Melissa
Grade 1
Note omissions
of n's

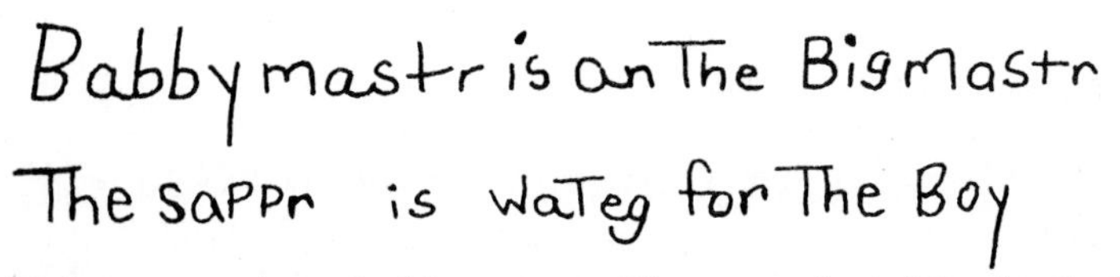

Babby mastr is on The Big mastr
The sappr is waTeg for The Boy

(Baby monster is on the big monster. The supper is waiting for the boy.)

working level she is exploring place, manner, and voicing. But if you ask her what she's doing—"Writing you a letter," she says!

Nasal Consonants: The Letters N and M

When children invent spelling they do so by breaking a word into its individual sounds and finding a letter to represent each sound. This point, we hope, has been made abundantly clear. But if children represent sounds they hear, how do we account for the peculiar case of N and M? These sounds quite often go unspelled, even by children who have otherwise demonstrated a keen ear and an inventive hand. Note, for example, the omission of the N's in

YUTS A LADE YET FEHEG AD HE KOT FLEPR.

Surely a child resourceful enough to think of using the letter Y for the sound *w* and the letter H for the sound of *sh* could find a spelling for an *n* sound if she wanted to. Notice, too, that *n* and *m* sounds are often spelled by children in some words. Sometimes on the same paper *n* and *m* will be spelled in one spot and left out in another, as in Figure 4–7.

What factors might there be in the *position* of the *n* and *m* sounds in words that would lead to their being spelled in one place and not spelled in another? Study Figure 4–7 again and see if you can answer this question. The factor that decides whether an *n* or *m* sound will be spelled or not is what follows it. If a vowel comes after an *n* or *m* sound or if either comes at the end of a word, these consonants will be spelled. Accordingly, the N is spelled in NIS ("nice") and SNAK ("snack"), and the M is spelled in SMIL ("smile").

On the other hand, when the sounds of *n* or *m* are followed by some other consonant, they often go unspelled. Thus, the letter N is omitted from YET ("went"), AD ("and"), FEHEG ("fishing"), and YUTS ("once"). Knowing where the N's and M's are omitted, however, does not explain why they are. We might venture a guess that the following consonant somehow overshadows the N or M, so that the child doesn't *hear* it, and hence, omits it. But is it the case that he doesn't hear the sound? We can easily test this out. Just ask a three-year-old to point to your "lap," and then to point to your "lamp," and see if he can distinguish the two. If he can, he can hear the *m* sound. The same test could be made with the words "land" and "lad," "crowd" and "crowned," "stained" and "stayed." If the child can tell the difference between the two words, he can hear the *n* and the *m* sounds. As it turns out, children can hear *n* and *m* in these environments well before the age when they begin to create invented spellings.

If they know how to spell *n* and *m* sounds in other positions, and they can hear these sounds when they are followed by consonants, then why don't they spell them in such cases? How *do* we account for the spellings YET for "went" and YUTS for "once"?

When we pronounce the *n* sound, we place the tongue in the same spot where *d, t, j,* and *ch* are made: the fleshy ridge behind the front teeth. In fact, when the sound of *n* is followed by any of these latter consonants, it is impos-

Sound	Letter	Examples
m	M	LAP (lamp) BOPE (bumpy) LEP (limp) STAP (stamp)
n	N	RAD (rained) WET (went) GOWEG (going) CADE (candy) AJLS (angels)

Table 4–4
N and M before other consonants

sible to tell from the activity inside the mouth whether the *n* is present or not. You can demonstrate this by repeating these pairs of words over and over: "witch–winch," "plant–plat," and "dote–don't."

We *hear* the *n* sound in these words, though—so how is it made? Hold your nose and say these pairs again. When *n* is present in a word, the air is resonated out through the nose while the *n* and the vowel preceding it are pronounced. When *n* is followed by a consonant made in the same place, the nasal resonance is the only feature of the *n* that is heard.

Since the nasalization is more of an influence on the vowel than on the consonant, many beginning spellers seem to assume that what they hear in "plant," "went," and "once" is a peculiar vowel, not an extra consonant. As we shall shortly see, children adjust early to the idea that a single vowel letter may spell variations of a vowel sound. Thus in YET for "went," the E may be intended to stand for both the sounds of *e* and *n*.

The sound *m* works the same way, except that it is made on both lips, where *p* is also made. When *m* occurs before *p*, as in "lamp," it is typically not spelled, because the *m* then acts as a nasalization of the vowel preceding the *p*. You can demonstrate this by pronouncing "lap–lamp," "stomp–stop," and "chip-chimp."

Some common examples of omitted nasal consonants—N and M—are presented in Table 4–4.

Invented Spelling of Long Vowels
"Long vowels say their names." That useful piece of first-grade lore is true enough. Judging from their writings, though, this rule need not be pointed out to many children; they know it already (see Figure 4–8). Of course, when long vowels occur in words, correct spelling usually will not let them stand alone and still say their names. They can in "A" and "I" and also in "he," "she," "go," and "so." But "stay," "late," "bone," "see," and the like require that the vowels be *marked* to indicate their longness. Inventive spellers leave off these markers, and this is one indication that they are inventing. The spellings that result are like those shown in Table 4–5.

Invented Spelling of Short Vowels
Short vowels do not say their own names or provide any other very good hint as to the way they should be spelled. Nevertheless, children often do figure out a consistent strategy for spelling short vowels. This strategy, like the

Figure 4–8
Ronnen
Grade 1
Note long
vowel spellings

MI Parit
Mi Parit is olwas clrfol
he lics to fli he lics to CrPe
he olwas lics to Pla.

(My parrot is always colorful. He likes to fly. He likes to chirp. He always likes to play.)

Table 4–5
Long or "tense"
vowels

Sound	Letter	Examples
$\bar{a}$	A	LADE (lady) PLA (play) TA (they) NAM (name)
$\bar{e}$	E	PLES (police) MNEKDE (manicotti)
$\bar{i}$	I	MI (my) FLI (fly) TRID (tried) SLIDEG (sliding) BIT (bite)
$\bar{o}$	O	JOD (Jody) DOT (don't)
$\bar{u}$	U, O	SOS (shoes) NTU (into)

omission of nasal consonants, reveals a surprising ability to hear and to make judgments about speech sounds.

In the samples in Figures 4–9 and 4–10, how are the children solving the problem of spelling the short $\breve{i}$ sound? These two children consensed on a spelling of E for the $\breve{i}$ sound. Why did they?

JOD ETS sPrng.

(Jody. It is spring.)

TheLaTisOGeKeG

(The lady is drinking.)

Figure 4–9
Jody
Grade 1
Note spelling of $\breve{i}$

Figure 4–10
Kindergartner
Note spelling of $\breve{i}$

The best explanation for children's representing the *ĭ* sound with the letter E is provided by Charles Read.[2] Read's explanation starts with the letter-name strategy for matching speech sounds with written letters. When children spell "fish" FEH, they use the letter E for the sound of the letter's name, which is long—*ē*. They use the letter name E because they perceive a similarity between the *long sound of ē* and the *short sound of ĭ*.

Let's see how inventive spellers solve the problem of spelling the short *ĕ* sound. As in the word "pet," the short sound of *ĕ* does not have an exact match in the names of any letters of the alphabet. Actually it *is* contained in the letter names for F, L, and S; but children rarely use consonants for vowel sounds in this way. Note in Figures 4–11 and 4–12 how these children spelled the short sound of *ĕ*. The letter these children used, we see, was A. Again, our hypothesis is that they used the letter A for the long sound in its name.

In children's invented spelling, short vowels are sometimes spelled correctly, presumably because children learn or are told their correct spellings in some words. But when they are spelled incorrectly, the most frequent substitution is E for short *ĭ*, A for short *ĕ*.

These substitutions create spellings that look very little like adult spellings for the same words. They sometimes lead us to the erroneous conclusion that children don't know what they are doing when they produce

Figure 4–11
Susie
Grade 1
Note spelling
of ĕ

Susie Lewis

Do You have A Dog. no I dot Do You no.
Butt I Wosh I had One Do You have A Cat.
Yes I Do have A Cat Butt he ran away -
All I have is a hurse I dot have A Pat.
My Dad Wot lat me have A Pat. the end

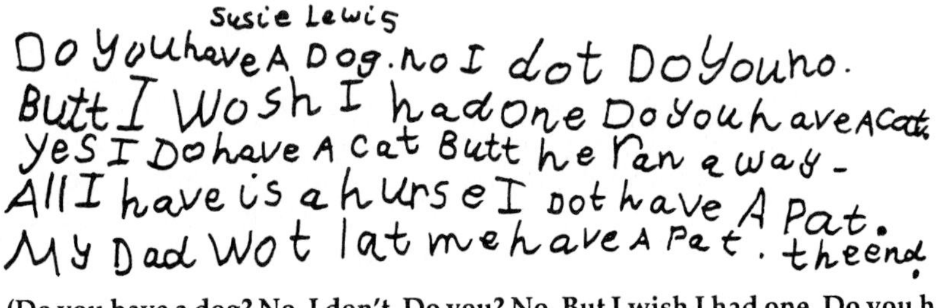

(Do you have a dog? No, I don't. Do you? No. But I wish I had one. Do you have a cat? Yes, I do have a cat but he ran away. All I have is a horse. I don't have a pet. My dad won't let me have a pet. The end.)

Figure 4–12
Brian
Grade 1
Note spelling
of ĕ

My fe his rad

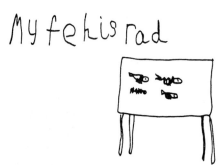

(My fish is red.)

spellings like ALVADR for "elevator." What are they thinking? By what process do they arrive at these spellings? Again we must consider the way speech sounds are made, and again our source is Charles Read.

How Vowels Are Produced

This time, let's consider vowels. If you open your mouth wide and vibrate your vocal cords, you will make a vowel, probably "ahhhh." If you pronounce a drawn out "ahhhh" and switch abruptly to "eeee," note what happens in your mouth. You may be aware of two things: first, your jaw raised slightly on "eeee," but even more obvious was the raising of the tongue in the front of the mouth. Now try this: pronounce "aaahh," and then change *very, very slowly* up to "eeee." You probably heard some other sounds you could recognize as vowels in between. What were they? Where was the tongue when they were made?

Pronounce the *u* sound of "fruit," stretching it out. Then shift to "eeee" again. Now back to *u*. What does your tongue do? You may have noted that it went up at the front of the mouth for "eeee," but that it went up at the *back* of the mouth for $\bar{u}$. If you didn't feel it go up in the back for $\bar{u}$, try saying $\breve{oo}$ (as in "took") in alternation with $\bar{u}$ (as in "new"): $\breve{oo}$–$\bar{u}$; $\breve{oo}$–$\bar{u}$; $\breve{oo}$–$\bar{u}$. This should help you become aware of a movement of the back of the tongue up toward the back of the roof of your mouth.

We make vowels by holding the tongue in certain positions as voiced air passes through the mouth. Essentially, the placement of the tongue is along two planes—it can move from front to back and from high to low; or into intermediate positions between high and low and front and back. We could diagram the positions of the tongue with a grid, as in Figure 4–13.

Let's demonstrate the *front* vowels. Try saying these sounds, gliding smoothly from one to the other: $\bar{e}$ (as in "beet"), $\breve{i}$ (as in "bit"), $\bar{a}$ (as in "bait"), $\breve{e}$ (as in "bet"), $\breve{a}$ (as in "bat"): $\bar{e}$, $\breve{i}$, $\bar{a}$, $\breve{e}$, $\breve{a}$. Do it three times and pay attention to what your tongue does. Now try it in reverse: $\breve{a}$, $\breve{e}$, $\bar{a}$, $\breve{i}$, $\bar{e}$. You probably noticed your tongue started high and went low in the first series, and that it started low and went high in the second series. You also may have noticed that this movement took place in the front of the mouth (although $\bar{e}$ is somewhat further forward than $\breve{a}$).

Note that the sounds $\bar{e}$ and $\breve{i}$ were positioned next to each other—that is, from $\bar{e}$ the next position you came to in the first series was the $\breve{i}$ sound, as you went from high to low. The sounds of $\bar{a}$ and $\breve{e}$ were also quite close in the position of the tongue. In the vowel grid in Figure 4–13 these vowels appear close together.

Actually, they are even closer than the vowel grid makes them appear. The sounds of $\bar{e}$ and $\breve{i}$ are formed in almost the same place in the mouth. They differ in what has been called tenseness/laxness. Hold your fingers against the flesh on the underside of your jaw and alternate pronouncing the vowels, $\bar{e}$–$\breve{i}$, $\bar{e}$–$\breve{i}$, $\bar{e}$–$\breve{i}$. You may feel the muscles in the floor of your mouth becoming

Figure 4–13
Diagram of
tongue
positions as
different
vowels are
produced

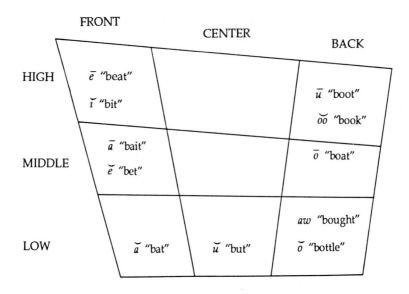

tense with the pronunciation of $\bar{e}$ and lax with pronunciation of $\breve{\imath}$. You should feel the same tensing and laxing with $\bar{a}$ and $\breve{e}$, respectively. Some language scientists consider $\bar{a}$ and $\breve{e}$ to be alike in the place in which they are sounded and different mainly in tenseness and laxness.[3] That is, they are tense and lax versions of the same vowel. The same is said of $\bar{e}$ and $\breve{\imath}$. The child who wrote FEH for "fish" and LATR for "letter" must have sensed this pairing of the tense and lax vowels by position.

To recapitulate the argument, children who are inventive spellers represent sounds in words according to the similarity between the sound in the word and the sound of the name of some letter of the alphabet. All of the vowel letters of the alphabet have long vowel sounds in their names. All of these long vowels, it turns out, are produced by tensing the tongue and floor of the mouth. Therefore, all the vowels you think of as long are also tense: $\bar{a}$, $\bar{e}$, $\bar{o}$, $\bar{u}$—we'll get to $\bar{\imath}$ in a minute! No short vowel sounds have *exact* matches with the names of any vowel letters, for a good reason. All short vowels are *lax*—produced by relaxing the tongue and floor of the mouth—while the sounds of all vowel letter names are *tense*. If you are getting confused, pronounce these sounds and check for tenseness:

$$\bar{a} \qquad \breve{e}$$
$$\bar{e} \qquad \breve{\imath}$$
$$\bar{o} \qquad \breve{o}$$
$$\bar{u} \qquad \breve{oo}$$

The vowels marked long should have felt tense, though $\bar{o}$ and $\bar{u}$ tense the tongue more than the floor of the mouth. The vowels marked short should have felt lax.

When children seek to spell a long or tense vowel, they have no trouble finding a letter to represent it, as we have seen, because the names of the vowel letters A, E, I, O, U are long or tense themselves. But when they want to spell a short or lax vowel trouble ensues because there are no short or lax letter names. The strategy most children employ in such a case is to *find the long (tense) letter name that is made in the same place in the mouth as the short (lax) vowel they wish to spell.*

This is sometimes called the vowel pairing strategy, so-called because it pairs in spelling the tense and lax vowels that are pronounced in the same position in the mouth. It results in some other strange matches beside $\bar{e}$–$\breve{\imath}$ and $\bar{a}$–$\breve{e}$, although these two are the most consistent. Another match that is often seen is *o* for $\breve{u}$: as in BBGON ("BBgun"). Still stranger is the case of the long $\bar{\imath}$ sound.

The long $\bar{\imath}$ is actually made up of two sounds: $\breve{o}$ and $\bar{e}$. If you pronounce it slowly, you will feel your tongue start low and back and then move high and front while the vowel is still being made: $\breve{o}$–$\bar{e}$. Children sometimes notice this short $\breve{o}$ or broad $\ddot{a}$ (as in "ahhhh" with a physician's tongue depressor) element contained in the letter name I, and make use of it to spell $\breve{o}$ (as in BIDM for "bottom" and WIS for "wants").

Why do the spellings produced by children's vowel pairing strategies ($\bar{a}$ with $\breve{e}$, $\bar{e}$ with $\breve{\imath}$, etc.) appear strange to us? For a very good reason: Although standard spelling pairs vowels, it pairs them differently from the matches that inventive spellers work out for themselves. Standard spelling pairs long and short A: $\bar{a}$, as in "bay," with $\breve{a}$, as in "bat." It pairs long and short I: $\bar{\imath}$, as in "bite," with $\breve{\imath}$, as in "bit." It pairs them because they are represented in spelling by the same letter—not because they sound the same or because they are made in the same place in the mouth. The pairing of $\bar{a}$ and $\breve{a}$, $\bar{\imath}$ and $\breve{\imath}$, $\bar{e}$ and $\breve{e}$ are second nature to us adults, simply because of our years of reading and writing experience. But this system of pairing vowels does not seem natural to beginning spellers.

Table 4–6 summarizes the vowel pairings that Read identified, with examples from writings we have collected from children.

Syllables without Vowels

Children who produce invented spellings often show surprising acuity not only in learning speech sounds but in categorizing them together on the basis of very subtle features. Why is it, then, that they leave out so many vowels, as in Figure 4–14?

We note two things in the circumstances of the vowel omissions: They happen before certain consonants—L, R, M, S—and they happen in certain places, mostly the ends of words, in unstressed syllables. The consonants before which vowels are omitted sound much like vowels themselves. The sound of R is made without any complete closing of the shapers in the mouth and consists largely of the vibration of the vocal cords to make themselves heard. The sound of L is made with the tongue against the roof of the mouth;

	Sound	Letter	Examples
Table 4–6 *Pairing of lax (short) vowels with letter names*	$\breve{e}$	A	FAL (fell) RAD (red) PAT (pet) TALUFO (telephone)
	$\breve{i}$	E	FEH (fish) HEM (him) BET (bit) VESET (visit)
	$\breve{o}$	I	WIS (wants) BIDM (bottom)
	$\breve{u}$	O	JOPT (jumped) MOD (mud) SOPR (supper) FOTIME (funtime)

Figure 4–14
Six-year-old
Examples of
R's for
syllables

THe Mo. MOST R. UVES MAD AT Tre PRSIN.

(The mad monster was mad at the person.)

the vibrated air is passed around the sides of the tongue for the L. The sounds of M and N both close off the mouth, but pass the vibrated air out through the nasal passage. All of these consonants are *voiced;* that is, the vocal cords vibrate while they are being made. All of them also allow the vibrated air to pass uninterrupted out of the mouth or the nose. Hence, of all the consonants, they are the most like vowels—because vowels are uninterrupted passages of voiced air.

When vowels occur in syllables that are unstressed, they are said to be *reduced.* Say these words aloud: "table," "wonderful," "lentil," and "infernal." The last syllables you probably pronounced all the same way—*ŭl*—even though they were written four different ways. In normal speech, the individual vowels in these unstressed syllables are unrecognizable—they are all reduced to a common *uh.*

When the vowellike consonants occur in these unstressed syllables where one cannot hear any distinct vowel, children tend to let the vowellike quality of the consonant serve for whatever vowel is needed. By children's logic, any vowel letter that they *did* write in such a place would say its name clearly—giving us 'litteel" if they wrote LETEL or "bottoam" if they wrote BIDOM. This is not what the children intend, so they leave the vowel out. Some common examples of syllables without vowels are given in Table 4–7.

Choo Choo Chran
Sometimes invented spelling diverges from standard spelling because children perceive oddities of pronunciation that adults do not. Words like "tree," "train," and "trick" are commonly pronounced as if they began with "chr."

Sound	Letter	Examples
ŭl	L	LETL (little) BISECL (bicycle) TABL (table) AJLS (angels)
ŭr	R	TEHR (teacher) GRAMOTR (grandmother) PECHRS (pinchers) SOPR (supper)

Table 4–7
Syllables
without vowels

We read *tree* and say "chree"—but we adults don't believe we say "chree" because we have seen the "tr" in print and we have a strange hidden conviction that what we've been seeing is what we've been saying. But children are not easily taken in. They will sometimes spell TR as CHR.

They will do a similar thing with DR. When we pronounce "drink," "drive," and "dragon," we often say "jrink," "jrive," and "jragon." When children spell these words the way they hear them, they often use letters G or J at the beginning of the word.

Often, too, they omit the letter R after the T or D. Children seem to have a bias toward simplicity in their pronunciation.[4] They *say* "jink" for "drink." It may be that the bias for simplicity carries over into spelling, too. We notice that many consonant blends get reduced to a single letter even when they *could* be puzzled out by the letter-name strategy.

Figures 4–15 and 4–16 show some samples where the sounds of DR and TR have been dealt with imaginatively by the children.

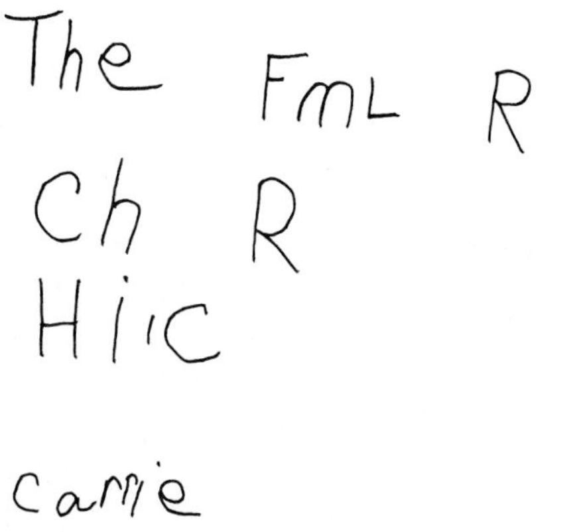

The FmL R
Ch R
HiiC

Carie

(The family are drinking Hi-C.)

Figure 4–15
Carrie
Kindergarten
Note spelling of "drinking"

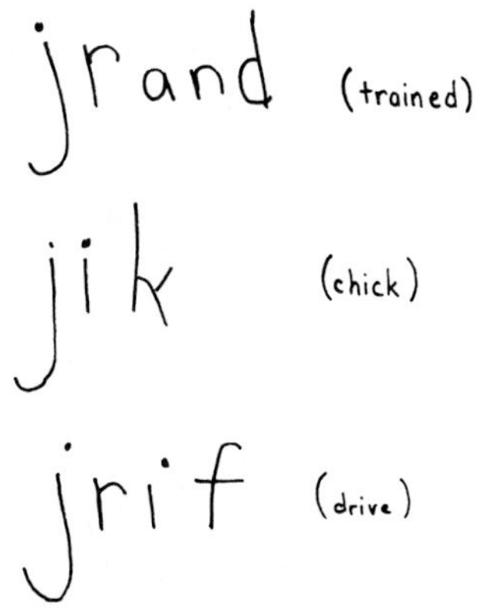

jrand (trained)

jik (chick)

jrif (drive)

Figure 4–16
First grader
Note spelling of "trained" and "drive"

The Developmental Dimension
of Invented Spelling

We have covered the most important aspects of children's invented spelling with the letter-name strategy. The spellings we saw in this chapter are of the most inventive sort that children produce. The children who wrote them were acting mostly on their own intuitions about spelling; learned spellings showed up less frequently than invented ones. In the next chapter this condition will be reversed. Learned spelling will dominate the children's writing, though invention will still be in evidence as children employ learned spelling patterns in novel ways. The result will still be spelling errors, but the errors will be influenced more by learning and less by intuition than those we encountered in the present chapter.

This next type of spelling, which we will call *transitional* spelling, is a developmental step beyond the letter-name spelling. On that subject, however, there is a developmental aspect of letter-name spelling that has been lurking in the background of the present discussion. The reader will have noticed that some of the spelling samples displayed in this chapter were more complete, more filled out, than others. Consider again the following two samples by Daryl. The first was written in September of his first-grade year, the second, two months later.

1. I L N GLEAD TXS ("I live in Goliad, Texas")
2. A MAN ROB SOS THE PLES FID HEM. ("A man robbed shoes. The police found him.")

Daryl used the letter-name strategy to produce invented spelling in both sentences. But in the second one he represented considerably more speech sounds with his letters than he did in the first. This reflects a widely observed characteristic of children's invented spelling: Early in their career as spellers, children represent far fewer speech sounds or phonemes with their letters than they do later in their development.

As we see in Figure 4–17, when a child begins to spell by phonemes, he does not advance instantly to producing well-formed spellings. Spelling words phoneme by phoneme, or *phonemic* spelling, at first seems to restrict the quantity of a child's written production. Whereas before he may have scribbled volubly and produced pages of mock writing, his first efforts at phonemic spelling yield only a trickle of production—usually only a letter or two for each word he wishes to spell. Clearly this reduced production indicates that the task of phonemic spelling is hard for the child and that he must really work at it. What is so hard about phonemic spelling?

There are at least three sources of difficulty: the need to segment words into phonemes, the need to have a stable "concept of word," and the task of choosing a letter with which to represent the phonemes.

Figure 4–17
Kindergartner
Early phonemic
spelling

Vis isspe

(This is spring.)

Segmenting Words into Phonemes

To anyone who can read this book, the idea of breaking a word down into its smallest sounds or phonemes may not seem to be an unusually difficult task. Our experience with reading written words over the years has made it natural for us to see words as bundles of phonemes—if we understand phonemes to be the sounds to which individual letters correspond. Certainly there are exceptions in the correspondences, but the very fact that we can recognize exceptions and irregularities in the match between letters and speech sounds is an indication that we have a working sense of the sound units to which letters correspond.

Our experience with print may be misleading, however, because even though letters on the page are distinctly recognizable units, the speech sounds to which they correspond are not. When we say "bat," we do not say "buh," "a," "tuh" rapidly together. No matter how quickly we pronounce those three sounds, we can never run them together to say "bat." Laboratory experiments have been conducted to test this point. Using sophisticated hardware, scientists have taken words like "bat" and mechanically broken them into their smallest components. Then they have tested to see if people could recognize the parts of the word. Invariably, people had no difficulty recognizing the vowel sound, but when the vowel sound was removed from either consonant, the consonant was unrecognizable—people reported hearing a "chirping sound" instead of a consonant![5]

The explanation is that we produce many phonemes together when we speak in a process called *coarticulation*. If we are able, on reflection, to separate phonemes out of the speech we hear, it is only because we have a sense of what we are looking for; the phonemes do not come to us separately. The task of recognizing the individual phonemes that make up a word—called *phonemic segmentation*—is more of a complex perceptual operation than it appears. It does not simply consist of recognizing separate items; it also includes the act of deciding how they might be separated.

For children, segmenting words into syllables is not very difficult. But segmenting words into phonemes usually is.[6] In any group of five-year-olds, there may be a few who are able to segment phonemes, a larger number who can distinguish only one or two phonemes per word, and a like number who cannot break a word down further than a syllable, if that.

The Concept of Word

In order to spell, a child must develop a concept of what a word is and the ability to think about words.[7] Like phonemes, words come to us all run together in undifferentiated strings. There is not usually any clue in the speech stream we listen to as to where one word leaves off and another begins. As in the case of phonemes, we usually attend to the meaning of words rather than to their sounds. Thus, a bilingual person may not be able to remember in what language a particularly interesting comment was made to her. The idea will be remembered but the words somehow fall away. But for the child to be able to spell a word, the word must have some reality for him as a unit; he must be able to make it hold still in his mind while he operates on it. For in order to spell a word, the child must

1. say the word mentally to himself;
2. break off the first phoneme from the rest of the word;
3. mentally sort through his repertoire of letters and find one to match with that phoneme;
4. write down the letter he has decided on;
5. recite the word again in his mind;
6. recall the phoneme he has just spelled, subtract it from the word, and locate the next phoneme to be spelled; and
7. match that phoneme with a letter of the alphabet, and so on, until all of the phonemes are spelled.

The child must have a very stable image of the word in his mind to be able to switch back and forth between the sound of the word, its phonemes, his repertoire of letters, and the motor act of writing each letter.

We can illustrate the importance of the concept of word in carrying out the tasks of spelling with an analogy. Suppose that your first assignment in an astronomy class is to make a chart of fifty stars in the sky. You go outside on a starlit night, armed with drawing paper and pencil, and look up. You spot a bright star. You look down at the paper to see where its mark should go. You look up to verify its position, but alas! Which star is it? So it goes— every time you isolate a star from the thousands of others, you lose your place in the transition from sky to paper and back.

But suppose later on you studied the constellations. Now when you looked into the sky you could quickly orient yourself to the patterns of stars in the sky. Every time you looked down at your paper you could quickly reorient yourself by the constellations.

For the beginning speller, we expect that a concept of word is akin to our ability to recognize constellations. It serves the same important orienting function when he attempts to spell.

Letters to Represent Sounds

After phonemic segmentation and the concept of word, the third source of difficulty for a beginning speller is deciding which letters should represent the sounds she has isolated in a word. At first, inventive spellers are very creative in finding these letter-to-sound matches. And although they are capable of sophisticated thinking in deciding on these matches, they are also largely unconcerned with being correct. The experience of reading, however, shows them again and again that their inventions are not the ways of the adult world, and they begin to be aroused to the need to spell words in a standard fashion. There is one strain of continuity in this new concern with standard spelling: The inventive speller continues looking for patterns of regularity—for rules that will enable her to generate standard spellings for words—in the same way she was able to generate letter-name spellings for them during the beginning stages we have just considered. The task of coming to grips with standard spelling is the topic of the next chapter. In it we learn more about both children's learning processes and the written language they are trying to master.

Conclusion

All of the spelling forms and spelling stages we have considered in this chapter have one important feature in common: they result largely from children's invention, from their untutored assumptions about the way spelling works. In succeeding chapters we will see what happens as children begin to learn the patterns of standard spelling. For now, a pair of questions remains to be answered about invented spelling.

Do all children invent spelling? If every child spontaneously wrote out invented spelling at the kitchen table, the phenomenon would be as widely known a writing behavior as baby talk is a speech behavior. But they don't and it's not. Many children do not explore writing before they enter school, and there they usually practice writing only words they have memorized. However, if these children were to write words whose spellings they had not memorized, it is probable that they would employ the strategies we have described in this chapter.

Should all children invent spelling? We raised this question in the first edition of this book in 1982. At that time our answer was, "Yes, children will learn to spell and write fluently if they are encouraged—but not forced—to express themselves in writing as soon as they feel the urge, and as best they can." We based that answer on our teaching experience and on anecdotal evidence from many teachers. The educational community has had much more experience with invented spelling since 1982, and virtually all of it supports the value of encouraging children to invent spellings for words.

ENDNOTES

1. This term and the term *letter-name strategy*, discussed in the next section, are taken from James Beers, "Developmental Strategies of Spelling Competence in Primary School Children," in Edmund H. Henderson and James W. Beers, eds., *Developmental and Cognitive Aspects of Learning to Spell* (Newark, DE: International Reading Association, 1980).
2. Charles Read, *Children's Categorization of Speech Sounds in English* (Urbana, IL: National Council of Teachers of English, 1975).
3. Ronald Langacre, *Language and Its Structure, Some Fundamental Concepts,* 2d ed. (New York: Harcourt Brace Jovanovich, 1973).
4. Jill DeVilliers and Peter DeVilliers, *Language Acquisition* (Cambridge: Harvard University Press, 1979).
5. A. M. Liberman, F. S. Cooper, D. Shankweiler, and M. Studdert-Kennedy, "Perception of the Speech Code," *Psychological Review* 74 (1967): 431–461.
6. I. Y. Liberman et al., "Explicit Syllable and Phoneme Segmentation in the Young Child," *Journal of Experimental Child Psychology* 18 (1974): 201–212.
7. Darrell Morris, "Beginning Readers' Concept of Word," In Edmund H. Henderson and James W. Beers.

CHAPTER 5

Learning
Standard Spelling

Susie wrote the writing samples shown in Figure 5–1 during the fall of her first-grade year. The writing in Figure 5–2 she wrote in the spring. The difference between her spelling at the two times is striking. Her first efforts are strange to the eye, while her later ones are familiar; she seems to have moved out of some exotic, foreign way of writing and into English writing. Her later words look like they *could* be English words.

The first sample shows many of the creative leaps as well as the limitations that occur when a child who is not yet a reader—or is just learning to read—tries to spell. Letters are used for their letter-name sound values; syllables are spelled without vowels; sounds that are normally spelled with digraphs are spelled with a single letter; and several sounds aren't spelled at all.

The second sample shows a child who can read, who is now learning from print about spelling. Some words ("can," "play," "home") are spelled correctly. Others (BILLEY, MINIT, THER) are spelled plausibly. And some (WITHE, COMEG) are spelled oddly, indicating that the child has not quite mastered some conventions of English spelling.

Figure 5–1
Susie
Grade 1
Susie's letter-
name spelling

(She is picking her flowers. Yellow flowers by her flower house. She is wearing a blue dress. Her flower house is white.)

Figure 5–2
Susie
Grade 1
Susie's
transitional
spelling

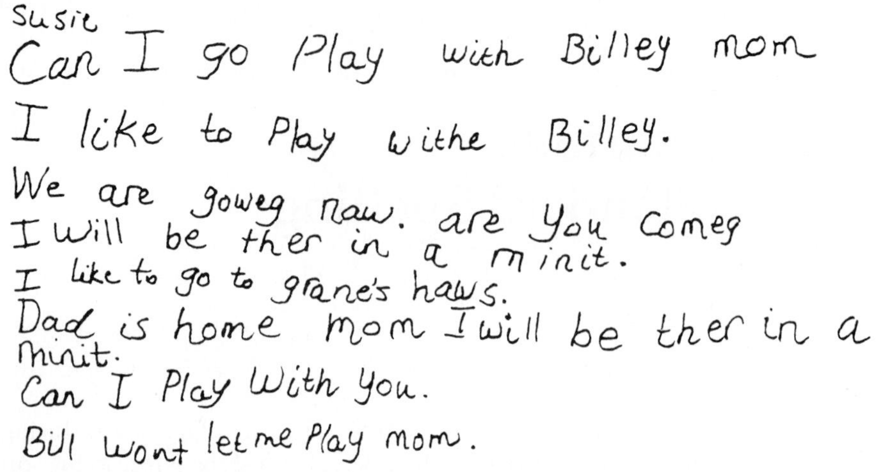

Susie
Can I go Play with Billey mom
I like to Play withe Billey.
We are goweg naw. are You comeg
I will be ther in a minit.
I like to go to grane's haws.
Dad is home mom I will be ther in a minit.
Can I Play With You.
Bill wont let me Play mom.

(Can I go play with Billy, Mom? I like to play with Billy. We are going now. Are you coming? I like to go to Granny's house. Dad is home, Mom. I will be there in a minute.
Can I play with you?
Bill won't let me play, Mom.)

Once a child begins to learn to read and she moves beyond the letter-name phase of invented spelling, the challenges of spelling change. No longer is she concerned only with finding a matching letter for each sound she hears. Now her task is to recognize

1. the spellings of consonant digraphs;
2. patterns that mark vowels as long or short, and mark some consonants as hard or soft;
3. that certain grammatical endings (-ed, -s, -ing) *have* to be spelled certain ways, though they may be pronounced variously;
4. there are often several likely ways to spell a given sound pattern (cream, creem, creme) but one *correct* way in each word;
5. there are some spellings that don't work the way we expect them to, because of pronunciation variations, or *phonological rules*;
6. there are other spellings that don't behave the way we expect them to because of choices made centuries ago by the first writers of modern English (we call these *scribal traditions*).

Before we describe these aspects of English spelling in detail, and then discuss the ways that they show up in children's spelling, we should say a word about how English spelling came to take its present form.

How English Got Its Strange Spelling

The alphabetic system of writing was introduced into England by the Romans. They spoke and wrote Latin, of course, but their writing system and alphabet were used to write the Anglo-Saxon or Old English language that was spoken on the island. Old English manuscripts have been found dating back to the eighth century, A.D.[1]

England does not occupy a large piece of geography, nor are there many natural barriers on the island. But early peoples living in different regions had very limited contact with each other. Thus, each region had a markedly different dialect of English. When speakers of these dialects occasionally came together, their dialects influenced each other in strange ways to give rise to new ways of speaking. Gradually, the whole language was propelled forward with changes of speech and usage unevenly spread across the land. By the time the printing press was imported to England, the language had evolved into what is called Middle English—the language of Chaucer.

There were great varieties in Middle English, but we know that when Middle English was written down, most letters, especially vowels, had one pronunciation; and almost all the letters that were written in a word stood directly for a sound.

Up until 1476 each scribe had had his own style of spelling, but in that year William Caxton set up the first printing press in England. The printer became the final arbiter of spelling, and variations of spellings for individual words greatly diminished. Caxton selected the London dialect of Middle English as the basis of his spelling, and succeeding printers usually followed his example.

In the few centuries before Caxton, England had been invaded and ruled by the French from Normandy. Though French was widely spoken, Latin was the language of the church, the school, and the court. Through the seventeenth century, literate people read more Latin than they did English, and also a good deal of French. At this time, when occasional attempts were made to reform the spelling of English, the reforms actually moved spelling away from sound so that English words would look more like their Latin and French cousins. *Dette*, for example, was changed to "debt" in order to make it resemble the Latin form *debit*.[2]

To complicate matters further, it seems that many of the early printers were from Germany and Holland. Some were not good speakers of English or French, and so they introduced several peculiarities into our spelling out of error! They gave us "yacht," for example, for *yotte*.

From the fifteenth century through the eighteenth, the English language changed so much that a speaker from the later period could not have understood a speaker from the earlier one. But spelling changed relatively little during the same time. The seventeenth and eighteenth centuries saw several efforts to reform English spelling along phonetic lines. The most influential man of letters of the eighteenth century, however, would have none of it. Dr.

Samuel Johnson published his famous *Dictionary* in 1755 and established from that time to this the historical, or etymological, basis of English spelling instead of the phonetic.

English spelling is today considered "historically phonetic"; that is, it is spelled roughly the way it sounded 500 years ago. In all these years many differences have occurred between spelling and sound. There are two such differences that stand out above all the others.

One source of difference between spelling and sound is the Great Vowel Shift. In Old English there was not the same distinction between long and short vowels (by which we really mean tense and lax) that we have today. But in Middle English, vowels came to have released pronunciations when they occurred in unstressed syllables. The letter E was at that time pronounced $\bar{a}$ in stressed syllables and $\breve{e}$ in unstressed syllables. Thus the word "bete" would have been pronounced "bāteh." The letter I was pronounced $\bar{e}$ in stressed syllables and $\bar{\imath}$ in unstressed ones, giving bēteh for "bite." The respective pronunciations for the letter A in stressed and unstressed syllables were *ah* and $\tilde{a}$.

Between the fifteenth and sixteenth centuries a very peculiar thing happened. The pronunciation of each of the above vowels in stressed positions was changed around, while the unstressed vowels kept their original pronunciations. The stressed letter E went from $\bar{a}$ to $\bar{e}$; stressed letter I went from $\bar{e}$ to $\bar{\imath}$; and stressed letter A went from *ah* to $\bar{a}$. Thus, the two vowel sounds that were represented by each vowel letter became remote from each other, as we can see in pairs such as "mate–mat," "bite–bit," and "Pete–pet."

The second major change that occurred in the relation between spelling and pronunciation was the appearance of silent letters. Words in Old and Middle English had almost no letters that did not stand for some sound. Thus "bite" was pronounced "beeteh," and "light" was pronounced "lixt," with the *x* having a sound akin to the *ch* in "loch" and "Bach." But with changes in pronunciation, the last vowel sound in "bite" dropped off, and the *x* sound in "light," "right," "bright," "sigh," and similar words ceased to be sounded. The spellings for these silent sounds stayed on, however. They came to indicate that the preceding vowel had its long or stressed pronunciation, since the first syllable in a two-syllable word was always automatically stressed. Today they serve as *markers*—letters that are silent themselves but serve to indicate the pronunciation of neighboring letters.

Some Learnable Patterns of Modern English Spelling

To account for the relationship between spelling and sounds of words in modern English, it is necessary to consider the historical background of the relationship. But that does not mean that children must become historians of language. Rather, it means that they must be able to sense patterns of spelling that are old in origin but that can be perceived today as generalizations governing the relation between spelling and sound.

In modern English spelling we can identify four separate types of patterns, all of which emerging spellers must contend with as they seek to learn the system. We will refer to them as *rules*, though we must emphasize that they were never deliberately planned as rules, and they are rarely explicitly taught in the fashion in which we will describe them. The patterns we will treat are *marking rules, phonological rules, scribal rules*, and *morpheme conservation rules*.

Marking Rules in English Spelling

As we noted in the previous section, the system of cues that tells us which pronunciation to give vowels and certain consonants was not deliberately designed as a system. Nevertheless, the result is a highly general and, hence, learnable set of patterns that can be summarized as follows:

1. *Vowel + consonant.* When a vowel is followed by a consonant, that vowel has its short (or lax) pronunciation. *Example:* mat.
2. *Vowel + consonant + e, i, or y.* When a vowel is followed by a consonant, followed by any of the above three vowels, the vowel has its long (or tense) pronunciation. The same is true when two vowels are written before a final consonant. *Example:* sale, sail.
3. *Vowel + consonant + consonant + e, i, or y.* A vowel can be insulated from the marking influence of e, i, or y by doubling the intervening consonant. *Example:* mat, matted versus mat, mated.

While it is true that some reading and spelling curricula teach these rules explicitly to young children, children who approach learning to write as a process of discovery find the rules out for themselves, as we shall presently see. As they do, they encounter three kinds of challenges. First, they must discover that there are some letters that make no sounds of their own and serve as markers. Second, they must discover how these markers work. Third, they must learn to coordinate the adding of grammatical inflectional endings with the marking rules; that is, word endings such as *-er, -est, -ing,* and *-ed* have the effect of marking the preceding vowels long. A child who is learning to add these onto words for grammatical reasons may not realize that they function as markers, too.

To make matters still more complicated, some consonants—notably *c* and *g*—also have variant pronunciations that are signaled by markers (e.g., *sag, sage*). Inflectional endings, of course, have a marking effect on these consonants as well (hence, *wag + -ing* goes to *wagging* and not *waging*).[3]

Children and Marking Rules. To use marking rules correctly, spellers must coordinate several things at once. To be able to spell "mat," for example, they must

1. remember that the letter A in English spelling properly spells the sound ă;
2. recognize that a vowel letter occurring before a word-final consonant will have its short pronunciation; and
3. recognize that if the first two conditions are met, then no further marking is necessary.

Beginning spellers do not always coordinate all three considerations at one time. In Figure 5–3 note the spelling of "pick" is PIKE. Elaine correctly paired the vowel sound ī with the letter I (she has moved beyond the letter-name match, by which she would have paired the sound ī with the letter E).

Figure 5–3
Elaine
Grade 1
Note vowel
marking
problems

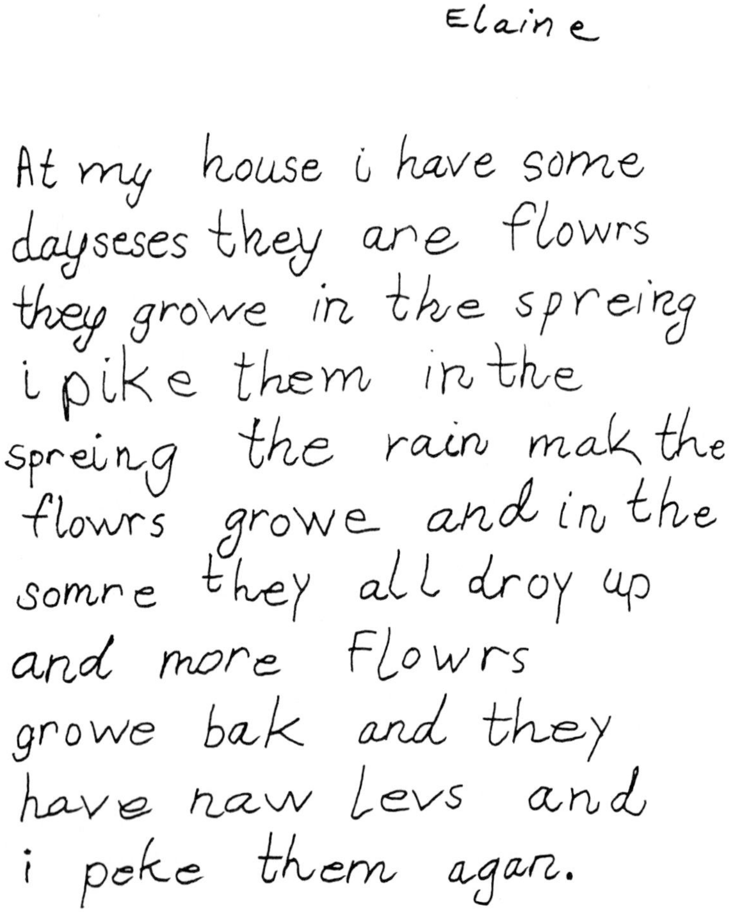

Elaine

At my house i have some dayseses they are flowrs they growe in the spreing i pike them in the spreing the rain mak the flowrs growe and in the somre they all droy up and more flowrs growe bak and they have naw levs and i peke them agan.

(At my house I have some daisies. They are flowers. They grow in the spring. I pick them in the spring. The rain makes the flowers grow and in the summer they all dry up and more flowers grow back and they have new leaves and I pick them again.)

She also demonstrates an awareness of markers—hence, the silent E she places after the K. But she appears not to know precisely when she should use markers and when the environment (i.e., the two consonants around the vowel) can do the work of marking for her.

But the reader may see that there is another problem. PIK does not spell "pick" (except in advertisers' spelling!). The letter K in word-final position follows a scribal rule: K can never stand alone after a single vowel without a vowel following. We cannot have PIK, or BAK, or LOK, or DUK. The letter K needs to be accompanied by a preceding C in all such cases. The reason for this goes back to the Middle Ages. At that time it was standard practice to double final consonants after a preceding *short* vowel—"egg" and "ebb" still follow that pattern. But the scribes of the period had an aversion to writing

Figure 5–4
Teri
Grade 1
Note the
marking of ā.

(Can you see snow flakes(?) They are very pretty. They make me think of Jesus when he was little and Mary, his mother.)

the two letter K's together (we don't know why). So they developed the device of substituting CK for KK. The practice of doubling final consonants to mark a short vowel is long past, but CK is still with us, as a scribal rule.[4]

Elaine may have seen that PIK was not what she wanted, and she may have therefore been put in search of a way of marking PIK to make it right. It would be logical, though incorrect, for her to arrive at PIKE.

GROWE is another interesting extension of the silent letter E marker. By a certain logic, she is well motivated to put it there. The letter W is, after all, a consonant whose influence on the word is easily felt in the rounding of the lips. By the normal pattern, a vowel between two consonants GR-O-W would have the *short* pronunciation without a final E marker. So Elaine's E, by this logic, is marking the O long.

Teri has overextended the marking strategy, too (see Figure 5–4). But her overextension is just the reverse of Elaine's. She has correctly noted the common juxtaposition of the letters C K, but she employs it for the long vowel marker instead of the short one. This pattern is apparently strong with

Figure 5–5
Elaine
Grade 1
Note marking problems

Elaine

I have a ducke. I can drcke
wottre. She has baby ducklings.
Theye foloe her in a strat line.
Theye leve in a barine.
Thaye are yellow. Theye can
tack a bathe and The
sun is out. and we play a
lot with Theme.

(I have a duck. I(t) can drink water. She has a baby ducklings. They live in a barn. They are yellow. They can take a bath and the sun is out and we play a lot with them.)

Teri, since she uses it both for FLACKS (flakes) and MACK (make). The word WENE, on the other hand, has been given a long vowel marker, even though the E is short.

   Figure 5–5 shows another by Elaine. She shows very clear signs of experimenting with marking as a strategy in invented spelling. Her use of a silent E is not just a half-remembered feature from some other words. From her handwriting, it appears that she first wrote "duck" and later appended an E to it—perhaps to make it look more like the words that followed! DREKE is a move toward institutionalizing the omission of N before other consonants. With the N omitted, the spelling DREKE probably comes closest to standard spelling of what is left. WOTTRE is another case of an earlier invented

Figure 5–6
Darla
Grade 1
Note marking
problems

Darla

here are the dogs

Ouce a pon a time we bote a
little kitten and you no how
they are win there little
They are little rascules.
But this one loved to climb
tree and scach pepple He was
a mean rascule.

(Once upon a time we bought a little kitten and you know how they are when they're little. They are little rascals. But this one loved to climb trees and scratch people. He was a mean rascal.)

spelling that has an overlay of standard practice. At an earlier stage, the letter R would have represented the final syllable by itself. Elaine seems to have sensed that a consonant cannot spell a syllable by itself, so she has inserted a vowel—but in a secondary position, which is what she may have thought it deserved. Meanwhile, she seems to recognize the need to double the consonant at the syllable boundary in order to keep the preceding vowel short.

Note that "take" is marked the reverse of the correct way, TACK. Note, too, that this marking business is still not second nature: She spells "straight" by the old letter-name strategy, STRAT.

Marking rules develop as a concept. The concept is applied very generally as a strategy for spelling words when the spellings have not previously been memorized. Sometimes these markers create spellings that can quite easily be read and understood by adults. For example, Darla's paper (Figure 5–6) is easily readable, but she shows some uncertainty with marking patterns. RASCULES (rascals) and PEPPLE (people) are marked in a fashion just the opposite of standard spelling.

Scribal Rules in English Spelling

Even when marking rules are taken into account, there are many words in English whose spellings appear to violate the normal relation between letters and sounds.

These irregularities can often be traced back to the influence of the medieval scribes. The scribes, acting as the manual forerunners of the printing press, had a monopolistic influence on spelling, just as printers were to have later. Occasionally, they made spelling changes to reflect changes in pronunciation. Sometimes their changes moved spellings toward greater consistency across classes of words. HWIC (which) and HWAT had their initial letters reversed to conform to the CH and SH spellings of words like "church" and "ship."

The scribes made some spelling changes to correct confusions among words brought about by the peculiar style of handwriting used in formal documents during the Middle Ages. The Gothic style of the period stressed a repetition of heavy vertical strokes, which reduced the means of discriminating between letters. An example can be seen in the text reproduced in Figure 5–7.

The spelling of the word "love" demonstrates the effects of two scribal changes. "Love" violates our expectations of regularity in two ways. First, it has a letter E at the end. This E looks like a marker for a preceding long vowel, but the vowel heard in "love" is short. The second irregularity is the sounded vowel: The vowel we hear in "love" is usually spelled by U, not O. How do we account for these anomalies?

The final letter E is there because since the early Middle Ages it has been unallowable for an English word to end in a letter V. This strange prohibition came about in the days when the letters U and V were not regarded as separate letters. Until the seventeenth century, the letter U or V could be written interchangeably for the vowel or the consonant sound. But confusion could be avoided if word-final V, when it stood for the consonant, was followed by the letter E. Thus "you" was spelled YOU or YOV. But "love," which had earlier been spelled LOU or LOV, came to be spelled LOUE or LOVE. In the seventeenth century, the vowel *u* and the consonant *v* were each stably identified with its own letter, but by then the silent E after V had become so entrenched that it is still with us 300 years later.

But what of the letter O in "love"? This vowel and the same vowel in "above," "some," "son," "one," "come," and "none" took its present form as a direct result of the Gothic script. In Old English, "love," "above," "some," and the others were spelled with the letter U.

The evolutions of their spellings were as follows:

Year			
A.D. 1000	lufu	bufan	sum
1200	luue	buuen	sum
1300	lou	abuue	summ
1400	love	above	somme
MODERN	love	above	some[5]

It seems that in all of these words the letter U was changed to O deliberately, because in the Gothic script, with its repetition of bold vertical lines, the letter U was difficult to distinguish from M, N, and, of course, from V. In the example of Gothic script in Figure 5–7 this difficulty is easily observed.

The Gothic script stayed in active use for centuries. Later typefaces alleviated the discrimination problem, but by the time this occurred, the letter O before V, N, and M was a solid fixture of English spelling.

Figure 5–7
Gothic script
u's are difficult
to distinguish
from m *or* n

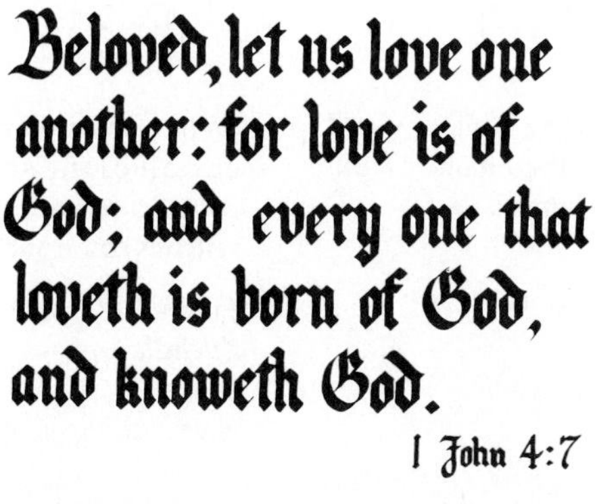

Beloved, let us love one another: for love is of God; and every one that loveth is born of God, and knoweth God.

1 John 4:7

Children and Scribal Rules.   Like the vowel pairings ($\breve{e}$–$\bar{i}$; $\bar{a}$–$\breve{e}$) we saw in Chapter 4, the presence of scribal rules in English spelling leads to divergences between children's invented spellings and standard forms.

These are apparent in spellings involving a final letter V, as we see in Figure 5–8. This child's spelling of the word "of " lays bare some of his thinking on this problem. His spelling UV by itself would be phonetically regular, but his addition of a final letter E shows he is aware that V's never occupy the word-final position without an E.

The scribal rule concerning U/O and V is a central issue in Michelle's paper (Figure 5–9). She, too, had arrived at the spelling UVE for "of," showing at once the tendency to spell the vowel phonetically with the letter U and remembering to "cover" the letter V with the following letter E. She used that spelling twice.

"Come," however, she spelled two different ways: CUM and CUME. The first of these spellings is phonetic. The second, strangely, contains the final letter E, perhaps because Michelle remembered seeing an E in the correct spelling.

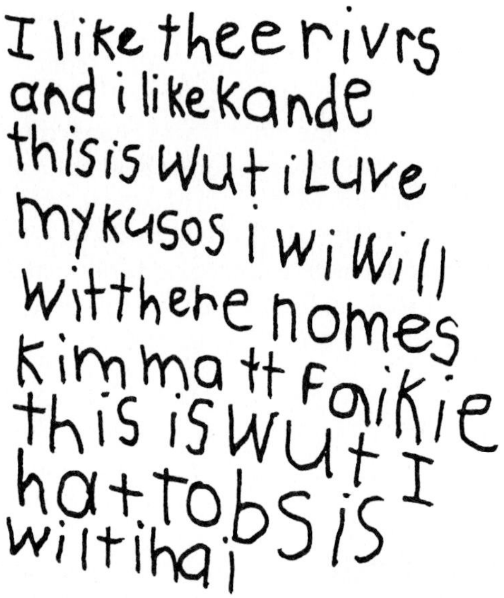

(I like the rivers and I like candy. This is what I love, my cousins, I will write their names: Kim, Matt, Frankie. This is what I hate: to be . . .)

Figure 5–8
Ralph
Grade 1
Note spelling of word-final v

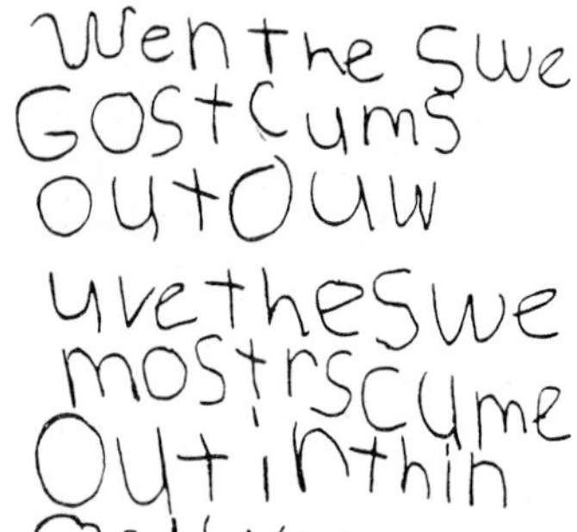

(When the swamp ghost comes out, all of the swamp monsters come out and then all of the witches come out.)

Figure 5–9
Michelle
Grade 1
Note spelling of "of"

Phonological Rules in English Spelling

Sometimes words change their pronunciation when they change their part of speech. Note the shift between "bath" and "bathe," between "teeth" and "teethe," between "strife" and "strive." These differences in pronunciation are reflected in spelling. But other such changes are not. Note the difference between "produce" (as a verb) and "produce" (as a noun; e.g., vegetables), "contract" (as a verb) and "contract" (as a noun; e.g., a document), "recess" (as a verb) and "recess" (as a noun).

Some sounds in words change their pronunciation when they occur next to other sounds. Say this sentence aloud, as you would to a friend: "I bet you can't eat the whole thing!" Chances are the end of "bet" and the beginning of "you" ran together as something like "betcha."

There are phonological rules that govern these sound changes. They work within words, too. When the sounds of *t* or *s* are followed by the sound *y*, the sounds blend to *ch* or *sh*. Thus we write *initial* but say "inishul." We write *special* but say "speshul." We write *fortune* but say "forchun." It is the coming together of the *t* or *s* and *y* sounds in each of those words that gives way to *sh* or *ch*. And that is a *phonological* phenomenon.

It is often the case that spelling is tied to a careful, overprecise pronunciation of a word. An accurate speller may need to work back from a relaxed pronunciation to an overprecise pronunciation and from there to the spelling.

It is one thing when the difference between the actual pronunciation and the spelled pronunciation is the same for everyone, as is the case with "special," "nature," "initial," and the like. The situation is more complicated when dialects are involved. Inhabitants of different regions and members of different social and ethnic groups sometimes have pronunciation patterns that differ strikingly from each other. These pronunciation differences have interesting effects on spelling.

Children and Phonological Rules. Young spellers have no way of knowing that "speshul" is a compact way of saying "spessyal" and that it's "spessyal" that the spelling is tied to. Nor do they know that "nachure" is a compact way of saying "natyure," and it's "natyure" that we are supposed to spell. So it is not surprising that their first untutored approaches to these spellings are phonetically based and incorrect.

Note how Stella (see Figure 5–10) went about spelling "nature trail." Remember that the sound of *t* and *r* rapidly produced results in an affricated (*ch*) sound (see Chapter 4). Not surprisingly, she heard the *ch* in "nature" also.

Stephanie's spelling of "especially " is also interesting (see Figure 5–11). To include the first syllable in "especially" indicates a careful attempt to spell the word, but the C and I in the middle of the word is simply not available even to the most careful reflection.

"Grocery" is another word whose individual sounds are often compacted and changed in normal speech. The letter C is often fricated (see Chapter 4)

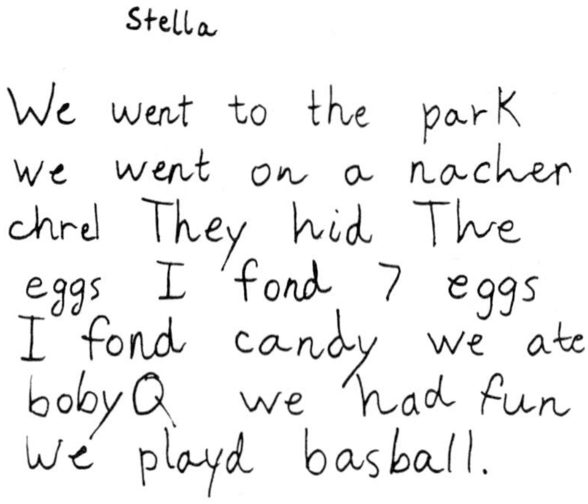

Stella

We went to the park
we went on a nacher
chrel They hid The
eggs I fond 7 eggs
I fond candy we ate
bobyQ we had fun
We playd basball.

(We went to the park.
We went on a nature trail. They hid the eggs. I
found 7 eggs. I found candy. We ate barbecue.
We had fun. We played baseball.)

Figure 5–10
Stella
Grade 1
Note spelling of "nature trail"

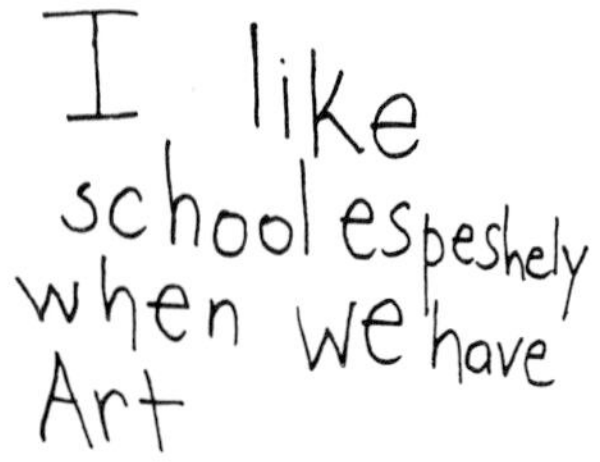

I like
school espeshely
when we have
Art

(I like school, especially when we
have art.)

Figure 5–11
Stephanie
Grade 1
Note spelling of "especially"

to yield GROSHRY. Susie's spelling of the word indicates the pronunciation
usually given in southern Texas (see Figure 5–12).

Susie's SH in "grocery" and Stella's CH in "nature" were clever, but not
surprising. We adults may sometimes forget what these words really sound
like—seeing print biases our ears—but children hear the sounds in words
very acutely as they are spoken. GROSHRY and NACHUR are good render-
ings of what these children hear in those words.

Figure 5–12
Susie
Grade 1
Note spelling of
"grocery"

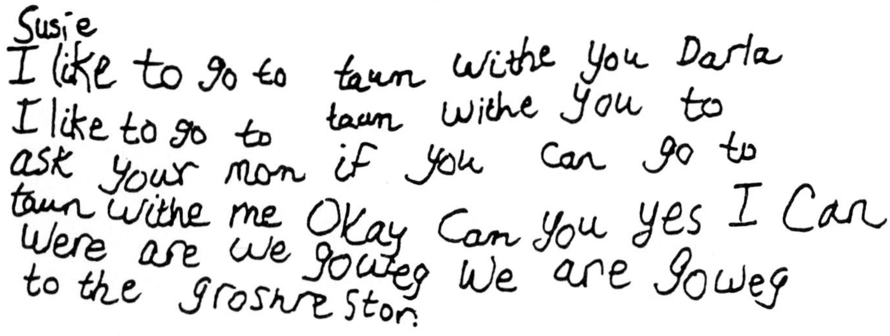

Susie
I like to go to taun withe you Darla
I like to go to taun withe you to
ask your mon if you can go to
taun withe me Okay Can you yes I Can
Were are we goweg We are Goweg
to the groshre Stor.

(I like to go to town with you, Darla. I like to go to town with you, too. Ask your Mom if
you can go to town with me. Okay. Can you? Yes, I can. Where are we going? We are
going to the grocery store.)

Figure 5–13
Susie
Grade 1
Note spelling of
"jewelry"

On the holaday.
I went to my gramows house
and we went to mexeco and
I got a dyolreybox and I
honeted ester egg and I got
elem and my bruther fawd
three and my sistder got elevn.

That is us
ester
egg

(On the holiday. I went to my grandma's house and we went to Mexico and I got a jewelry box and I hunted Easter eggs and I got eleven and my brother found three and my sister got eleven.)

In Figure 5–13, Susie shows that her knowledge has gone a step further. In her spelling of "jewelry box" she demonstrates that she is aware that the sounds of *j* and of *dy* may alternate with each other. This awareness goes beyond having an acute ear for sounds. Her spelling demonstrates an awareness of phonological rules and of their relation to spelling.

Figure 5–14
Second grader
Regional
dialects affect
spelling

Onece there was two dogs
he chood on the sofa
and inee thang he can
git a hode uv.

(Once there was two dogs. He chewed on the sofa and anything he can get a hold of.)

A fine example of the influence of regional dialect on spelling is seen in Figure 5–14. This, too, comes from southern Texas.

Morpheme Conservation Rules in English Spelling

Morphemes are words, or else they are parts of words, that have meaning yet cannot stand alone. "Word" is a word and a single morpheme. "Words" is also a word, but is composed of two morphemes: *word* and *-s*. The letter S has meaning of a sort, because it shows that there is more than one of whatever it is attached to. There are dozens of these *bound morphemes,* thus called because they cannot stand alone: *–ed, –ing, –ly, –er, –ness, –ful, –ity, –ation, un–, re–, dis–, anti–* are some examples.

Morpheme conservation gets to the heart of the issue morphemes raise for young spellers. The problem is that because of speech habits, some morphemes are pronounced in a variety of ways. But because the different pronunciations all *mean* the same thing, they are usually spelled one way. In these cases we say that letter-to-sound regularity is ignored so that the identity of a morpheme may be conserved or maintained. And that is the morpheme conservation rule.

Let's return to *–s*. The *–s* actually represents two morphemes. One is a plural marker, as in "one duck/two ducks." The other indicates the number of the verb, as in "I duck/she ducks." But note the different sounds these morphemes can have:

Nouns	Verbs
cats	stacks
dogs	folds
foxes	presses

There are three possible sounds in *-s: s, z,* and *iz.* Which one it takes depends on the ending of the word it attaches to.

There is a phonological rule, that is, a rule of sound relationships, that summarizes the conditions under which *–s* will take its various sounds.

- Generally, *-s* takes the sound *s* after words ending in the sounds of *f, k, p,* or *t.*
- It takes the sound *z* after the sounds of *b, d, g* (as in "bag"), *l, m, n, r, v, w,* and all vowels.
- It takes the sound *iz* after words ending in the sounds of *j* (such as "page"), *ch, sh, s,* or *z.*

This rule is well known on an unspoken level to all native English speakers. (It is devilishly tough, though, for foreign speakers of English!) To demonstrate, try pluralizing these nonsense words:

- one *barch,* two _____
- one *pog,* two _____
- one *bort,* two _____

You undoubtedly produced the correct sounds for -*s*. The curious thing is that we can do this sort of thing automatically, without being conscious of knowing or using a rule. We may even be surprised that -*s* has three sounds. Is this because the three sounds of -*s* are psychologically the same to us, or because we have so often seen them share a single form in print? It is difficult to say. The task for children, however, is to learn that the various spoken forms have a single written form.

The past tense marker -*ed* is another morphemic ending. Like the ending -*s*, it has one usual spelling but three pronunciations. The pronunciations depend on the sounds of the word ending to which the -*ed* is attached.

To demonstrate for yourself the three pronunciations of -*ed*, put the following nonsense verbs into the past tense: Today I will *blog* my yard. Yesterday I _____ my yard, also. Today I *trock* my grass. Yesterday I also _____ my grass. But I won't *frint* the leaves. I _____ the leaves yesterday.

The three endings, as we hope you discovered, are -*d*, -*t*, and -*d*, respectively. Here is a summary of the distribution of the sounds represented by -*ed*.

1. Generally, -*ed* takes the sound of *d* after endings in all vowels and after the sound of *b*, *g* (as in "beg"), *j*, *l*, *m*, *n*, *r*, *v*, *w*, *z*.
2. Usually -*ed* takes the sound of *t* after endings in the sounds of *f*, *k*, *p*, *s*, *ch*, and *sh*.
3. Similarly, -*ed* takes the sound of *id* after endings in *d* or *t*.

Children and Morpheme Conservation Rules.   Since the sounds of *s*, *z*, and -*iz* all mean the same thing, it is convenient for readers that they be written in a standard way, with a letter S. Children, however, may not be aware that spelling in this instance ignores the various sounds of the -*s* element in favor of its meaning. Thus, they will spell the -*s* ending in a variety of ways that honor the sounds. Examples of this are found in Figures 5–15 and 5–16.

Figure 5–15
Ginger
Grade 1
Note spelling of
"hugs"

(I love my daddy. My daddy is nice, nice, nice. He hugs me when I go to bed. I have dreams.)

Elaine

Figure 5–16
Elaine
Grade 1
Note spelling of
"tadpoles"

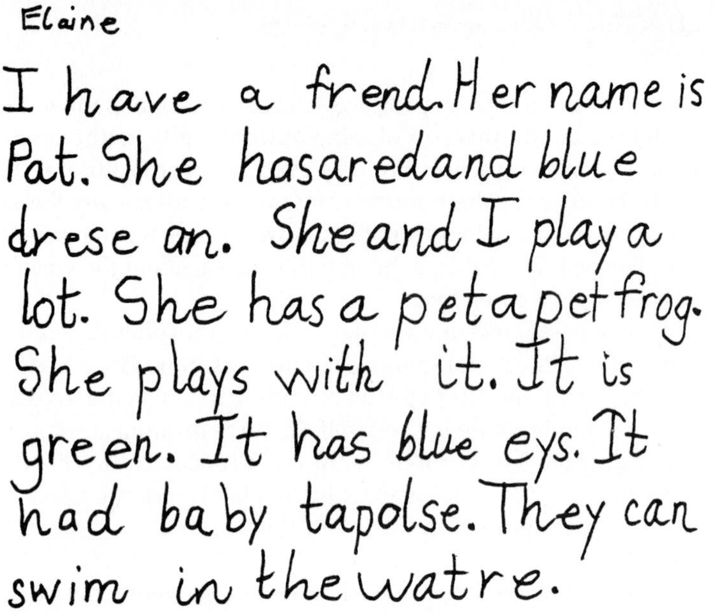

I have a frend. Her name is Pat. She has a red and blue drese an. She and I play a lot. She has a pet a pet frog. She plays with it. It is green. It has blue eys. It had baby tapolse. They can swim in the watre.

(I have a friend. Her name is Pat. She has a red and blue dress on. She and I play a lot. She has a pet, a pet frog. She plays with it. It is green. It has blue eyes. It had baby tadpoles. They can swim in the water.)

Figure 5–17
Ginger (left)
Grade 1
Note spelling of
"pushed" and
"rode"

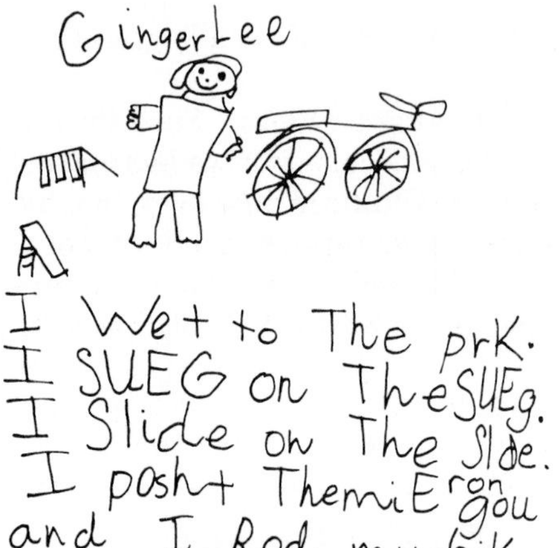

GingerLee

Figure 5–18
JoBeth (right)
Grade 1
Note spelling of
"lived"

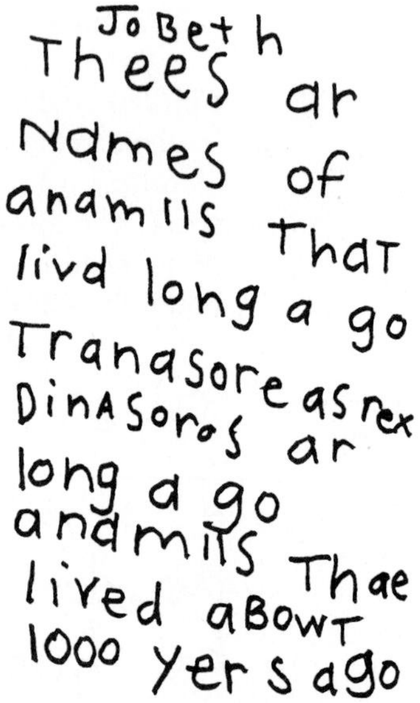

I Wet to The prK.
I SUEG on TheSUEg.
I Slide on The Slde.
I posht Themieron you and I Rod my bik. ten I Spetonit at m es has ter I camt Schoo.

(I went to the park.
I swing on the swing.
I slide on the slide.
I pushed the merry-go-round and I rode my bike. Then I sped on it at my house. Then I came to school.)

JoBeth

Thees ar Names of anamlls That livd long a go Tranasore as rex DinAsoros ar long a go anamlls Thae lived aBowt 1000 yers ago

(These are names of animals that lived long ago. Tyrannosaurus Rex. Dinosaurs are long ago animals. They lived about 1000 years ago.)

Figure 5–19
Teri
Grade 1
Note spelling of
"told"

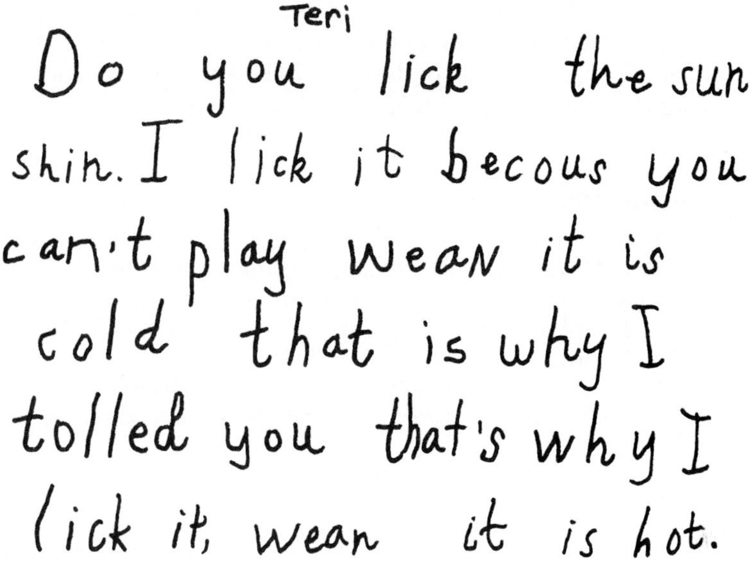

Do you lick the sun
shin. I lick it becous you
can't play weaN it is
cold that is why I
tolled you that's why I
lick it, wean it is hot.

(Do you like the sunshine? I like it because you can't play when it is cold. That is why I told you that's why I like it when it is hot.)

We have become accustomed as readers to seeing written words ending in *-ed* whose endings are pronounced different ways. We may even be surprised that these endings *are* pronounced different ways, since we have learned to associate them with one written unit: *-ed.* Children who have not learned that different pronunciations are associated with this one written unit, however, are likely to spell these endings different ways. Note in Figures 5–17 and 5–18 how these children treated the endings.

In Figure 5–19, Teri shows that she has become aware of *-ed* as a morphemic unit that must preserve its *–ed* spelling. She has not figured out how to graft it on properly to the rest of the word, though.

Conclusion

When children first begin to spell, they seem to perceive their task as one of breaking down their spoken words into individual speech sounds and matching each sound with a letter. As they move toward mature spelling, they must abandon the relatively simple phonetic approach to spelling and take on the complex patterns that are at work in our spelling system. Marking rules, scribal rules, phonological and morpheme conservation rules are involved in some of the more important patterns.

Children become aware of these rules and patterns through experimenting with spelling and comparing their productions with correctly spelled words. When children reach the stage of transitional spelling, well-considered teaching can help, too. This is the topic of the next chapter.

ENDNOTES

1. G. L. Brooks, *A History of the English Language* (London: Norton, 1958).
2. G. H. Vallins, *Spelling* (London: Andre Deutsch, 1965).
3. Richard Venezky, *The Structure of English Orthography* (The Hague, Netherlands: Mouton, 1970).
4. Vallins.
5. *The Oxford English Dictionary*, 13 vol. (Oxford: Oxford University Press, 1933).

CHAPTER 6

Making Progress in Spelling

Children's invented spelling changes as they get older. Early spelling strategies give way to later ones, and the changes in strategies are reflected in the way words are spelled. Observe in Figure 6–1 spellings of the words "dragon" and "purred" offered by five children at different levels of maturity.[1]

Though these spellings were taken at one time from different ages of children, most children pass through different stages of spelling in the order suggested here. That means that if we were to watch Brian over a period of about two years, we would see his spelling change so that it would resemble first Angela's, then Chris's, then Joyce's, and finally Lorraine's. To give these spelling strategies names, we would call Brian's spelling *prephonemic,* Angela's spelling *early phonemic,* Chris's spelling *letter-name,* and Joyce's spelling *transitional.* Lorraine's spelling is, of course, correct.

Our purpose in this chapter will be to place these stages of spelling in developmental perspective and to explain how you may accurately determine where a child is in his spelling development. Then we will describe the instructional goals that seem appropriate for a child at each stage of development and suggest several learning activities that have been found helpful at each stage.

Figure 6–1 *Developmental changes in spelling*	*Lorraine* *2nd grade*	*Joyce* *2nd grade*	*Chis* *lst grade*	*Angela* *Kindergarten*	*Brian* *Kindergarten*
	DRAGON	DRAGUN	GAGIN	J	MPRMRHM
	PURRED	PURD	PRD	P	BDRNMPH

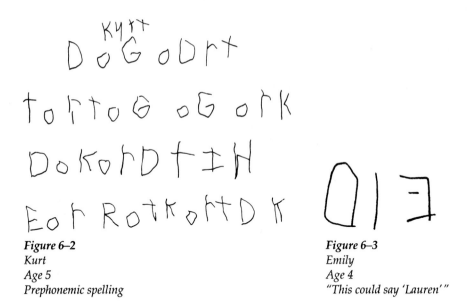

Figure 6–2
Kurt
Age 5
Prephonemic spelling

Figure 6–3
Emily
Age 4
"This could say 'Lauren'"

The Stages of Spelling Development

Let us begin by fixing the stages of spelling development firmly in mind.

Prephonemic Spelling

The characters in Figure 6-2 are examples of *prephonemic spelling.* They were written by Kurt at age five. At that time he formed letters accurately and wrote voluminously, but he had not yet discovered how spelling works. He had not discovered the phonetic principle, which is the notion that letters represent the speech sounds or phonemes in words. Hence, his letter strings *look* like writing, but they do not *work* as writing works.

When children string letters together without attempting to represent speech sounds in any systematic way, they are spelling prephonemically. This is the sort of spelling Brian produced in Figure 6–1.

Prephonemic spellers usually have not learned to read, but they appear to know a lot about written language. They know how letters are formed and that they are supposed to represent language, some way, as we see in the following anecdote.

Four-year-old Emily wrote what is shown in Figure 6–3 and said, "This *can* say Lauren—for make believe." (Lauren is her friend.) Then her mother wrote what is shown in Figure 6–4.

"*That* can't say Lauren," Emily objected.

"Why not?" asked her mother.

Figure 6–4
Ruth
Age 35
"This couldn't"

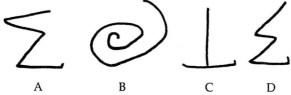

A   B   C   D

Pointing to the first letter, Emily said, "That's wrong." Pointing to Figure C, "That's upside down." Pointing to Figures A and D, "They're upside down."

Thus we see that Emily, a prephonemic speller, knows that letters can represent words, but only allowable letters can do this.

Early Phonemic Spelling

Figure 6–5 shows examples of early phonemic spelling, so called because the children have attempted to represent phonemes in words with letters. These children have discovered the phonetic principle—they know basically how spelling works. But there is a curious limitation to early phonemic spelling. The children write down letters for only one or two sounds in a word, then stop. Thus, spelling in which letters are used to represent sounds, but only very sparsely, is called *early phonemic spelling,* as in Figure 6–6.

The limitation seems to be related to the stability of the speller's concept of what a word is. The early phonemic speller cannot make words "hold still

Figure 6–5
Kindergartner
Early phonemic
spelling

MBEW WM L nt

My Baby was with me last night.

VL+n DAL ISOM+hR

Valentine   Day   is   almost   here.

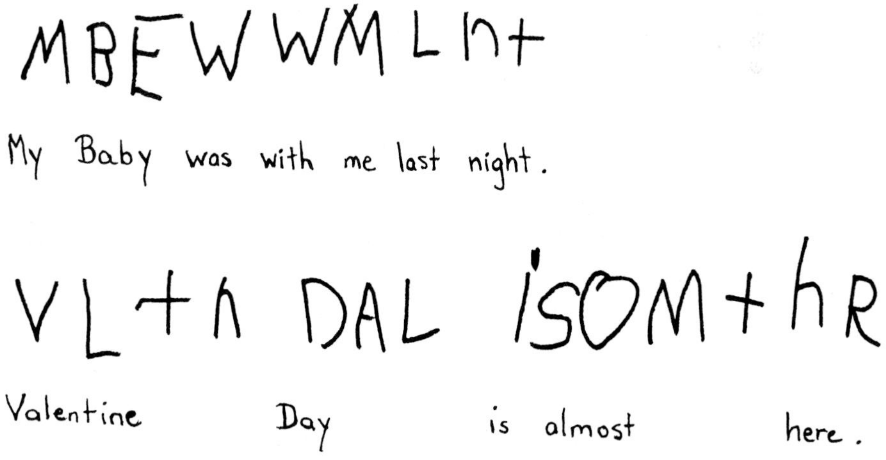

Figure 6–6
Daryl in
October
Grade 1

IL ngLeaDTXS

Figure 6–7
Daryl in
December
Grade 1

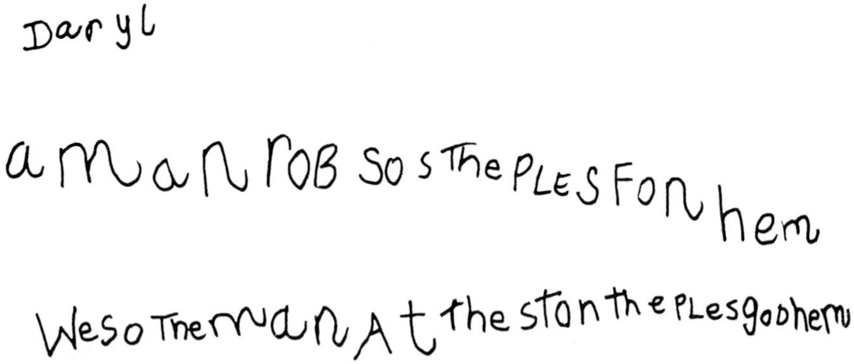

Daryl

a man rob so s the ples for hem

Weso The man At the ston the ples goo hem

(A man robbed shoes. The police found him. We saw the man at the store. The police got him.)

in his mind" while he examines them for phonemes and matches the phonemes with letters.

The transition from early phonemic spelling to the next stage, letter-name spelling, appears on the surface to be a matter of degree. A child represents more and more phonemes with letters until he is representing most of them. But the transition takes place rapidly. One month a first grader is producing early phonemic spelling, like Daryl's. Two months later he produces letter-name spellings (see Figure 6–7). The abruptness of this progress seems

Figure 6–8
Daryl (no
relation)
Age 5
Letter-name
spelling

He had a blue clth. It trd in to a brd.

(He had a blue cloth. It turned into a bird.)

to be the result of an underlying factor: most likely the concept of word has stabilized between the early stage and the later one.

Letter-Name Spelling

Letter-name spelling is the practice of breaking a word into its phonemes and representing the phonemes with letters of the alphabet (see Figure 6–8). The letters are chosen to represent phonemes on the basis of the similarity between the sound of the letter-names and the respective phonemes.

Letter-name spellers often are not yet readers. That is, they may begin producing letter-name spelling before they are able to read. But the concept of word and the ability to identify phonemes in words are important prerequisites for reading. Thus, when a child begins producing letter-name spellings she usually begins to read soon after. For a time she will read words written in standard spelling and write words in letter-name spelling. This leads, not surprisingly, to confusion when a child reads her own writing.

Before many months have passed the experience of reading will present the letter-name spellers with differences between their way of spelling things and standard spelling. When their spelling begins to change as a result of this influence, they pass to the next stage.

Transitional Spelling

Figure 6–9 shows *transitional spelling*. Words spelled by transitional spelling look like English words, though they are not spelled correctly. Transitional spellings employ many of the features of standard spelling—the silent letters for markers, scribal rules, and the rest—but employ them uncertainly. The conventional spellings for short vowels are normally employed at this stage,

Figure 6–9
Susie
Grade 1
Transitional
spelling

Can we go see the form
well we mite go later ohcaye
win will we go mom tsafter
noon ohcaye I will get redey
now no its not time yet ok
I will go play then ohcaye
can I go to Darlas house

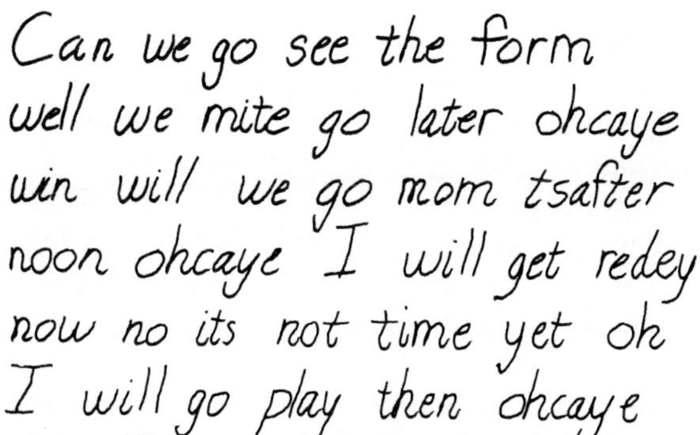

(Can we go see the farm? Well, we might go later. O.K. When will we go, Mom? This afternoon. O.K. I will get ready now. No, it's not time yet. Oh, I will go play then. O.K. Can I go to Darla's house?)

with occasional throwbacks to the letter-name strategies for spelling vowels. Words with irregular spelling patterns are usually misspelled by the children, and sometimes the misspellings have the effect of making the spelling of the word look the way it *should*.

Transitional spellings will be mixed in with correctly spelled words, whose forms the children have either accurately invented or memorized.

Children who produce transitional spellings often demonstrate that they have become aware of *features* of standard writing; particularly marking rules, scribal rules, phonological rules, and morpheme conservation rules. But they have not yet integrated all of these features into a systematic understanding of English spelling that works. In most cases, they will do so with practice.

Transitional spellers are readers. The source of the generalizations about spelling that they are beginning to manipulate is in the print they see around them. The path to correct spelling lies through more reading, more writing, and more attention to the way words are put together.

Correct Spelling

Few of us spell everything correctly. All of us resort at one time or another to a dictionary for the spelling of a troublesome word. Still, most literate adults have an accumulated body of knowledge about English spelling that enables them to spell an immense quantity of words with hardly a second thought. We couldn't have memorized them all. Most of the words we write we were never directly taught. Many of them we have occasion to write no more often than once every two or three years, yet we still spell them correctly without hesitation.

Young writers who have successfully dealt with the issues raised in this chapter—marking systems, scribal traditions, phonological rules, and morpheme conservation rules—will usually be correct spellers at a second-grade level. However, as their vocabularies grow in complexity, these young writers will be challenged to develop more sophisticated strategies in spelling, especially strategies that honor the family relationships of words (for example, relating *photograph* and *photography*, or even *separate* and *pare*, as in *paring knife*). Many won't cope all that well with this next round of challenges, which they will meet by about fourth grade. By fourth or fifth grade, children who are still using only the spelling strategies that we are calling correct in second grade will not be correct spellers; their spelling will look plausible but unlearned.

The ins and outs of more mature spellings are beyond the scope of this book.[2] For now, we can assure you that if you cultivate children's curiosity and an exploratory attitude toward spelling; if you are interested in words yourself and talk about patterns and oddities that you notice in the spelling of English words; if the children make friends with a dictionary; and if the teachers they meet in future years do the same things you do, the children will continue to grow through higher levels of literate spelling.

Now that we know something of the course of children's development in spelling ability, what can we do to help them along?

Helping Children Make Progress in Spelling

When children learn to spell, there are at least two kinds of learning going on: discovery learning and memorization. We have described this discovery learning throughout the book: first with the examples of children's language acquisition in Chapter 1; then in children's discovery of the graphic features of print, described in Chapters 2 and 3; and then in children's discovery of spelling patterns in their invented spelling, the topic of chapters 4 through 6.

But most children will not learn to spell correctly by discovery alone. Many children, first of all, need guidance to discover spelling patterns: they need words presented to them in groups, and they need to hear us comment upon the spelling patterns. Secondly, children need to be encouraged and taught to memorize the correct spellings of many words. Why?

Children need to have a store of correctly spelled words in mind from which they can infer spelling patterns, for one thing. For another, it is often unclear *which* pattern a word will follow: the word "read" could be spelled by many different patterns, including REED, REID, REDE, or REYED. Knowing these patterns helps, and the patterns can be learned by discovery; but knowing which pattern applies to a particular word requires some memorization. Also, memorizing is surely needed to learn irregularly spelled words such as "of," "was," "woman," and the like.

In the following sections we will suggest strategies for teaching spelling to children at each level of spelling development. We will concentrate on methods that nurture discovery learning and also offer explicit instruction where necessary.

For the Prephonemic Speller

Prephonemic spellers, you will remember, are children who string letters or letterlike marks together to look like writing, but whose letters bear no relation to sounds. Prephonemic spelling is common in kindergarten and early first grade. (Some children who have already discovered something of how letters represent sounds may revert to prephonemic spelling or scribbling when they are in a hurry to fill a page with print.[3] We are assuming in this discussion that each kind of spelling described is the child's most advanced way of spelling at that time. If you are not sure, ask the child to spell some one and two syllable words as best she or he is able.)

Prephonemic spellers may *not* know:

- that what we record when we write a message is a particular set of words.

read aloud. With this kind of support, the information that links a printed word with a spoken word is brought into focus for the child. Aspects of this information are things like: a word in print is a configuration of letters bound by spaces on both ends; words are arranged from left to right; more than one syllable may be a single word; and individual letters may resemble individual sounds heard in words.

There are several successful variations of the Lap Method. One is done with a poem or a song that the child has memorized. The teacher and the child sit down with a written version of the poem or song, which is ideally four to six lines in length. They read each line chorally, as the teacher points to each word. Then the teacher points to a single word and asks the child what it is. The teacher points to the first word in the line, then the last, then one in the middle. It is not likely that the child will be able to recognize the words pointed to. Instead she will have to recite the line to herself and guess what each word must be by its order in the written line. This gets her thinking about words as units of writing and gives her practice matching a word in her head with one in print.[6]

Taking dictated experience stories, a part of the language-experience approach to reading and language arts instruction, also helps develop the concept of words in print. Dictated accounts are done either with individuals or in groups. After the children have undergone an interesting episode—perhaps an encounter with baby rabbits or a field trip to the post office—each child is invited to dictate one sentence to the teacher as part of a group composition. A number of reading activities usually follow the dictation: The group reads all the sentences chorally several times; individuals volunteer to read words or sentences; the teacher points to a word in the line and asks a child to read it. In cases where the child knows by heart what the line says but cannot recognize the word, he is likely to work his way through the line, matching memorized words with units of print until he makes a match with the word in question.

The shared book method, as developed by Don Holdaway in New Zealand,[7] is nicely suited to helping young readers and writers learn about the relationships between print and speech. Holdaway's method uses big books, yard-high versions of children's books that are read in the children's presence by the teacher, who uses a pointer to touch each word as she reads. After several passes through the big book in the group setting, the children are handed standard-size versions of the book to read on their own. Holdaway and his colleagues began by creating their own big books out of whatever books were likely to be favorites with their particular children. Following their lead, commercial publishers now offer printed versions of big books for sale.

Many early phonemic spellers write their own names correctly, as well as the names of their friends, brothers, and sisters. Names can be used in learning activities to establish the concept of word. Write the child's name

Figure 6–10
Establishing
the concept of
word

JULIEJULIEJULIEJULIE

JULIE JULIE JULIE JULIE

several times on a strip of paper without leaving any spaces between the words. Then ask the child to help you separate the names. The child spells her name first, pointing to each letter. When she comes to the end of one spelling, she cuts the name apart from the one that follows. When she has cut the names apart, she may paste them on another piece of paper, leaving spaces between them (see Figure 6–10).

A similar procedure, involving whole sentences, is suggested by Marie Clay.[8] Have the child dictate a sentence to you, write it down, and read it back to him. Then read the sentence with him until he can read the sentence by himself. As you read the sentence each time, point to the words. When the child is able to read the sentence by himself (he is able to do this by memorizing, of course, not by actual reading), write the sentence a second time on a strip of paper. Now cut the words off the strip, one at a time, reading the sentence aloud minus the severed word each time. As a next step, the child can match the cut apart words with those in the sentence that left intact. A fairly easy task is for the child to arrange the cut apart words on top of the words to which they are matched. A more difficult exercise is to arrange the words into a sentence several inches below the sentence left intact.

Emily devised a similar activity when she was not quite four. She put pieces of thin paper on the covers of her favorite books and traced the titles. A sample of her work is found in Figure 6–11.

Another specific instructional goal we have for children who are early phonemic spellers is that they grow in their ability to segment spoken words

Figure 6–11
Tracing book
titles

HAND HANV
FHNDERS
THUMB

into individual phonemes. The most natural practice is to continue to spell the parts of the words of which they are more certain. Thus, their spellings may look like this at first: I W__T D__N __E P __ __ ("I walked down the path"). But in time, there will be fewer blanks left and more letters filled in as children gain practice in segmenting phonemes.

The final instructional goal we have for early phonemic spellers is that they be more willing to take risks. We have seen abundant evidence that making errors is a necessary part of learning to spell. We want children to pay attention to the print around them and see how it is put together and how it works. But we want just as much for them to produce their own writing, in which they try out spelling the way they think it is. We want them to formulate ideas about written language and act on them; then they will know what to do with the information they gain from examining other people's written language.

Unless children take risks and unless they are willing to make errors, their progress as spellers will be slow and inhibited, and their delight in making their own messages in print will be small. Children who are willing to invent spelling for words usually become correct spellers in a reasonably short time—and they also become fluent writers in the process.

Whether or not a child is a risk taker depends on a number of factors—his personality, the expectations of his parents, and the atmosphere of his classroom all contribute. There are several steps the teacher can take to help a child gain self-confidence and take risks.

Talk to the children and praise them for what they *know* about writing. If some children have discovered that writing goes left to right across a page, they may be congratulated for this discovery. If some have discovered that words have letters in them, and that the letters are mixed, this is something that the teacher can discuss with them. And if some have discovered that words are spelled by matching letters with individual sounds, this is a realization worthy of an adult's attention. Having an adult express interest in these issues as the children investigate them adds to the children's sense of accomplishment and reassures them that their efforts are worthwhile.

Parents and teachers should both understand the value of encouragement, practice, and freedom to make errors in learning to spell. If the teacher encourages invented spelling at school but does not share her position with the parents, confusion may result. Parents may be alarmed that children bring home papers with uncorrected spelling errors, or that children enthusiastically produce writing with spelling errors at home. Unless the teacher enlists the parents' understanding and support, they are likely to say discouraging things to their children, with the best of intentions. They may even question whether the teacher is doing her job, mistakenly equating the teacher's encouragement of early writing and invented spelling with a lax attitude that leaves errors uncorrected.

For the Letter-Name Speller

Children who produce letter-name spelling have developed a system of spelling that can be read by others who understand the system. Letter-name spelling represents the high-water mark of children's intuitive spelling development, and their spellings during this period are their most original. From this point on, children will become increasingly aware of the details of standard spelling, and their spelling will grow closer to that of adults.

Most children become letter-name spellers by Thanksgiving in first grade. Some begin sooner, and several may wait until late first grade to start using the letter-name strategy. Letter-name spellings will persist into second grade, though most second graders will use transitional strategies, especially in the second half of the year.

The insights letter-name spellers have about written language are the same ones needed to begin to read. And of course with more reading practice, these children will learn more and more features of standard spelling, until their spelling becomes transitional.

By now their concept of a word in print is beginning to stabilize, but exercises to develop this concept still further will continue to be helpful—both for their spelling and for their reading. Their ability to separate individual phonemes out of words has become highly productive. What they do not yet know is all the business on the other side of the letter-to-sound representation issue. They are just beginning to explore the rules by which letters represent phonemes.

They can find the phonemes, but so far their ideas of how these phonemes should be spelled stick closely to the names of the letters. They use letter-names as if they themselves were pieces of sound—building blocks out of which words can be constructed. They have not yet realized the complex rules for choosing letters to represent words.

If the disparity between their system and the complexity of standard spelling is pointed out to them too suddenly or too harshly, many children will lose confidence. If this happens, their progress into standard spelling will be delayed because they will not experiment with new forms enthusiastically. The greatest amount of progress may be gained if children at this stage are encouraged to continue writing—indeed, if they are given a steady agenda of interesting writing tasks. Their writing can be taken seriously for the sake of its message. The teacher or parents can talk about what the child wrote and not just her spelling—focusing on the message is likely to be more motivating than dwelling on the spelling.

If the letter-name speller is exposed to a good supply of interesting print, this should provide him with data from which he can, at his own pace, draw new conclusions about spelling. We should continue to read to him. We should continue to help him find favorite books, read them to him frequently, and encourage him to read them to himself. Read-along books can be highly beneficial at this stage, both for reading and for writing. Language-experience teaching—dictated stories that are reread together—bears even more fruit at this stage, both in the children's ease at finding words by the voice-to-print matching method and in the number of words the children can learn to recognize after a dictated story. They will now recognize words in the story days after they were dictated, a feat they could not do before.

Having children build a word bank—a collection of word cards for the words they recognized during the reading of a dictated story—is good practice. It's a good idea to check each child's word bank occasionally and see if she can still read all the words in her word bank. Any words that she cannot read should be taken out, placed in a separate envelope, and reviewed at a later time. The children can be encouraged to use their word bank cards when they are writing because they are always spelled correctly, and so constitute a source of correct spellings.

To help children sound out words and spell with more confidence, use a group brainstorming procedure. Choose an interesting word to spell and ask the students to help you spell it. Ask the students which sound they hear first. Then ask students to offer a letter to spell it. Discuss whether the letter makes sense or not. Then ask students to name the next sound they hear and suggest a letter to spell it.

Note that our goal is to have children hear sounds in words and match letters with them. We will accept reasonable guesses, even if they are not the correct spelling of the word, because we are trying to encourage the children to use invented (or temporary) spelling. Correctness will come later.

How do we describe this spelling to children? We like Elizabeth Sulzby's advice. If the children come up with ANEML, we say, "This is the way many children spell 'animal'" (or whatever word they are spelling). We go on to make it clear that adults spell the word a little differently and they will learn that adult spelling later.

Should we teach correct spelling to children at this stage? These are several considerations here. If we do teach them correct spelling, we must be careful not to undermine their willingness to write words the way they sound. The spirit of discovery is valuable for their learning; and besides, the act of inventing spellings actually helps children learn features of the sounds and writing system of English that will help them both in their spelling and even in their reading for some time to come.

By the second half of first grade, it may be advisable to make a "door dictionary"; that is, write frequently used words on gummed note papers and post them on the back of the classroom door or filing cabinet. Children may peel a needed word off the door, take it back to the desk to copy, and return it to the door. Alternatively, you may encourage children to make a personal spelling dictionary: a notepad with frequently used words in it, spelled correctly.

In the second half of first grade, you may safely require children to memorize a short list of words per week: five or six words, we would say. We prefer to group these words by *phonogram pattern*, especially those patterns to which we are calling the children's attention in their reading. (A phonogram pattern is a vowel and consonant combination. It is usually what is left over when we remove the beginning element from a word: the phonogram *at*, for example, is found in "that," "cat," and "rat.") You or the children may wish to add other frequently asked for words: "of," "love," "have," and so on. In the next section we describe several recommended procedures for having children study words.

Care must be taken, however, not to limit the children's writing to the words on the spelling lists or in the spelling dictionaries. It would be sad, indeed, if a preoccupation with these correctly spelled words undermined their confidence in their ability to think out spellings for themselves. Their willingness to try spelling on their own is necessary for them to move beyond memorization and learn the system of English spelling.

For the Transitional Speller

Children who are transitional spellers are adept at breaking out phonemes for words and finding letters to spell them. They are moving beyond the intuitive one-sound, one-letter spelling of the previous stage. They have begun to take note of the way standard spelling works and are trying to gain control over the patterns they perceive in standard spelling.

Transitional spelling emerges gradually from letter-name spelling; it is certainly not a gear-shift change. Letter-name spellers are learning to read, and as they read, standard spelling patterns make their way into the children's spelling. When we see many of these standard spellings—*ch, sh,* and *th* digraphs; vowels with their correct short sound; silent letters; and the like—we say that these children have become transitional spellers.

As we observed in Chapter 5, the patterns of standard spelling are many and complex. It takes time, curiosity, and much exploration for a child to master these patterns. Children need to be led gradually to learn the patterns at work in standard spelling, and it is best if they learn these in the context of meaningful writing, though isolated activities are sometimes helpful.

Inductive approaches often work well for helping children learn spelling patterns. In these, children compare the spellings of several words in light of their pronunciation, meaning, part of speech, and origin. Then they are led to formulate their own generalities about the patterns that appear to be at work.

Word sorts are teacher-made or homemade activities that help children notice and form concepts about spelling patterns. Word sorts are a categorizing exercise in which children are led to group words together that share a common feature. This exercise gets them thinking about spelling features of words, and it works with words the children already know.

The procedure works as follows. The teacher or the children write down a collection of words on small pieces of tagboard. If the teacher is using the language-experience approach, the words used are those in the children's word banks. If he is not using the approach, then he or the children can jot down fifty words or so from the children's sight words on word cards. It's important for all of the participants in an activity to know the pronunciation and meaning of every word used.

With an individual or small group of children, the teacher starts off the activity by dividing the cards among the participants. Then he puts a card in the center of the table. He asks the children to read it and to put any words they have in hand that *begin with the same sound* on the table below the guide word. (Sometimes the teacher uses a picture of an object for a guide word, so the children cannot depend on a visual match between the first letters of the guide word and the words in their hands.) The teacher makes sure that the participating children have several cards in hand that match the guide word, as well as some that do not.

Besides working with beginning sounds, the activity can be centered on long and short vowel sounds; other vowel sounds, such as diphthongs and R-controlled vowels; grammatical endings, such as -*ed* or -*s*; words that end in a *v* sound; words that undergo phonological changes; words with similar prefixes and suffixes; compound words; and many other features. The activity can be directed toward any word feature—including similarities of meaning and nuance—that the teacher intends. In fact, word sort activities often bring to light interesting word features of which the students and the teacher may have been unaware.

Word sorts have the potential for helping children to construct concepts about spelling patterns and enabling them to display the concepts they already hold.[9] Children at this stage of spelling profit from games and exercises that play on the spelling patterns of words. There are many games that play on children's recognition of allowable sequences of letters—letter sequences that typically spell words. Boggle, Perquackey, and Spill 'n Spell are games of this type. In all three, the players roll out letter cubes and try to identify English words within a specified time limit out of the letters that surface. Word hunts, Hangman, and Password are more games that encourage children's efforts to think of spelling patterns in English. All are worthwhile, both in the classroom and at home.

Beyond exploring spelling patterns, should transitional spellers be taught to spell? The answer is certainly Yes. As Ruell Allread remarked,[10] children can learn a great deal about numbers and quantities from playing with different sized cans and sorting buttons—but the day will surely come when they must memorize the multiplication tables. There are correct spellings that must be learned. This fact does not take away from invented spelling. On the contrary, when children have been encouraged to use invented spellings, have written prolifically, have developed a curiosity about words, and have discovered many of the spelling patterns of English, they will surely learn correct spellings more easily than children whose learning has been controlled by teacher or textbook. But if these children are to spell correctly, they must still be challenged to learn correct spelling.

How should spelling words be taught?

From second grade on, select twelve to fifteen words each week for the children to learn. Which words? Many teachers prefer to choose words from the children's reading, writing, or science activities. The advantage to this approach is that children certainly benefit from studying the correct spellings of words they will read and write anyway. But there are disadvantages, too. Topically chosen words may be of only momentary usefulness—children may read and write them only while the unit is being studied. Surely children should study those words they will use the most in the long run. Another drawback is that fifteen topically chosen words may show fifteen different spelling patterns, which won't call attention to spelling patterns at all and will put a heavy burden on memory.

Some sort of compromise seems best. Choose three or four words from children's reading and writing, words they will use a lot and that build on spelling patterns that seem useful to learn. For each of these words, think of two or three other words that share the same spelling pattern. These, too, should be words that children use frequently. This method should give you nine or ten spelling words. If this seems like too much work, use a basal speller; most spellers choose their words by the criteria we have just set out.

You can round the list out to fifteen by asking the children to nominate words that they want to learn that week or adding words that you've seen children misspelling. You can personalize the list by having each child choose five words each week to learn. (Just make sure these words are spelled correctly before the students set about learning them!)

Use the test/study/retest method. On the first day of the week, call out the words on the list and have each student attempt to write the correct spelling. Then call out the correct spelling of each word, and have the students strike through any incorrect spelling and write the correct spelling beside it. Or, have the students pair up and call out the words to each other.

Advise the students to study the words they misspelled for a retest at the end of the week. If some students spell most of the words on the list correctly the first time, or if they get them all wrong, you should substitute harder or easier words as appropriate. If you're using a basal spelling series or borrowing words from one, choose lists from a different grade.

Have students study their misspelled words using the multisensory study technique. This method was modified from Grace Fernald by Bradley and Bryant.[11] Advise the students to study the words using these eight steps:

1. *Look* at the word and *say* it aloud.
2. *Read* each letter in the word.

3. *Close* your eyes, try to *picture* the word, and *spell* it to yourself.
4. *Look* at the word. Did you spell it correctly?
5. *Say* each letter of the word as you *copy* it.
6. *Cover* the word and *write* it again.
7. *Look* at the word. Did you write it correctly?
8. If you made any mistakes, *repeat* the steps.

Use all of the interesting techniques you can to have children practice writing these words correctly. Computer software companies have programs that motivate children to practice spelling words, and some can be programmed to use your word lists. Software that can generate crossword puzzles using your spelling words is also available. Check with your librarian or media center director.

Conclusion

Making progress in spelling is like making progress in playing chess. Both require enthusiastic commitment not only of the memory but of the intellect as well. It is unnatural to think of spelling this way. After all, spelling and multiplication tables are two subjects that are still learned by rote at school.

A certain amount of memory work in spelling is necessary, it seems, to spell the truly exceptional words accurately. However, the active study of words, with a mind for learning how they came to be spelled the way they are and how they resemble and differ from other words, seems to be just as necessary for accurate spelling.

Those who undertake word study are often surprised at the patterns and clues they find for predicting the spellings of words. Even when some words fail to fit patterns, they become more memorable as exceptions if the normal patterns are well fixed in mind. The memory thrives on associations; reasoning and reflecting on spellings thus makes memorization easier.

The teaching of spelling in school should therefore include plenty of discussion and exploration of words—including the patterns present in their spelling, the parts of speech they can be, and the meanings they can have. In the home, games that play on spelling patterns and word meanings should be encouraged, as should frequent trips to the dictionary.

ENDNOTES

1. J. Richard Gentry and Edmund H. Henderson, "Three Steps to Teaching Beginning Readers to Spell," in Edmund H. Henderson and James W. Beers, eds., *Developmental and Cognitive Aspects of Learning to Spell* (Newark, DE: International Reading Association, 1985).
2. For more information about the spelling of older students, see Edmund H. Henderson, *Teaching Spelling* (Boston: Houghton Mifflin, 1986) or Charles

Temple and Jean Gillet, *Language Arts: Learning Processes and Teaching Practices,* 2d ed. (New York: HarperCollins, 1988).

3. Elizabeth Sulzby, "Writing Development in Early Childhood, *Educational Horizons* 64 (Fall 1985): 1, 8–12.

4. For more information on little books, see C. McCormick and J. Mason, "Intervention Procedures for Increasing Preschool Children's Interest in Knowledge about Reading," in W. Teale and E. Sulzby, eds., *Emergent Literacy* (New York: Ablex, 1986).

5. James Moffett and Betty Wagner, *Student-Centered Language Arts and Reading* (Boston: Houghton Mifflin, 1978).

6. Darrell Morris, "Beginning Readers' Concept of Word," in Henderson and Beers.

7. Don Holdaway, *Foundations of Literacy* (Portsmouth, NH: Heinemann, 1978).

8. Marie Clay, The Early Detection of Reading Difficulties, 2d ed. (Portsmouth, NH: Heinemann, 1979).

9. See Charles Temple and Jean Wallace Gillet, "Developing Work Knowledge: A Cognitive View, *Reading World* (December 1978); Jean Wallace Gillet and M. Jane Kita, "Words, Kids, and Categories," in Henderson and Beers; and Elizabeth Sulzby, "Word Concept Development Activities," in Henderson and Beers.

10. Allread made this remark to Charles Temple in August 1991.

11. Peter Bryant and Lynette Bradley, *Children's Reading Problems* (New York: Oxford University Press, 1985).

PART THREE

The Beginnings of Composition

Three-year-old Emily was intently watching her mother write. Suddenly, a pencil flew across the desk and her mother sighed over another rough draft that refused to work. "Oh, Mom," said Emily, "writing's such a cinch. All ya gotta' do is get the letters."

For Emily, and many other nursery and kindergarten children, that is what writing is all about for a while—"getting the letters." They have been exploring with pencil and paper, learning for themselves the distinctive features of alphabetic characters, and sorting out the relationship between the way words sound and their representation in print. "Getting the letters" and arranging them in some meaningful order are, in the early stages of development, prerequisites to becoming a writer.

In Chapters 2 through 6, we explored these developmental processes in depth. In the chapters that compose this section, we will explore the patterns that emerge in the way children frame their messages—in other words, their compositions. *Composition* literally means "putting together." We define composition as *putting together the elements of a message in a form that is understandable to a reader.* We will look at children's movement from writing that sounds like talk to writing that sounds like written language—writing that achieves some of the purposes for which adults use it: rethinking life, telling a story, describing something, explaining the steps in a process, or waging an argument.

CHAPTER 7

Functions and Forms
in Children's Composition

Perhaps she was inspired by the stories her mother had read to her. Perhaps she was tired of being always on the receiving end of the telling. At any rate, one day four-year-old Jessie sat her mother down and told her a story. It went like this:

> The rabbit was at his house and his mother told him to go to the well and fetch some water. But Bunny didn't go to the well because she was very curious. She went to the woods and picked some raspberries. So she said to herself, "Why don't I go and find Daddy? Have lunch in town and ride home with him. That will be more fun."
>
> She rode out with Daddy but then a great THUMP THUMP filled up the whole air. It was a real big air-walking giant. She really was frightened. She ran to the house and said, "Mamma, help!" And she hid them both. And they lived happily ever after.

We can learn several things about children's composition by looking carefully at Jessie's piece.

Children can compose before they can write. If Jessie's story is evaluated according to our definition, it is clear that she made up a composition and she did so without writing anything down. (Her mother *wrote* down her words, but Jessica composed the story.) Whether in making up stories, telling true accounts of family happenings, or fantasy play with other children, young children compose before they write.

This point is worth making because it shows us the continuity between speech and writing. At four, Jessie is a prolific talker. She is also a fluent composer of stories, so long as speech is the medium. At five and six she will begin to write, but it will be years before she will be able to write as fluently as she can talk. Jessie's speech is a laboratory for composition before she begins to write. And it should continue to serve as a laboratory as she develops writing fluency. We will want to encourage her to continue her oral composition, to continue telling stories. Otherwise the task of transcribing ideas onto paper may become the bottleneck that chokes off her creativity. Drawing pictures and talking about them, dramatizing bits of story ideas, acting out play scenarios, and simply telling stories will keep her growing as a composer as her skill and speed at transcribing ideas slowly develops. Later, she will be able to compose more skillfully on paper than in speech—as she learns to write, reconsider, and hone her thoughts in print.

Children incorporate in their compositions bits and pieces of what they have heard and read in the works of others. In Jessica's story, we hear echoes of "Peter Rabbit," "Jack and Jill," "Curious George," "Jack and the Beanstalk," and Pete Seeger's rendition of the African folktale, "Abiyoyo." The story is her own creation, yet she created it out of images, characters, actions, and themes that come from the literature she has heard, as well as from her family life.

There's nothing unusual about the amount of borrowing she has done. Like all writers, children find resources for composing in the stories they hear and read—and not just stories but other catchy uses of language, too—and they learn from their peers as well as from professional writers.

In composing, children are challenged to juggle the interests of self, audience, topic, and purpose in their writing. Although Jessica's story is ostensibly about a character called Bunny, when the action switches from going to the woods and picking raspberries to finding Daddy in town and riding home with him, we get the sense that the fictional character is being shoved aside and Jessica, the real four-year-old girl, is taking center stage. When young writers are composing, they seem driven by a powerful urge to put themselves and their interests in the foreground.

Another challenge writers encounter lies in respecting the audience's need to know. If a child wants to write a story about Bunny, how much can she assume her readers know already? She doesn't want to tell them obvious things, like what a rabbit is; on the other hand, she *should* tell them what this particular Bunny is like. These are difficult questions for young writers, presumably because their young minds cannot easily imagine other people's points of view. Piaget[1] used the term *egocentrism* to describe the young child's assumption that other people know what she knows and can see what she sees. (Perhaps the best example of this occurs when a five-year-old says "Look at this!" yet holds his book so that only he—not you—can see it.) Young people gradually overcome egocentrism as the people around them assert their needs to be considered, especially their need for information.

"Hold the book so I can see it, silly!"

"Wait. Did Bunny ride in the truck?"

The best remedy for egocentrism in writing is to write frequently for real audiences who can ask questions and make comments about the work.

Compositions follow familiar patterns, or forms. When Jessica sat her mother down and began to talk, it was clear that she intended to tell a story. She demanded and received complete attention, her eyes twinkled, she put on a sing-song voice and an exaggerated delivery: "But Bunny didn't go to the well because she was veeerrry curious!" None of these signals comes through in the written version of the story, though, and if we had been given no introduction, we might for a moment have stayed in the dark about what sort of writing we had before us. But by the time we reached the end of the first line, it would have occurred to us readers that rabbits who live in houses with talking mothers are the stuff of fiction. Once we had used these details to pigeonhole the work, we had a sense of what other sorts of events to expect.

Readers rely on *form* to make sense out of what they read. Whether the words before you are a story, a letter from a friend, a summons to appear in court, an advertisement, or the instructions for operating a lawn mower makes a big difference in the way you read them. In our society, the forms taken by texts that serve these different purposes are somewhat conventionalized, and they are, for the most part, easily recognizable. It will be our purpose for the rest of this chapter to lay out and describe the forms of composition that most frequently come up in children's writing.

Self, Audience, Topic, and Purpose: A Menu of Writing Forms

To put the self into the piece, or not? To tell the audience a lot, or a little? To write about one thing, or many? To address our topic with an expression of feeling about it, or as a story, or to explain or describe, or as an act of persuasion? There seem to be many choices to make whenever we compose in written language. Those who work with young writers need some way to handle

Figure 7–1
JoBeth
Grade 1

Figure 7–2
Annabrook
Grade 1

A

ohe Dog.
Oetc there wues
a Dog named
Sip. he
witeto the
soo. And he
100kt at the
Fish,
like ing his lips
tain he Sol
a cat named
Nip. named

B

Whats
you'r name,
my name
is Nip. I
came to look
for you. And
fish. oh!
thar ovr
thar.

C

Oh thank
you. Oh I Love
You. And
I love you.
We will be
mirred by the
Pig. And they
kisод,

AAAA
Choo
ooo
I LOVE
You
I LOVE
you

D

wy are
you, I meen
wy did you
want me.
Oh I just
wantid to
sing for
you.
And I whnt-id!
too sing for
You too,

the complexity. We find such a means in the work of James Britton, an English educator who has studied and written insightfully for years about young people's development as writers.

Britton has a system for describing different acts of writing that takes into account the writer's self, her audience, her purpose, and the form she uses.[2] The system divides acts of writing into three major categories, for which we will use the term *modes*: the *expressive mode*, the *poetic mode*, and the *transactional mode*. (Britton used the term *voice* for what we are calling *mode*.) Figures 7–1, 7–2, and 7–3 provide examples of each mode.

The sort of writing in Figure 7–1 seems to come naturally to young writers. The author has put herself directly into the piece, in center stage. The reader, if any is contemplated, might be assumed to be anyone who is interested in the author: the piece is written as if to a friend. The purpose of the piece seems to be to *express JoBeth's feelings*. We may say that JoBeth has written in the "expressive mode," about which we will say more later.

The second mode of writing in Britton's scheme is the poetic. The term *poetic* is a little misleading here. It comes from a Greek word *poeien*, which means "to create." Hence, poetic writing is not limited to poetry but is any written work whose function is creative, to generate understanding and enjoyment beyond itself.

Consider the story in Figure 7–2. The work is not intended to express the writer's likes and dislikes, at least not directly. The story does not stand or fall on the readers' knowledge of or interest in Annabrook. The function of this piece is to stand as a work of delight, much like a picture hung on the wall.

Figure 7–3 shows a piece of writing with a clearly different purpose. In this piece the writer is in the background; it is the topic as well as the reader

Figure 7–3
Missy
Grade 2

Missy

firstyou get on your bicyle andput your left hand on one bar. And you put your right hand on the other bar.Then put your left foot on one pedle.And yourother foot on the other pedle.And then you put your but on the seat and you know how to ride a bike.

that are brought most prominently into the piece. Something is expected of the reader: he is supposed to learn how to ride a bicycle. Britton calls writing of this kind *transactional* because it conducts or transacts some real-world business between the writer and the reader.

In the transactional mode the writer may wish to persuade, describe, explain, or give directions. Note that it doesn't matter who the writer is in Missy's piece in order for the piece to achieve its purpose. Moreover, the truth of the statements can be verified by simply getting on a bike and seeing if, by following her directions, we can ride the thing.

Conclusion

To summarize, when children make messages on paper, they normally use language in one of three modes:

1. *The expressive mode.* This is language that is close to the self, used to reveal the nature of the person, to verbalize his consciousness, and to exhibit his close relation to the reader. Expressive language is a free flow of ideas and feelings.
2. *The poetic mode.* Language is used as an art medium in the poetic mode.
3. *The transactional mode.* This is language concerned with getting things done. It involves giving information or instructions and attempting to persuade and advise others.

Britton's three modes capture the basic varieties of young children's writing fairly well. In terms of children's development as writers, it appears that most children write first, and continue to write most easily, in the expressive mode. Gradually they also gain control over poetic writing and transactional writing.

In the next three chapters, we will explore children's writing in each of the three modes. As we shall see, writing often falls in transitional points between expressive and transactional and poetic. But let us begin with expressive writing and see how it works and how a child moves out from it.

ENDNOTES

1. Jean Piaget, *The Language and Thought of the Child* (New York: New American Library, 1974).
2. James Britton, *Language and Learning* (Harmondsworth, England: Penguin Books, 1970).

CHAPTER 8

Writing in the Expressive Mode

A basic function of writing is to put the writer in touch with her own thoughts. What we call here the expressive mode is purely and simply self-expression through words. It does not need or take into account an audience. While writing in the poetic mode seeks to entertain or to delight the reader, and writing in the transactional mode seeks to inform or persuade, writing in the expressive mode seeks only to express. It is for the writer's own benefit.

Writing in the expressive mode is very much like talking to yourself. We find it in very young children's writing (see Figure 8–1). We find it in diaries and journals (see Figure 8–2).

We find it recommended by therapists to adults who have lost track of themselves and by group leaders to would-be novelists as a way of bringing to light the rough stuff of the subconscious.

The spontaneity of the expressive voice in children marks their writing as childish but also gives it strength.

Writing in the expressive mode can sound a lot like talk. It is even common for children to put dialogue into their early writing, apparently because the give-and-take of dialogue is more familiar to them and easier to maintain than a long message by a single speaker (see Figure 8–3). Sometimes the other partner in the dialogue is the writer's intended audience. Sometimes it is some other character.

Jeff's writing, which follows on p. 131, allows him to relive his hockey experience. He is not thinking yet about how to make the experience clear to an audience, but when he's ready to do so, he'll have the raw material at hand. In the meantime, he has re-created the experience for himself.

Figure 8–1
Alex
Kindergarten

(Oooh. I love camping but not itching.)

Figure 8–2
JoBeth
Grade 1

Sant paTriks
day is comeing in
to weeks. my
Teachr hasant
GoT a chance
To PuT up The
Pichers for it.
I Like it
Becose We Get
to edT Goas
and Turky BuT
The BeST ParT
is. you GeT TO
GeT FaT.

A

Boy is this
boring.
S.t. Paterics
day is intwo
Months if you
Thank thats
not Boring
Tell Me What is .

B

No Geting
To eat turcky.
No Pillgrims.
No indeins
No inethang.
Like I say
if you Dont thank
that's Not Boring Whdt
IS

C

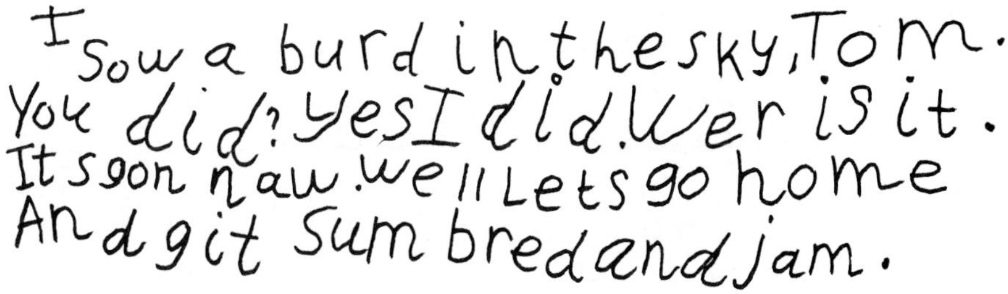

Figure 8–3
Susie
Grade 1

I sow a burd in the sky, Tom.
You did? Yes I did. Wer is it.
It soon naw. Well Lets go home
And git sum bred and jam.

IT IS TIME TO GET UP
YOU'RE KIDDING I DO NOT WANT TO GET UP TO GO TO
HOCKEY
BUT YOU HAVE TO
OKOK
FIRST YOU HAVE TO GET DRESSED
LET'S GO
GO GO GO GO GO GO GO
SPRINT AT THE BLUE LINE!
THAT IS THE END OF THAT DRILL
NOW WE WILL HAVE TO SCRIMMAGE
GO DEVON! TWEEEEEEEEEEEEEEET
SWITCH UP! NICE GOAL.

Jeff, Age 7

Much writing relies on monologue, not dialogue, and for many children this represents a profound shift to a very different way of using language. Children may need experience in drawing language out by themselves, without an interlocutor. Some researchers believe that children should be encouraged to engage in dramatic play in the classroom because it allows them to practice language that is decontextualized from here-and-now reality, in which language relies heavily on gesture. Such play requires them to elaborate, as we do in writing: "Go, messenger, and tell the queen her royal dinner is ready." At the same time, language use within dramatic play is supported by more than one interlocutor, making it a sort of intermediate activity between conversation and the monologue of writing.[1]

James Britton encourages teachers to draw out children's contributions to conversation by asking questions: "Yes, and then what happened?" "Was there anything else you saw?" and so on.[2] Having children write in a journal is another means of drawing out monologue; even first graders can be encouraged to keep journals. Figure 8–2 shows an example of one first grader's monologue. This piece is from a diary that JoBeth, a first grader, and the rest of her classmates were keeping at school.

Another loose form of expressive writing is what Susan Sowers, a researcher at the University of New Hampshire, calls an *inventory*. Inventories

Figure 8–4
Tyler
Grade 1

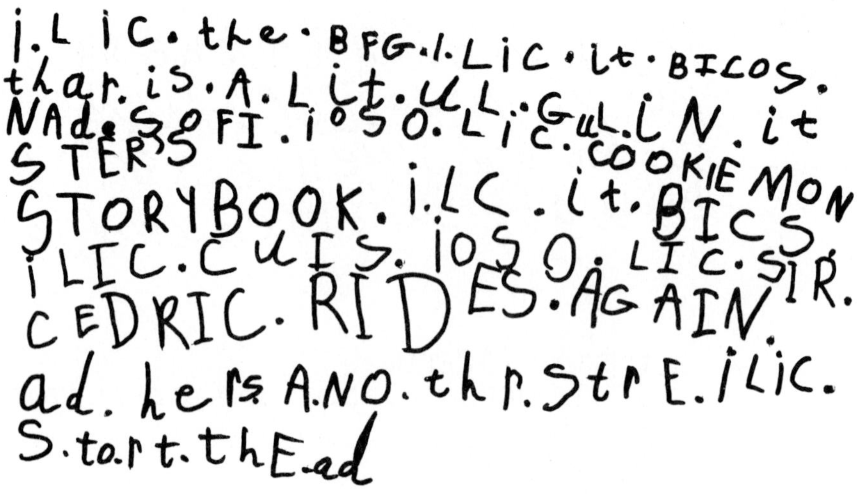

i.L iC. the. BFG.i.LiC.it.BICOS.
that.is.A.Lit.ULL.GuLN.it
NAd.SoFI.i°So.Lic.Gull.N.it
STERS
STORYBOOK.i.LC.it.BICS
COOKIE MON
iLIC.CUIS.io So.LiC.SiR.
CEDRIC.RIDES.AGAIN.
ad.heRs A.NO.th r.Str E.iLIC.
S.tart.thEad

(I like the B.F.G. I like it because there is a little girl in it named Sophie. I also like Cookie Monster's Storybook. I like it because I like cookies. I also like Sir Cedric Rides Again. And here's another story I like: Stuart. The End.)

Figure 8–5
Tyler
Grade 1

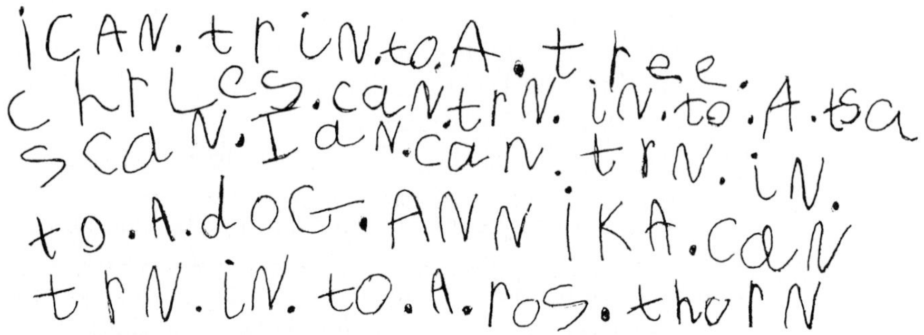

iCAN.tr iN.to.A.tree.
chrLes.caN.trN.iN.to.A.tsa
scaN.IaN.caN.trN.iN.
to.A.doG.ANNIKA.caN
trN.iN.to.A.ros.thorN

(I can turn into a tree. Charles can turn into a trash can. Ian can turn into a dog. Annika can turn into a rose thorn.)

are collections of things a child has or knows or likes. Tyler's first piece (see Figure 8–4) lists all the books she likes just now. Figure 8–5 lists what her friends can turn into in their sleep.

Transitional Writing: Expressive Traces in the Other Two Modes

Since expressive writing comes naturally to children, we do little to promote it as such in school. In fact, as soon as children begin to share their writing, both teachers and their peers help push them toward the other two modes of writing by giving them audience reactions.

Figure 8–6
John
Grade 2

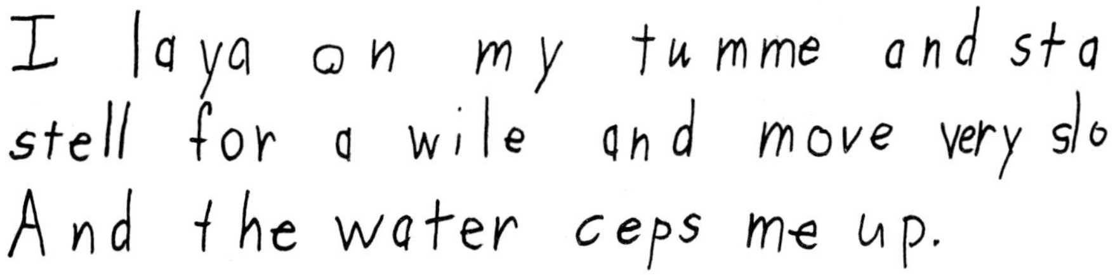

I laya on my tumme and sta stell for a wile and move very slo And the water ceps me up.

The three modes—expressive, poetic, and transactional—are in no way exclusive. Most writing will combine all three.

In Figure 8–6, John relives the experience of floating on his tummy, and so will be able to explain to someone else how to do it. You might call this piece expressive/transactional.

Eric fantasizes the experience of being a snapping turtle under water. This is make-believe written down. Call it expressive/poetic since he then uses this piece as lines in a play. The audience is able to share his experience through his words.

> I AM SINKING INTO THE MUD. ALGEE GROES ON MY FACE. GREN PLANTS FLOTE BY MY EYES. WHEN I AM REDDY I WIL SWIM SWIFLY TO THE SURFIS AND I WIL SNAP!
>
> *Eric, Grade 2*

The features of expressive writing linger even when young writers intend to write in other modes. The loosely structured conversational tone and the tendency to put the self and the self's interests on center stage pop up in pieces that might have been expected to tell stories, give explanations, or make arguments. Note, for example, the piece written by Debbie in response to her teacher's instruction to write an argument (see Figure 8–7). Debbie's intention was to write an argument, and she clearly succeeded. Yet the language she used has the give-and-take structure and bouncy rhythm of conversation, as if she had rehearsed her spiel by arguing with herself in the mirror.

Whether children are writing directions for hatching hens' eggs or creating a story, their delight in authorship may lead them to come out from behind the pen and enjoy the limelight of being read. And suddenly the reader's attention will be shifted away from the topic or the plot to some deeply felt emotion or new awareness of the author's.

Children, and adults for that matter, approach the transactional and poetic modes only as they begin to think about the things their audience—the people who read their work—may need to know, and as they begin to consider the structural requirements of the different forms of written composition. Britton points out that young children are not able to comply fully with all the expectations readers of transactional or poetic writing have of the writer, nor

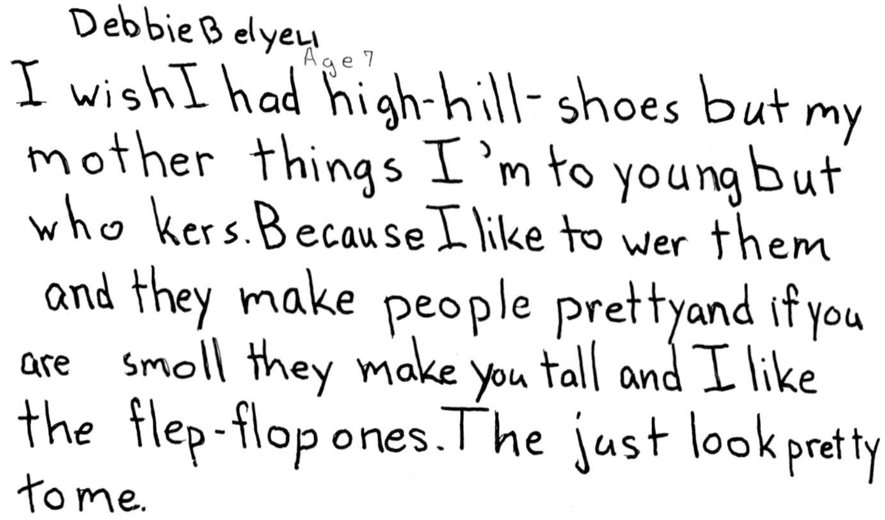

Figure 8–7
Debbie
Grade 2

Debbie B elyeu

Age 7

I wish I had high-hill-shoes but my mother things I'm to young but who kers. Because I like to wer them and they make people pretty and if you are smoll they make you tall and I like the flep-flop ones. The just look pretty to me.

would we want them to. It is by *attempting* to meet these expectations that children gradually gain control over the different modes of writing.

In any case, the fact that young writers put themselves visibly into their writing and use direct conversational language shows that they are keeping alive their own *voice*, the expression of their own personal stake in their topic.

As Debbie, the author of the "high-hill" composition, shares her work with teachers and peers, and as her writing efforts and reading experience help her become aware of her audience and the various structures that may shape written composition, she will produce more consistently structured examples of the transactional and poetic modes. For now, remnants of the expressive mode come into her writing, even when she is trying to address other purposes. When they do, her writing will have plenty of personality, but a slightly disorganized and digressive style.

Conclusion

Expressive writing is the bedrock on which other forms of writing are built. It is through expressive writing that the child begins to see language as a pipeline to his own inner self.

When children are ready to share their work and are strong enough in their attachment to writing to take the heat of others' comments, the class and teacher can help them move into the other two modes without fear of losing their own voice.

ENDNOTES

1. Lee Galda, "Narrative Competence: Play, Storytelling, and Story Comprehension," in A. D. Pellegrini and T. Yawkey, ed., *The Development of Oral and Written Language in Social Contexts* (Norwood, NJ: Ablex, 1984).
2. James Britton, *Language and Learning* (Harmondsworth, England: Penguin Books, 1970).

CHAPTER 9

Writing in the Poetic Mode

Gradually, throughout the primary grades, but usually beginning quite early in the first-grade year, young writers become sensitive to their readers and listeners. They shift from the purely expressive mode to a form of writing deliberately shaped to interest the reader. This is what we call writing in the poetic mode.

Although jokes, riddles, poetry, song lyrics, and play scripts all fall within the poetic mode, the most popular and most difficult form of poetic writing is the story. Many stories are make-believe written down to be shared, as in Figure 9–1. Other stories are personal narratives straight out of

Figure 9–1
John
Grade 1

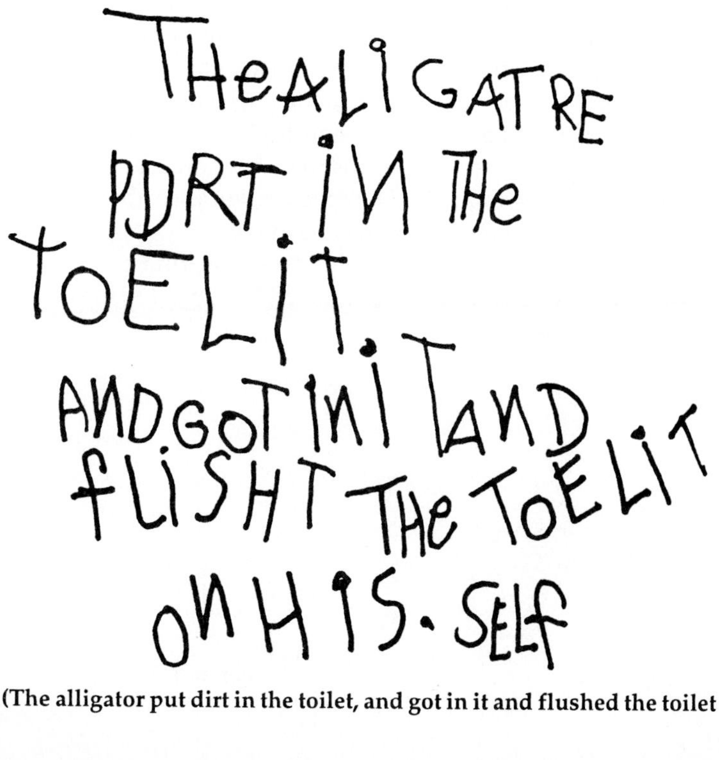

THEALiGATRE PDRT iN THe ToELiT. ANDGOTiNi LAND fLiSHT THe ToELiT oN HiS. SELf

(The alligator put dirt in the toilet, and got in it and flushed the toilet on his self.)

reality but shaped into a story form in order to catch the listener's interest. Sara's story is one of these.

> ONE DAY I WAS SITTING ON THE FLOOR WITH MY BROTHER AND SISTERS. WE WERE WATCHING MR. ROGERS. MY BROTHER AND SISTER WERE SUCKING THEIR THUMBS. I WASN'T SUCK-ING MY THUMB. BUT IT ENDED. I SAID MOM! IT ENDED. SHE SAID WHAT MOVIE DO YOU WANT TO WATCH. WE SAID FROSTY. WHEN WE GOT TO THE PART WHEN FROSTY MELTED THEY HAD TEARS IN THEIR EYES.
>
> *Sara, Age 6*

In the first pages of this chapter, we will sketch out the developmental sequence of children's ability to organize their thoughts into stories. Next we will follow two quite different young writers as their skills develop through the first and second grades. Finally we will focus on classroom practices that help children grow as writers within the poetic mode.

Stages

First, a warning: While developmental stages provide a useful guideline for those who work with young children, the ability of a child should never be judged by one piece of work. The clarity of each story reflects the writer's awareness of audience. It also reflects his concentration span, the distractions in the room, how tired his hand is, and the amount of helpful curiosity shown by his listeners. Because there are so many variables, a child may write a one-worder on Monday and be up to a full page on Tuesday, or vice versa.

Stage one is marked by seemingly random words (see Figure 9–2). Writing at stage one often seems to be triggered by whatever the child feels safe spelling (see Figure 9–3). Some reassurance about the acceptability and strategy of invented spelling may be in order.

At stage two, one idea leads to another, a phenomenon Arthur Applebee calls *chaining*.[1] Often the child can fill some of the gaps verbally. (See Figure 9–4.)

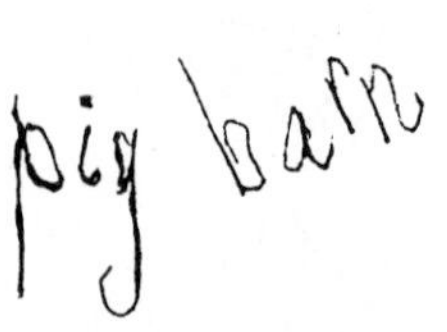

Figure 9–2

Figure 9–3

Figure 9–4
Alex
Grade 1

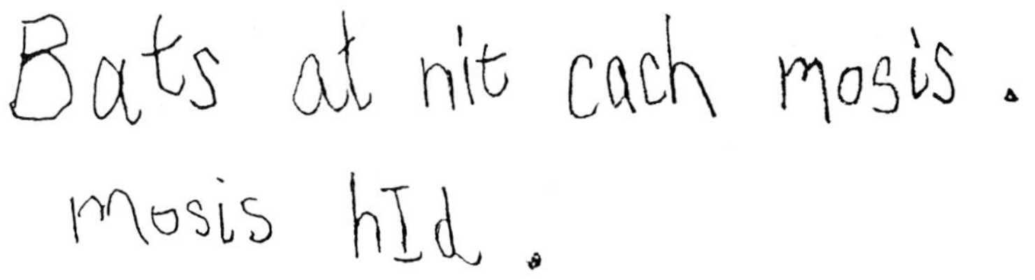

Bats at nit cach mosis. mosis hId.

Words and phrases begin to cluster around some central idea in stage three. Applebee calls this *centering*. Laura's writing is an example of stage three.

> I HAVE A FROG. HE IS MY FAVORITE FROG. I LIKE HIM. I LIKE YOU FROG.
>
> *Laura, Age 6*

In stage four, children's writing is semi-structured. Laura produced this more complex piece of writing the day after she wrote her "I have a frog" piece.

ONE SUNNY DAY I WOKE UP. I WENT OUTSIDE. I FOUND A FROG. I WANTED TO KEEP IT. I PLAYED WITH HIM. THEN I PUT HIM BACK. HE WAS HAPPY. WE HAD DINNER AND WENT TO BED. I COULD HEAR MY MOM AND DAD WASHING THE DISHES.

Laura, Age 6

Stage five is characterized by structured writing. (See Figure 9–5.) Children's ability to structure an entire story in an interesting way increases rapidly when they share work with each other and give each other comments. This will be discussed more fully at the end of this chapter.

Another factor that clearly influences children's ability to structure stories is the quantity and quality of stories read or told to them. Most stories have the following elements:

- a setting (time, place, etc.)
- one or more characters
- a strong wish on the part of the main character, *or* a problem
- resolution to the wish or problem

How do children understand these elements, and how do they incorporate them into their stories?

It seems that much of their ability is intuitive. The following first lines of stories were all written by first graders, none of whom had had formal instruction in story structure. (We standardized the spelling and punctuation.)

> THERE WAS ONCE A GIRL WHO WAS VERY POOR AND HER FATHER LIVED IN ANOTHER WORLD . . .
>
> *Daisy, Age 6*

Figure 9–5
Josie
Grade 1

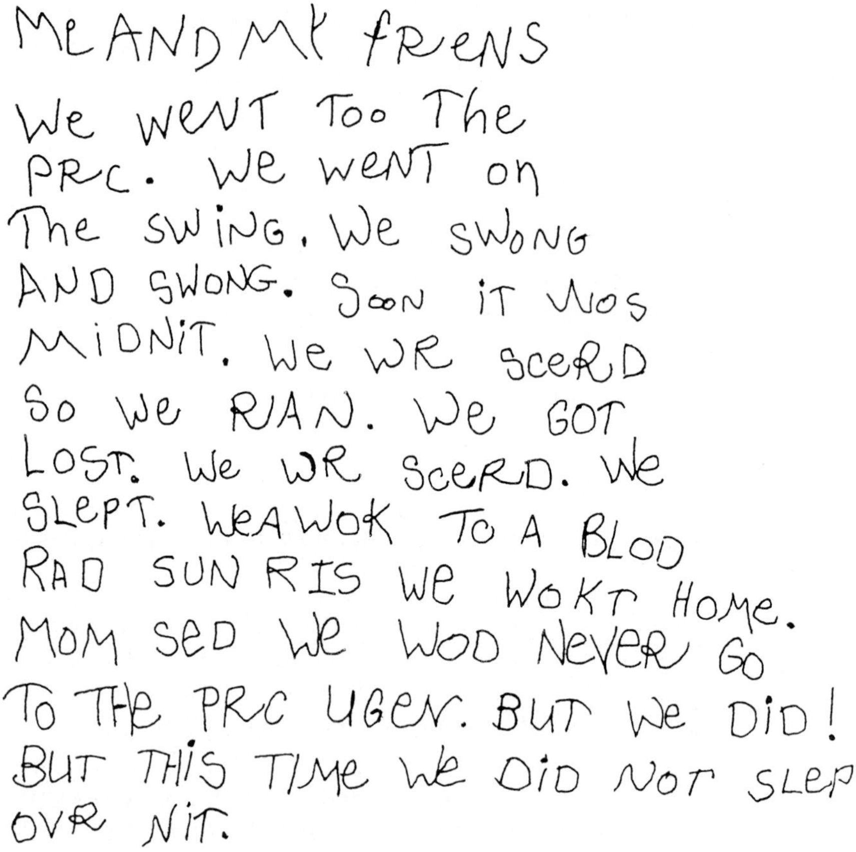

ME AND MY FRENS
WE WENT TOO THE
PRC. WE WENT ON
THE SWING. WE SWONG
AND SWONG. SOON IT WOS
MIDNIT. WE WR SCERD
SO WE RJAN. WE GOT
LOST. WE WR SCERD. WE
SLEPT. WEA WOK TO A BLOD
RAD SUN RIS WE WOKT HOME.
MOM SED WE WOD NEVER GO
TO THE PRC UGEN. BUT WE DID!
BUT THIS TIME WE DID NOT SLEP
OVR NIT.

A STORM BLEW UP. NOBODY COULD EXIST IN THIS STORM, THE
PEOPLE THOUGHT. BUT THEY THOUGHT WRONG...

Rebecca, Age 6

GODZILLA IS HEADED TOWARD TOKYO AND HE IS FLYING
FAST...

Hugh, Age 6

"NOW LET'S SEE SOME REAL WORK!"
"WHAT KIND OF WORK?" ASKED CHARLES.
"ART WORK," SAID REBECCA.

Rebecca, Age 7

"HMMM, I WONDER HOW MUCH MISCHIEF I CAN CAUSE
TODAY..." THOUGHT WITZ.

Jeff, Age 7

THE CUBS WOKE UP TO A BLOOD RED SUNRISE. THEY SLIPPED
ON THEIR HIKING BOOTS AND THEIR HEAVY BLACK COATS
AND TIP-TOED OUT OF THE KITCHEN . . .

Jessica, Age 6

Without any instruction, by some storyteller's instinct, each of these
children has established character, setting, and challenge. Where do children
get these ideas? From life, from books, from each other, from their imagination? How do they learn to shape, present, and develop their ideas? We get
some idea by observing the development of two young writers, Joey and
Sarah.

Joey's Works: A First Grader
Learns to Write Stories

Joey was a first grader in Angell Elementary School, in Berkeley, Michigan, a
community near Detroit. He was a confident and prolific writer. His work
folder had entries dating from the third week in September; most had big,
colorful pictures and full sentence captions. He spelled some words correctly—"love," "like," "is," and "can"—and he didn't hesitate to invent spellings
for other words: "dinosaur," "rocket," "blast off," and others. For the first six
weeks of school, the form his early writings took was almost all expressive.
He used two familiar features from this form: the *love/like inventory* that Susan
Sowers noted in the New Hampshire studies[2] and dialogue, which uses the
language of conversation as a model by which to structure writing. Figures
9–6 and 9–7 are examples of his early work.

In late October he began to write pieces with fictional topics (he continued to write other kinds of pieces, too—mainly expressive pieces, notes to
friends, and expository and descriptive pieces). We decided to use the presence of such fictional topics as a criterion of story-ness and chose twenty-two
pieces that met this criterion for analysis.

Figure 9–6

Figure 9–7

REB WC KAN PLEZ GO to BAES
BAES KAN GO TO SES LEA. BAES
KAN PLEZ GO TO SES REB. BCS
I LE K. BES. BCS. LER. QET. AE A.
LEA. LEK. ME BCS. LEE R. QET. LEE,

The first piece with a fictional topic is seen in Figure 9–8. He established his (sort of) fictional topic with a nice drawing of a rocket, then went on to write "A USA rocket is taking off." But what to do next? A problem in all story writing is how to give structure to the work. By what principle does one stretch out word after word to fill lots of space, as professional writers do?

Figure 9–8

a USA rakit
is taken foo
0987654321O
BIAS OOP

Figure 9–9

Goibal   Goibal
Hiou   is   Taet
lakre dig and
Eat Goibal
Goibal.

Figure 9–10

MR. Bump I'm
MR Bump
Why are you Calling me?
MR. Noes Be Kas
I want you.
Joey

Joey solved the problem with the device of repetition, by reciting the count-down sequence. It doesn't take his story very far, but it is vivid and appropriate to the topic of rockets, and it fills the page nicely.

He did a similar thing in his next piece, about a turkey (see Figure 9–9). A drawing of the turkey anchored down his topic. For structure he relied on the repetition of turkey sounds and a dialogue: "Gobble, gobble. Who is that turkey, big and fat? Gobble, gobble." Again, this strategy addresses the topic vividly, though it doesn't approach being a plot yet; there is nothing to propel the story forward.

There is something new in this piece: the conventionalized sentence structure of story language. "Who is that turkey, big and fat?" is not the syntax of speech, but it has the cadence of the storyteller's language.

The next piece uses a storybook character, Mr. Bump (see Figure 9–10). Here is a fictional character, taken from a series of books for children. Having introduced him, now what? Around what structure will the writer organize more sentences about him? The solution again is found in dialogue, this one between Mr. Bump and Mr. Nosy. This dialogue seems to follow its own logic rather than to develop any story. Applebee would say that the sentences are *chained* (each one suggests the next) but not well *centered* (they don't develop to any point).

The next piece introduces another character from the same book series, this one Mr. Bounce (see Figure 9–11). The structure used here is one of

Figure 9–11

Figure 9–12

he is borsting off
10. 9. 8. 7. 6. 5. 4. 3. 2. 1.
bost off So
off they go

off the rocket gos
in the rocket are
sem astronaut

Figure 9–13

The cios are
moing the srep
are baing
the bratis sir
Is sining so brat
worje ius up and
Miare and Joeshs

action, relating all of the things that Mr. Bounce does. He bounces all over the place, bounces out of the window, and has to go to the B.R. (bathroom?). But these actions still do not develop into a plot, and again we would say, in Applebee's terms, that the events are chained but very weakly centered—we hear of things that Mr. Bounce does, but the actions do not develop any point.

In mid-December Joey returned to the theme of rocket launching (see Figure 9–12). The last time he wrote on this topic he simply announced the topic and then wrote out the countdown sequence. This time he adds another line that uses the diction of an eyewitness reporter—"Off the rocket goes"— and then a piece of description—"In the rocket are some astronauts"—that might eventually lead into the development of a plot, but doesn't yet.

The use of description is taken much further in this next piece (see Figure 9–13). Now his use of description has become almost lyrical. "The cows are mooing, the sheep are baaing. The brightest star is shining so bright, wakes Jesus up and Mary and Joseph." The details are nicely focused around the topic of the Nativity, and the little bit of action Joey has written into his piece gives it the quality of an animated tableau. But it is still a tableau, not a developed story; there is still no problem, no effort, and no solution.

After Christmas recess Joey took a giant step forward (see Figure 9–14). Joey consciously imitated the fairy tale form, and in so doing used the conventionally phrased story opener, "Once upon a time." But he did more. The undifferentiated actions that had characterized his earlier stories

Figure 9–14

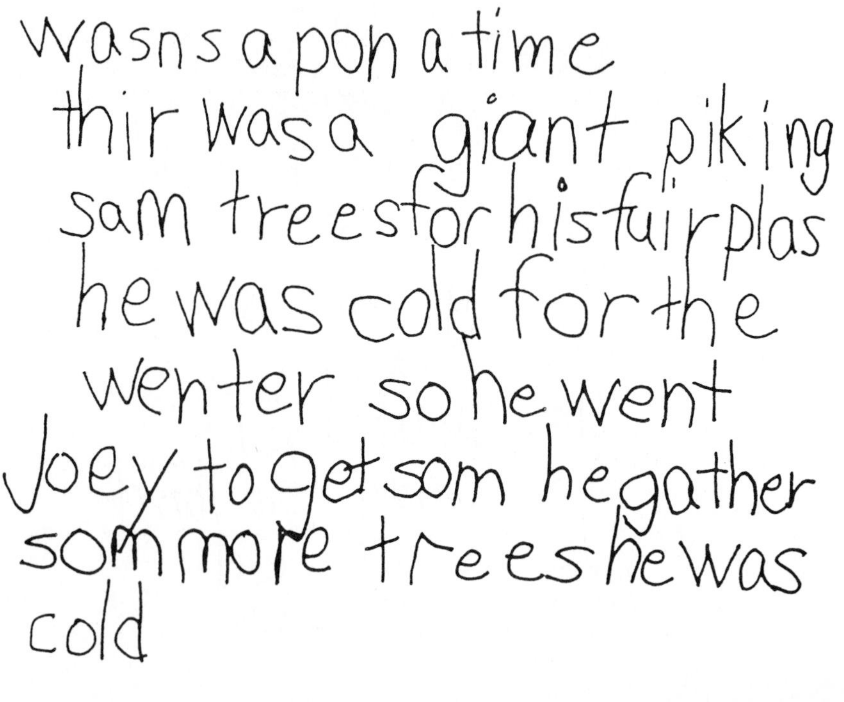

Wasns apon a time
thir was a giant piking
sam treesfor his fuir plas
he was cold for the
wenter so he went
Joey to get som he gather
som more trees he was
cold

Figure 9–15

ET was landing
on erth his shp was
big it had many laes
bt was in it it was
landing that nithe

he now divided into a problem and an effort to solve it—"He was cold for
the winter so he went to get some trees for his fireplace."

Another piece from late January showed a slight development over his
earlier work (see Figure 9–15). To this point his pieces have tended to feature
action or description, but not both. But now in writing about ET's landing, he
integrates good description—"His ship was big. It had many lights"—with
more action—"ET was landing on earth . . . It [the spaceship] was landing
that night." A pattern is emerging here: A story element will first appear in
and dominate an early piece of writing before it is combined with one or
more elements in another piece of writing, sometimes weeks later.

Early in February Joey appears to be consolidating his move to separate
problems or causes from actions or efforts. Now it is explained that the boy is
running because the ghost is chasing him (Figure 9–16). In early February
Joey wrote a Valentine piece. For the first time he added to his work of the
previous day (see Figure 9–17). This piece shows several new developments.
His first day's effort was essentially an expressive piece. The tendency to
write a love/like inventory came through strongly—"I love my Dad, I love
my Mom, I love my sister." On the second day he turned the piece into a
story. He used himself as the character—the first time he'd done that in his
fictional pieces . He also used his drawing to convey the action in the story,
something he didn't do again, to such an extent, after writing this piece.

Figure 9–16

the ghost was chasing
after the boy the boy
was scrared the boy
ran fast as he can.

Figure 9–17

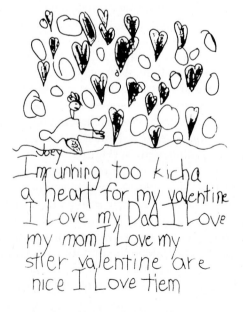

I'm running too kicha
a heart for my valentine
I Love my Dad I Love
my mom I Love my
stier valentine are
nice I Love tiem

oh no I'm in tralbel I
don't know what to
do hela, hela, hela
I min tralbel yes I
am what shaed a
I do hela hela me

Figure 9–18

A heart fairy is
coming I'm running
to get a heart
hi fairy can I
have a heart yes
you can thankyou
vevrymuch, you're
waelkkcome!

Finally, in this piece he used directly quoted speech to express some of the action; before when he had quoted dialogues, these tended to digress from the thrust of the story.

The next week, in his "heart fairy" piece (Figure 9–18), he again used himself as a central character, though he introduced a novel character in the heart fairy. This piece continued to observe the division between problem and solution (or we might say goal and attempt, or justification and action). It also used dialogue to carry the plot further, something Joey had not done successfully before.

The Leprechaun piece, again, has Joey as the central character (see Figure 9–19). The structure has become something like introductory action + problem-raising action + reaction. The actions have a definite time sequence to them: (1) "I found a Leprechaun," (2) "I touched it," (3) "I begin to turn into a Leprechaun," (4) "Oh no, look at me. I'm a Leprechaun."

This is the second piece (the first being the Valentine story of a month before) that he wrote in the first person. Before, his choosing the first person seemed to invite him to lapse into the digressive love/like inventory, that familiar feature of expressive writing. Now the expressive urge seems to have settled on the *reaction* in the piece: "Yaaaaaaaaaay, I'm a Leprechaun. . . . Good. I'm happy."

Figure 9–19

I fond a LePRECHAUN Hat I tocht it I Begin to tiun into a LEPRECHAUN oh no look at me I'm a LEPRECHAUN ya.

xaaaaa aaaaa aa aa I'm a Leprechaun. Goodde I have some mich that's Good I'm happy. the end by Joey

The short piece in Figure 9–20 uses the picture to portray some of the action, to show what the problem is. It also uses dialogue successfully to carry the story forward. It lacks explanation to support the dialogue.

The Cobra piece (Figure 9–21) is a further development along a line that began with the Valentine and continued with the Leprechaun. We readers are still plopped right into the middle of the action from the first sentence, an effect we call *introductory action*. But this action, too, is broken into parts that

Figure 9–20

PaPa smurf sind don't tach that posan. all riht sind smurfet

Figure 9–21

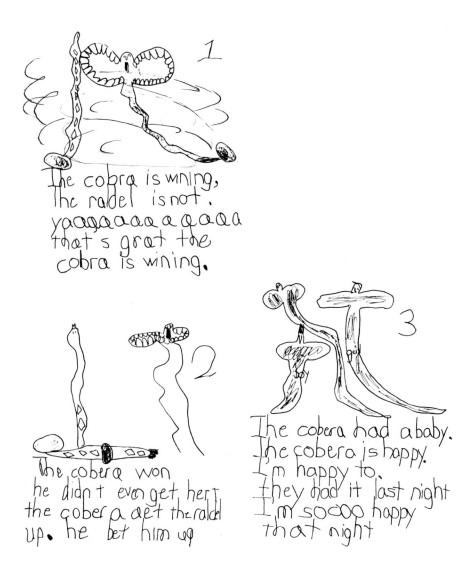

The cobra is wining,
the radel is not.
yaaaaaaa a aaaa
that's grat the
cobra is wining.

the cobera won
he didn't even get hert
the cobera aet theraldel
up. he bet him up

The cobera had a baby.
the cobera is happy.
I'm happy to.
they had it last night
I'm soooo happy
that night

allow some development in time—"The cobra is winning. The rattle is not. . . .
The cobra won."

The action, again, is followed by reactions—"That's great, the cobra is
winning." It's not clear just who is cheering, but again this appears to be a
throwback to the expressive urges in his Valentine piece.

Ten days later Joey wrote the mouse piece (Figure 9–22). This piece had
a nice story shape. It began with the familiar introductory action, the combination *setting* and *initiating event* of story grammar—"My raccoon found a
mouse." It continued with an *internal response*—"He liked him"—then went
on to a sort of undifferentiated main action—"He invited the mouse to his

Figure 9–22

myraccoon fond amosue
he liked him so he
invaded the mosue.
to his home themosue
was glad,the raccoonis
happy.

Figure 9–23

The trace fomers won
the batle.
Of the dekeperon. the
place car shot the
bose with a lazer
gun. Trace fomers

Figure 9–24

I said wheres the Beef?
Jon said what?
Come on over.
oh oh here comes
my dad.
I beter go home
right now. I said Jon
Hi dad. Hi Joey
I'm going to play
alrit. dont get in
troble.

home." Then followed two reactions—"The mouse was glad. The raccoon is happy."

Joey wrote only one story in April. It was about Transformers (see Figure 9–23). The topic didn't seem to inspire him, and the form of his story showed no development over what he was able to do weeks before.

In early May he managed to work the then-popular expression "Where's the beef?" into his story (Figure 9–24). The rest of the piece is structured around a dialogue that strays completely from "Where's the beef."

The next week, still working on fitting sayings from the popular media into his writing, Joey wrote "beat it" (see Figure 9–25). This time he succeeded admirably by using techniques he already knew. He opened with his familiar introductory action, but this time, instead of using his punch line right away, he let his introduction set up a context for it—"I ran away with the radio, and some cookies." He used some descriptive detail, something else he had known how to do for months—"It was a half moon . . ."—and then slipped his punch

Figure 9–25

I ran away with the radio. and some cookies it was a hafe moon that night. on the radio the song was Beit Just Beit.

Figure 9–26

Figure 9–27

line in as part of the description—"On the radio the song was 'Beat it, just beat it.'"

With this piece, he achieved another dynamic tableau, this one with sight and sound and action. But note that he still hasn't combined his real descriptive power with plot development—the pieces with elaborate descriptive detail don't yet develop any sequence of initiating events, goals, actions, and reactions.

The next week Joey goes again to the popular media for story characters, but his piece about Care Bears—like the ones about Smurfs and Transformers—fails to take off (see Figure 9–26).

Can we make the generalization that popular media characters fail to trigger very imaginative stories? This seems to be true of one-dimensional characters—Smurfs, Care Bears, Transformers, and He-Man. But E.T. seems to be the exception. His appearance was the occasion of Joey's experimenting with something new: integrating Rebus-like drawings into his text (see Figure 9–27). Still, the experiment didn't seem to lead him where he wanted to go. He didn't use this technique again that year.

The next week he wrote his roller coaster paper (Figure 9–28). It is the longest piece he wrote all year, with the longest text and the most detailed drawings. This piece contains a surprising number of elaborations over previous works. It has his first use of a title—"My roller coaster." His introductory action is finally split into an introductory description—"My roller coaster is a fun ride"—followed by an action—"Everybody takes a ride on it." There is specifying detail—"The kids are Toni and Justin and Fred and Malisa

Figure 9–28

1

My roller coaster
My roller coaster
is a fun ride.
tvrey body takes
a ride on it.
The kids. are loni
and Justin and
fred and malisa
too. It isfun very
fun

2

Time to go
home kids ahhh
I have to eat.
Thats bad
bye-bye kids
bye Joey.
You can play to
moyro bye-bye.

3

The next day,
they had lots of
fun.
Thay loved the
four lops to lops
thay went on and
and on and

Figure 9–29

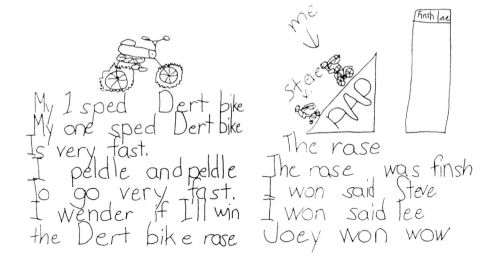

My 1 sped Dert bike
My one sped Dert bike
Is very fast.
I peldle and peldle
To go very fast.
I wender if I'll win
the Dert bik e rase

me
Steve
RAP
finsh line

The rase
The rase was finsh
I won said Steve
I won said lee
Joey won wow

too"—but this time the detail doesn't overshadow the development of the story.

In continuing the story, he put in dialogue that carried his story forward ("Time to go home, kids" "Ahhh"). This time, too, it was clear who was doing the reacting; and the reaction was part of the plot: His friends expressed disappointment over going home, so Joey explained that he had to eat, and invited them back another day.

Joey's last story turned out to be the best developed. He seemed to integrate into it almost everything he had learned about writing stories his first-grade year (see Figure 9–29). He began with a title, and for the second time used his two-part introduction (description + action). But in this story he went on to put in a problem: He was in a race, and he wondered if he would win it. Now, he had put problems and solutions into his stories before, but this time he went a step further. He used dialogue, something he had also included many times, to *delay the solution* and hence to create suspense:

The race was finished. "I won," said Steve.

"I won," said Lee.

"Joey won. Wow!"

And he finished off with a one-word reaction.

So at the end of Joey's first year of composing, we find a piece that culminates his development very nicely. It combines in one story elements that had made their debut in isolation. We saw topics introduced, followed by descriptions. We saw personal reactions. We saw problems. We saw dialogues. We saw story language. But only in the final piece do we see them all together.

Sarah's Works: Literature
Influences Story Development

We've seen in Joey's writing over the course of the year a spirit of eager ex-
perimentalism and growth in his ability to generate longer and longer texts,
by using such devices as problem + comment, problem + solution + comment, description, and dialogue. Some figures and phrases from popular cul-
ture that struck his ear made their way into his compositions: E.T., Care
Bears, "Where's the Beef," "Beat It," and "Mr. Bounce."

Let us look now at Sarah. Unlike Joey, Sarah seems to have assimilated a
good deal of literature into her writing. We meet her in mid-first grade and
follow her development through grade two.

In December of first grade the children in Sarah's class were passing
around *Lollipop,* by Wendy Watson:

> One time Bunny wanted a lollipop
> and Mom said "No"
> and Bunny kept wanting and wanting
> and Mom said "No"
> and Bunny kept wanting and wanting
> and Mom said "NO!"[3]

During writing workshop one day Sarah wrote "Julie" (Figure 9–30).
"Julie" is not a close borrowing from *Lollipop,* but it does incorporate two of
that story's features. The repetition of "wanting and wanting" is reflected in
"nobody, nobody" and "happy, happy, happy." Also, the use of capitals to
signal strong emphasis is repeated in "nobody, NOBODY," and "HAPPY
HAPPY HAPPY."

Figure 9–30
Sarah
Grade 1

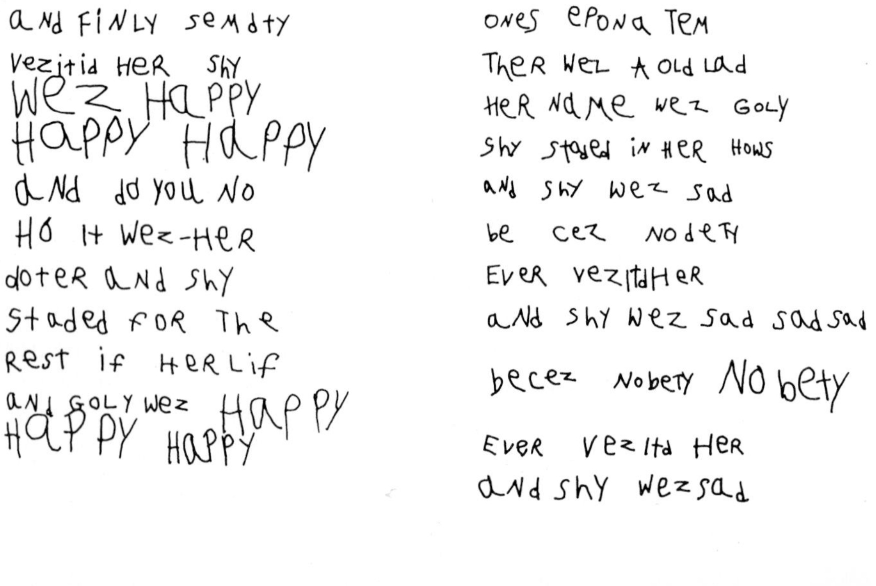

And FINLY seMdty
Vezjtid HeR SHY
WeZ HaPPY
HaPPY HaPPY
aNd do you No
HO It Wez-HeR
doteR aNd SHy
Staded foR The
Rest if HeRLif
aNd GoLy wez HaPPy
HaPPY HaPPY

oNes ePoNa TeM
TheR Wez A old Lad
HeR NdMe wez GoLy
Shy Staded iN HeR Hows
aNd Shy Wez Sad
be cez NodeFy
EveR vezjtdHeR
aNd Shy Wez Sad SadSad
becez NobeTy NObeTy
EveR Vezjtd HeR
aNd Shy Wezsad

Sarah wrote "The Changing Boy" (see below) in the fall of her second-grade year. We can discern in it two influences from the literature she had heard and read. First, as her class was in the midst of a unit on Africa, she had listened to many African folktales, as well as parts of a story by the Nigerian novelist, Amos Tutuola, who writes in a folktale style:

> I lay down near my bag of food. I used the bag of juju as a pillow, while I put my heavy matchet and bow and arrows of poison closely to my right hand. . . .
>   As I opened my eyes and sat upright with great fear, I saw a horrible black being who squatted very closely to me. . . . His head was bigger than necessary with two fearful eyes. The two eyes went deeply into his skull. The hair on his head was so long that it covered his breast. It was muddled together as if it was rubbed with a large quantity of thick grease. . . .
>   Without wasting a sixtieth of a twinkling, I continued my journey.[4]

Tutuola's story carries on for nearly two hundred pages with a wonderful spirit of one magical thing following another, a spirit that seems to have infected Sarah's story, "The Changing Boy."

A second influence is the character who changes his identity. Such characters are commonplace in folklore. Note the following sequence from "Taleisen," one of many such tales Sarah heard that year. This segment tells of the escape of the hero, Gwion Bach, from the witch, Caridwen:

> And she went forth after him, running. And he saw her, and turned himself into a hare and fled. But she changed herself into a greyhound and turned him. And he ran towards a river, and became a fish. And she in the form of an otter . . . chased him under the water, until he was fein to turn himself into a bird of the air. She, as a hawk, followed him and gave him no rest in the sky. And just as she was about to swoop upon him, and he was in fear of death, he espied a heap of winnoed wheat upon the floor of a barn, and he dropped among the wheat, and turned himself into one of the grains. Then she transformed herself into a high-crested black hen, and went to the wheat and scratched it with her feet, and found him out and swallowed him. And, as the story says, she bore him nine months, and when she was delivered of him, she could not find it in her heart to kill him. . . . So she wrapped him in a leathern bag, and cast him into the sea to the mercy of God, on the twenty-ninth day of April.[5]

Sarah seems to have adapted this idea of the metamorphosizing hero in her "Changing Boy."

The Changing Boy

It was a stormy night. I was walking home when I came to a shack. It was so stormy that I went inside and what did I see but a bag.

I was so curious that I opened it. I heard a voice say, "Thank you. I was just going to ask you to do that."

I looked inside the bag. There were lots of bones. The voice said, "Put me together."

I was very curious so I put him together. It was a huge skeleton.

"Now I will eat you!"

I ran right out of the shack and into a cave and put a rock in the door. All of the sudden the light turned on. I saw a witch and a bunch of spiders.

"Here is another boy. Shall I turn him into a spider, too? These spiders were once boys, but they got turned into spiders because they did the same thing as you and I will turn you into a spider, too!"

And she pulled out of her pocket a wishbone and said

POOF!

and I felt myself change. I was a spider.

Then she fell asleep. With no sound at all I took the wish bone and ran out of the cave. When I got out I changed back into a boy.

Then a hand grabbed me and took me to a house. But it was just a hand that went down the chimney and attached to a lady. She kissed me. Oh, she stunk! We watched TV. Then she rocked me. Then a HUGE DOG came into the room and ate me. I could hear the lady yelling, "Alfred, you know little boys have to be cooked before eating!"

Then I remembered the wishbone. I said

POOF!

Finally I was home in bed and sound asleep and happy, too.

The End

Sarah, Age 7

In January of her second-grade year Sarah's teacher told the story "Don't Count Your Chickens Before They Hatch."

One summer morning a woman named Petina walked down a country road on her way to market carrying a large jug on her head, carefully set on a little cushion. She had just finished the milking and was thinking how lucky the customer would be who would buy such fresh and foaming milk. "I will ask three pennies for it, and perhaps my customer will give me one extra, because it is such a fine day," she thought. "With four pence I can buy four eggs, maybe more, and I will set them under my hens and when they hatch I can trade them for a little pig. After I fatten him up I'm sure someone will want to trade him for a young calf. When my calf becomes a fine bull he will win prizes, gold pieces with which I will buy fine gowns, and weddings for my children with musicians . . ." Petina skipped with pleasure at the thought, but alas, when she did, the jug slipped and crashed on the ground, splashing milk everywhere.[6]

Sarah set out deliberately to write a piece with a similar structure. She wrote "Amanda."

> Once there was a little girl named Amanda. She was walking down the street with a cake on the top of her head yelling, a cake for sale! If I sell this cake I will get lots of money for it. Then I will buy myself a farm with all of the animals I like. But when everyone saw her with a cake on her head they laughed and laughed. One little boy laughed so hard he tipped over backward, dropping the eggs he was holding and knocking Amanda off her feet so there was a mess of eggs and cake. Amanda feeling very sad. Not rich. Just the same.

Sarah managed to capture both the form and the sense of the story of the milkmaid. At the same time, she put her own stamp on the plot, adding the boy whose laughter makes him drop eggs in her path and cause her to fall. The piece is derivative, but it has a complex structure and a sense of irony that are rare in second-grade writing. Sarah's imitation of the original is sufficiently different in detail to suggest that she has used the structure of it to generate her own story, rather than imitating the original detail for detail.

By May of her second-grade year, Sarah was able to sustain the writing of one story over several sessions. Her story about Rudie's adventures at summer camp had to be excerpted because it is four chapters and twelve pages long!

Rudie Goes to Summer Camp

Rudie was at school when his teacher gave him a note and said to give it to his mother. Rudie did. It said:

Dear Mrs. Vernen,

I think you should get your son in with a few more boys by sending him to camp.

When Rudie arrived at camp . . . at cabin 15 . . . he was greeted by a man named Chip. He told Rudie he was the first one. He could have his choice of beds. Rudie picked the bottom bunk of one of the beds. Chip said he was going to go greet the others. While Chip was doing that, Rudie yanked the sheets down from up above him and draped them down over the opening.

The last one in was Mike. He walked in glumly. All the beds were occupied but the one up above the strange, mysterious bed. Mike had no choice. He climbed the ladder to the top bunk.

"Hey! There's no sheets on this bed" he yelled.

"What's going on in here? Rudie, is that you in there?" Chip tore the sheets down. . . .

"Now it's supper time," said Chip. "Kids, you're at table 15."

"Ugh! That number again!" mumbled Rudie.

"What is this stuff?" asked Rudie when they got to the table.

"It's my famous stew. It's very good," said Mike, who had not even tried it.

"Since you like it so much, have mine." Rudie scraped his plate onto Mike's plate.

"Rudie, leave the table!"

"Gladly," said Rudie.

Sarah, Age 8

By now, Sarah's reading consisted of longer books, too. She was especially fond of Beverly Cleary's books about Ramona, a very normally maladjusted schoolgirl to whom painfully funny things happen with regularity. Ramona's adventures show a child's-eye view of a world designed by well-meaning but not very perceptive adults. Without imitating Ramona's adventures point for point, Sarah uses many of those stories' features to create a story that is very much her own. The realism of the Ramona stories is evident in her Rudie story; so is the irony of having adults planning your life without consulting you. Ramona's wry verbal humor, too, seems to have rubbed off on Rudie. Even the outer form of the Ramona books—a story sustained across several chapters—is reproduced in Sarah's writing.

In these two children, Joey and Sarah, we have seen the earlier and later phases of developing story writing. In the earlier development represented by Joey, it is possible to see each feature enter into his writing and gradually become elaborated and diversified into different features. Much of this development appears to come from the inside: Joey's cognitive and linguistic development controls much of the agenda, while the influence of the writing and language he sees and hears around him are only indirectly and sporadically reflected.

In Sarah's writing, the relative importance of her conceptual development and of the influence of the texts she hears and reads has become more of a blend. Her power over the forms and features of stories has continued to grow. But her development follows no single track now. The course of Sarah's story development has diversified, and the pathways are as many and various as the stories and authors who have captured her imagination. Sarah has become able to take in the stories she hears and reads as raw materials for her own creations.[7] She has thus become an active participant in the conversation of authors, the conversation we call literature.

Developing the Poetic Mode in School

Joey's and Sarah's teachers and many others have struggled to create an atmosphere and a system in classrooms where children view themselves as writers. In these process classrooms, as they are called, children are given time, encouragement, a ready audience, feedback, and occasional mini-lessons on such points as writing exciting leads and using quotation marks.

The process approach to the teaching of writing is based on a belief that the driving force behind young children's learning is their own interest in life, coupled with their desire to express themselves. Advocates of process writing also point out that too much instruction stifles a child's urge to express herself and dissipates her learning energy and sense of purpose. Instruction is given at the point of need; in other words, a child is taught the use of a semicolon when one is needed in her particular piece of writing.[8] The process approach to writing has been introduced into many public schools across the country and has been shown to be very successful. Because it has worked as a way of teaching writing to young children, it is taking root. We think it is one of the best things happening in schools today.

Therefore, it is with some trepidation that we include in this book experiments in "teaching" story writing. In the classes where these exercises were used, the teacher felt that a majority of students was at a "point of need" as far as organizing and deepening stories was concerned; and she felt that instruction around these challenges would be most beneficial to children in groups, where they could learn from each other. Having carefully established writing workshop or free writing time as an opportunity for children to choose their own topics and work on their own initiative (see Chapter 11), she was reluctant to give any assignments during that time. Therefore, she established a separate writing instruction time at a different point in the day, for assignments, discussions, games, and so forth, designed to enrich the children's writing. We include these exercises and some of the writing that resulted from them because they begin to answer some interesting questions.

Story Grammar

What happens when children are given exercises in inventing and shaping stories in addition to their free writing time? As children progress as writers, they are sometimes frustrated by a sense that their stories are not as complete as they would like them to be, or they feel caught in a rut of sameness and begin to lose interest in writing. When several of her students seemed to be at this point, one first- through third-grade teacher decided that sharing story grammar with them might help.

> *Teacher:* How many of you remember the story of the Three Billy Goats Gruff? Everybody? Great. [Writes the word "setting" on the board.] Who can tell me the setting of the Three Billy Goats Gruff?
> *Child:* What's a setting?
> *Child:* Like a set. A backdrop.
> *Child:* Mountains.
> *Child:* There's a stream.
> *Children (together):* And a bridge. And under the bridge is hiding the mean troll . . .
> *Teacher:* Right. You've got it. The setting is the place where the story takes place. And also part of the setting can be the time when the story takes place. When did the Three Billy Goats Gruff happen?

Child: Never.
Child: Once upon a time.
Child: No. It was in the spring when the grass was high.
Child: If it never happened you wouldn't have a story.
Teacher: Who are the characters in the story? [Writes the word "characters."]
Child: Ch-
Child: The goats; and the troll.
Teacher: Anybody else?
Children: [after a pause] No. Just the goats and the troll.
Teacher: [Writes the word "problem."] Do these characters have a problem? Let's take the goats. Do the goats have a problem?
Child: They are hungry, and they want to go over the bridge and eat grass.
Child: And they are scared too, because the troll under the bridge will kill them.

Figure 9–31
Sarah
Grade 2

characTeR: sepT. 11
          Dolls aNd marcella

Pro Blem:
          They a re HuNG ry aNDThey
          CaN't Rech The Pantry Door
SoLUSHUN:
          RaG GEDY ANN
HelD U P JUMPING up JackTO The
  DOOR He SliD uP HiS Stik
        aND uNlockeDThe Door
seTiNG:
          PaNtery

          SheGot GraPe
          JaM ON HeraND
          sheHaD To Get
              WashD.

Child: Yeah. Smash 'em.

Teacher: [Writes "solution" on the board.] So what's the solution for these goats? Let's act it out.

The children grew familiar with the terms *setting, character, problem,* and *solution,* which is simplified story grammar, by discussing stories they already knew, stories they wrote themselves, stories they read on their own. Figure 9–31 shows the homework of a second grader who was asked to analyze a Raggedy Ann story.

During writing workshop time, both the teacher and the children began using these simple story grammar terms in conferring with each other. Here are some random excerpts from conferences in that class:

Child: Can a robot be a character?

Child: Sure, if he's a thinking robot . . .

Teacher: I have this wonderful setting for my story, but I can't seem to get beyond it. I'm having a hard time thinking of characters . . .

Child [to another child]: Teri's nice. She's a good character. But what's her problem? You say she's sad because she's adopted. But then

Figure 9–32
Sarah
Grade 2

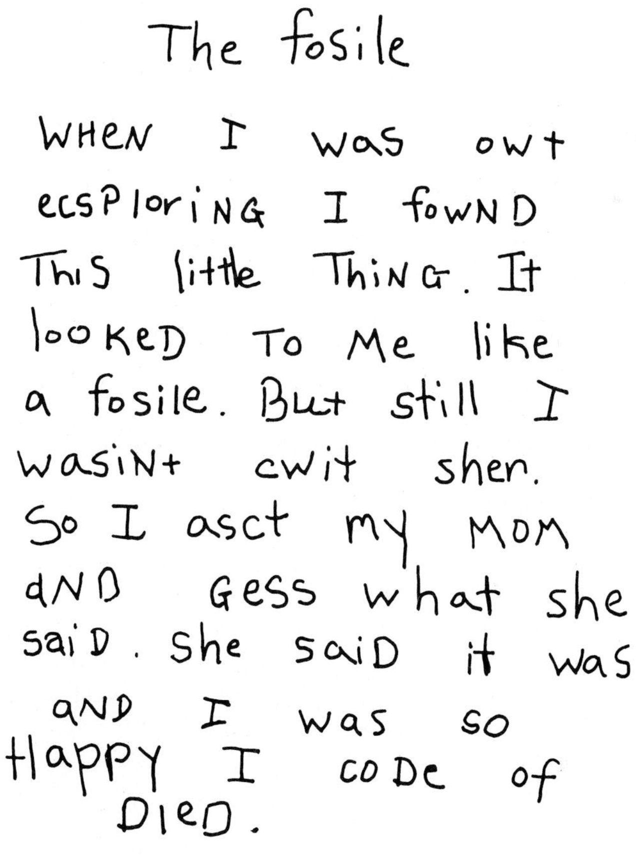

The fosile

WHeN I was owt ecsPloriNG I fowND ThiS little ThinG. It lookeD To Me like a fosile. But still I wasiNt cwit sher. So I asct my MoM aND Gess what she saiD. She saiD it was aND I was so Happy I coDe of DieD.

when she finds a ball she gets happy. So maybe she wasn't sad because she was adopted. Maybe it was just an excuse.

The children seem to use story grammar concepts mainly in two ways: to discuss their own and each others' stories more fully, and as a criterion of completeness. That this criterion was internalized seems to be reflected in the children's writing, as seen in a journal entry written during writing workshop time (see Figure 9–32). Sarah was able, on her own, to successfully incorporate the elements of story grammar.

Elizabeth provides the reader with all four elements of story: a vivid setting, a character whose mind and even skin the reader enters, a problem the reader is compelled to share, a solution that makes the reader feel relief.

First Station

It's hot in the desert; Tom works hard in slavery. The sun is out and shines on the sand. Tom is barefoot. One day he decides to escape.

He made sure no one was looking and started to run. He ran and ran and didn't stop until he came to a pile of leaves and a couple of sticks. He made a roof and lived four days under that roof.

He was eating a fish and he heard a horse neigh. Could it be true, someone was coming to get him? He ran behind a bush. The horse stopped. Tom peeked through the bushes. The man said: "I see you. Come on out of there. Hop in." It was a friendly voice . Well, it really made Tom feel good. So he climbed in and the man said: "Where to?"

"Anywhere in the North," said Tom.

Elizabeth, Age 8

Teaching with story grammar is a tricky business. For some children the use of structure terms, even such simple ones as *problem* and *solution*, can discourage creativity. This happens when a child feels that the teacher thinks structures are more important than what she wants to say. Structural terms are only useful to help the child clarify features she has already become aware of and is trying to control. With very new writers, in particular, it may be better not to mention structural terms at all. The teacher's job as writing coach is to discern the structure inherent in the story the child is writing and talking about, and to ask questions that help the child make it clear to the reader.

Outer Actions and Inner States: Souriau's Dramatic Roles

Although it is certainly not true of the above stories, some stories children write, when viewed through the grid of story grammar, show curious gaps right where they should specify some *psychological* action: an internal response, a goal, a reaction. Compared to stories adults tell, children's stories seem to be heavy on action, light on reflection.

Here is a great story by a second grader, which serves to illustrate our point.

The Knight

Once there was a knight named Stanley. He had a suit of steel. He had to fight a dragon, but before he got to the dragon's castle there was a dangerous woods and a dangerous river that he had to cross. He would begin the next morning because it was night time. The next morning he got on his horse and rode away. Soon he came to the woods and there he saw a monster. The monster, whose name was Hckee. Hckee had a green body with 1000 eyes and 1000 legs and 1000 arms with two horns. Hckee ran at Stanley with a sword. Quickly Stanley jumped to the side. Hckee ran right into a tree and Hckee just turned right into a pile of mud. Stanley hopped on his horse and rode away. Soon he came to the river, and Stanley looked at the river. There was no danger. But just then he saw danger: the waves were fire. Stanley hopped on his horse and jumped across the river and landed hard. Stanley rode for a little more. Then Stanley got off his horse and went to sleep. In the morning Stanley got on his horse and rode away. Soon he came to the dragon's castle. Stanley got off his horse. Stanley went across the drawbridge; the drawbridge closed behind Stanley. Stanley was trapped. Stanley took his sword and cut off the dragon's head.

The End

Orion, Age 7

The usual claim is that psychological action, being internal, is not obvious to children, so they leave discussions of characters' inner states out of their stories.[9] Or, perhaps they are aware of inner states but not used to talking about them. Or it may be that the stories they hear and the television shows they watch are heavy on action and light on discussions of inner states—so they simply might not associate talk about inner states with stories. We believe that children can get better at discussing the psychological dimensions of stories—goals, motives, and inner reactions—and that this ability is what keeps the writing and discussing of stories endlessly interesting. Children are quite able to consider how events make people feel or to take motives into account in deciding whether or not someone deserves blame.

The work of a French drama critic, Etienne Souriau, has provided us with one device for discussing the interplay of motives in a story.[10] Souriau analyzed scenes from plays, but his findings pertain to stories as well. Each scene, he maintained, is driven by the motivation of the character central to that scene, and each of the other characters play some role in relation to the motivation, either as helper, impediment, judge, etc.

Souriau claimed that we can make sense of what's going on if we think of the characters as sharing no more than six dramatic roles. To make it easier to note them symbolically, he assigned each role a sign from the Zodiac.

The first of these roles Souriau called the *lion force,* and represented it this way: ∿ . This is the person who will direct the scene, the main character or hero.

The second is the *sun* ☉ , or desired object: Who or what does the lion force want?

The third is *Mars* ♂ , the rival: Who is trying to stop the lion force from getting what he wants?

The fourth is the helper and is represented by the *moon* ☽. There can be any number of helpers, and they can help the lion force, or the rival, or anyone.

The fifth is the *earth* ♁ , or receiver of bounty: For whom does the lion force want the desired object? (Often this is the lion force him- or herself.)

The sixth is *Libra* ♎ , a sort of arbiter or judge: Who or what decides if the lion force gets the desired object?

All of this may sound a bit exotic, but what Souriau provides is a simple framework for looking at the complex interweavings of characters and motives. This is how Souriau's model was used during writing instruction time in one class. The first four character roles were written on the board, and the teacher explained the symbols to the class.

∿ Who is the main character?

☉ What does the lion force want?

♂ Who is trying to stop the lion force from getting what he wants?

☽ Does anybody have a helper?

Teacher: Do you all remember the story of "Jack and the Beanstalk"?
Children: (yesses, nods, yawns)
Teacher: Who do you suppose is the lion force in "Jack and the Beanstalk"?
Children: Jack!
Child: The Beanstalk (laughs).
Child: No, Jack.
Teacher: Does the Beanstalk want anything?
Child: The Beanstalk just grows.
Teacher: I think to be the lion force in a story you have to want something.
Child: In the beginning of the story Jack's mother could be the lion force. She wants Jack to go out and get some food.
Child: But Jack is the hero; I mean, that's who the story is about.
Teacher: Does Jack have a helper?
Child: The old man with the beans.

Child: Yeah.

Child: Well, also the giant's wife helped him.

Child: How about the Beanstalk?

Teacher: Who would the rival be?

Children: The giant!

Child: And *his* helper is the harp. The harp called out to wake up the giant so Jack couldn't steal it.

Teacher: What do you think we should put for the object? What did Jack really want?

Child: Gold.

Child: The hen.

Child: But he didn't know there was going to be any hen up there.

Child: Adventure.

Child: To get away from his mother.

Child: Money. Because remember he was starving. And he took money back to his mother.

Child: In a way the giant was Jack's helper because nothing much would have happened to Jack if the giant hadn't been there.

As a tool for analysis, for getting the children actively interested in and discussing the story, Souriau was already proving his salt.

Clarifying roles is an interpretive process: The discussions give a nice feeling of moving toward consensus, and yet it is also a divergent process. It is clear that in this class everyone didn't have to agree, that there were often several legitimate interpretations. Children were encouraged to give reasons for their interpretations, but not pushed. Discussions of stories conducted in Souriau's terms often seem more fun and lively than analyses of their simple structure. We think this is because the teacher always knows what the setting of a story is, or who the characters are, whereas in discussions of roles the children have ideas that differ from the teacher's that are valid and interesting and that give the teacher insights into how they see things. To start early with children on this sort of discussion can reassure them that it is quite acceptable and right to make their own interpretation of a story.

After the children seemed confident of the different roles, the teacher tried a game to see how these roles might help in writing stories. She produced two sets of cards. On one set she had written "people" labels: TRUCK DRIVER, TEENAGER, SKINNY GIRL, OLD MAN, MAGICIAN. At the children's request she included some animals, too—BROWN DOG and MOUSE. The class would draw from these all the characters for a story, except the sun (desired objects, as Souriau calls them). For "suns" she made a different set of cards: ADVENTURE, WEALTH, HEALTH, FAME, TO COMFORT, TO DISCOVER. These cards were all marked on the back with a ☉ .

Here's how the game was played. After telling the children that the group would make up a story together, the teacher asked a child to draw a card for the lion force. He drew TRUCK DRIVER. Another child was asked to draw a card to answer the question, "What does this truck driver want right now?" He drew FAME.

> *Teacher:* How do you suppose this truck driver wants to become famous?
>
> *Child:* He wants to be a rock 'n roll star. He practices singing while he's driving.
>
> *Child:* He wants to be in the movies because he thinks he's real handsome.
>
> *Teacher:* I wonder if anybody might try to stop him from getting famous. Matthew, want to draw a rival? (Matthew drew a MOUSE.) A mouse? How could a mouse stop a truck driver from getting famous?
>
> *Child:* He could run out in front of the truck, and then the truck would swerve off the road and run into a tree and that would be the end of the truck driver.
>
> *Child:* He could, well, if the guy was recording his song, the mouse could chew a wire or something . . .
>
> *Child:* Well, the mouse could just tell him, you're no good, you good-for-nothing truck driver, so forget it.

The discussion got very loud, the children were spilling over with ideas, everyone wanted to talk at once. The teacher then asked the children to take paper and pencil and write a story on their own, using the cards drawn. The three stories that follow were written by the children we quoted in the discussion, two first graders and a second grader (see Figures 9–33, 9–34, and 9–35). Note the variety in character motivation.

As children in a classroom develop throughout the year, both as people and as writers, it is hard to tell what progress can be attributed to a particular teaching practice, to general development, or to some outside event in the child's life. In the class where the Souriau game was played, several first graders who had never before written long or coherent stories were able to do so. Perhaps the game element encouraged them to rehearse their ideas out loud before writing; perhaps the cards served as reminders, as notes enabling them to hold their story in mind for long enough to write it down.

Some of the children spontaneously made "Souriau" into a party game, drawing the cards, and then splitting off into groups to make up stories and work them into skits to present to the whole class. These skits showed a strong awareness of character motivation, which did not always show up in the written versions produced after the skits. However, since the teacher had heard the children discussing motives at length while preparing the skits, she was able to remind them of these motives in the course of conferring about their stories. Many became interested in the challenge of showing character motivation to the reader.

Over the centuries, people who have become good story writers have picked up a sense of the structure and dynamics of stories not from Mandler

Figure 9–33
Johanna
Age 6

There once a truk drivr and he loved to make up sogs and he stopt his truk too sing the sogs to peple and they loved the sogs and they clapt and he sead i must be on me wae and he klimd in the truk and went and he stopt ugen in the necs tonwand he wod sing the same sogs and they clapt and he got in his truk and he went to bed and he wook up the necs moning at sun up and he had brekfis and sag sum moor sogs and he set to and old pepl came from the nesc town to here him and aftr the frset sogs a man came out to the crod and sead you cen sig on the t.v. he sead o.k.

Figure 9–34
Jared
Age 7

Once There lived a trucker
he wantid to be a rock star
his Dad was a rock star and he
wantid to be one to. one day
he was driveing along reacoding
a song and a mos star tid to choow
on the mike wirer. the truch
drirer didit no that The mouse
was doowing it. then wen he
was dun he trid to lisin to it
he siad wats the mader with
you! he siad in madnis. Then
he broke the mike
he was wery mad. I will never
bie a cheep thing lik thas
ugen! he went home and went
to bed. The neskt moning he went
to a moovy Thater he siad That
is what I what to be and so
he did and That is the End

Figure 9–35
Juan
Age 6

Juan
a trucke divre wotid to be
famise. but a mose wes afdr him.
and owen Day the mose Sende
gowe awaye your mom and dad
nevr levd you eneews.
yes they did.

and Johnson or from Etienne Souriau, but from reading and hearing stories. Daily storytime, books in the classroom and books sent home, time and encouragement to read and write stories will surely do more for the young writers coming along today than any direct instruction. However, the classroom observations above indicate that instruction strategies that encourage discussion and analysis of stories can help young writers enter and learn from the mainstream of literary tradition.

Poetry

It would be sad to conclude this chapter on writing in the poetic voice without some discussion of the writing of poetry. The Oxford English Dictionary defines poetry as: "The expression of beautiful or elevated thought in appropriate language, such language containing a rhythmical element." Often poetry is also understood to mean expressing strong sensory and emotional content in a few words.

Because of their wish to express what they truly feel, and because handwriting difficulties force them to economize on words, very young writers often create works of poetry. Joey's Christmas piece, for instance, could probably best be appreciated as poetry rather than as a truncated story.

> THE COWS ARE
> MOOING THE SHEEP
> ARE BAAING
> THE BRIGHTEST STAR
> IS SHINING SO BRIGHT
> WAKES JESUS UP AND
> MARY AND JOSEPH
> *Joey, Grade 1*

Influenced by haiku the class had been learning by heart, Chris wrote the following a few weeks into first grade:

HELLO THERE SLOW SMALL SNAIL

Around the same time another first grader (with some spelling help from her sister) wrote:

PEACHES ARE GOOD

She elaborated when asked if she could think of five good things about peaches (see Figure 9–36), and the result was published in the class paper as Rebecca's Peach Poem.

Sometimes it helps students to ask them whether they consider their piece of writing a poem or part of a story. It helps the author to look at his writing objectively, and it helps him realize that there is a difference between the two. It also makes it easier for the teacher to frame conference questions if she knows what the child intends.

Figure 9–36
Rebecca
Grade 1

a peach
furry
squishy
yellow
sweet
drippy

During writing workshop, one child, Sarah, was groping around for a topic and someone suggested dinosaurs. Sarah then wrote:

DINOSAURS,
OLD DEAD BONES
SAD END.

Sarah, Age 6

A year later she wrote:

The River
When calm and still it is
peaceful and nice and you
can just sit and watch it,
but when it is rough and
the wind is blowing
all the birds stop singing
and all you can hear is
the splashing of the waves,
but as the wind dies down
the birds start to sing again
and it's peaceful again.
        tweet
        eeeee

Although Sarah did not lose her poetic voice as she became a more fluent writer, many children seem to. Some teachers use form poetry successfully to help children find again the telegraphic intensity of expression they may have had when they were very young, or simply to focus in on the experience they want to convey. Haiku, cinquain, diamante—each form urges the child to condense her thought, to observe her subject. One teacher we know teaches children the haiku form as she encourages them to keep a nature journal. A drama teacher has her students write cinquains about the characters they will portray:

> *Cassius*
> Sly, sneaky
> hungry for power
> persuading, interesting, plotting, killing
> Evil
>
> *Elizabeth, Age 8*

After reading "Jack and the Wonderbeans" aloud, a teacher got the children as a group to write a cinquain about a particular character, drawing their attention to the story writer's evocation of the character and to the words that triggered it.

> Giant
> Hands like hams
> He comes tromping in
> Sniffing and snuffing and snorting
> Mean-eye.

Later, in workshop, a child writing a story about two sisters who couldn't get along began her story with these two cinquain portraits:

> Jenny
> mean, loud
> Think she knows everything
> Kicking, bragging, talking back
> a horse.

> Marie
> sweet, kind
> a real nice girl
> smiling, ready to help
> a friend.
>
> *Erin, Age 8*

After a discussion of strip-mining and its consequences, the class wrote the following diamante poem:

> Mountain barnyard
> Squawking, smelly
> I'm coming, chickens

> Hoeing, growing/standing, staring
> Nothing to say
> Dead, empty
> Slagheap
>
> *Group poem*

And during workshop, one of the same students wrote this on her own:

> *Generations*
> Children
> Lively, smart
> They are great
> Screaming, receiving/praising, knowledging
> They are O.K.
> Charming, elderly
> Parents
>
> *Elizabeth, Age 8*

Writing group or individual diamante poems about a character as he appears at the beginning and the end of a story can help draw the children's attention to character evolution.

> *Hansel and Gretal*
> Extra mouths
> Lost, scared
> Pushed out of home
> Captured, crying/planning, winning
> welcomed back home
> strong, smart
> Children.
>
> *Group poem*

Many children find it easier to be creative within some constraints, and judging from the popularity of poetry forms with rules governing meter, rhyme, syllables, and so on, that feeling has been shared by many writers throughout history.

Reading good free-form poetry in class, as well as form poetry, and calling the children's attention to examples of free-form poetry in their own work can help dispel the notion that poetry has to fit a particular form.

Take what Joey wrote one day in April:

I RAN AWAY WITH THE
RADIO AND SOME COOKIES
IT WAS A HALF MOON
THAT NIGHT, ON THE
RADIO THE SONG WAS
BEAT IT, JUST BEAT IT.

If an adult had written this we might say "What a wonderful beginning to a story," and wonder where it went from there. But we know Joey is not yet up to writing long stories, and we can also recognize that he has said a tremendous amount in these few lines. Taken as a poem, Joey's piece is complete, containing the evocation of a scene (the half-dark night), a sensory connection (cookies clutched in one hand, radio in the other, straining to see, with the music beating away), and a kind of ambivalence of mood (connection between I ran away and Beat It). Does he want to say how he felt, or would he rather leave it to the reader to guess?

Joey's piece makes a good poem partly because it is still so close to the expressive mode, though a reader who doesn't know Joey can certainly appreciate it. This is the sort of piece that can serve as a bridge for children between the purely expressive and the poetic modes. He probably wrote straight from the heart, without much thought of his readers, yet he chose his words so well that they can communicate to a wide audience. He could get a sense of this by reading it to a number of different people and asking them what they imagine when they hear it. Once he is able to appreciate how much he has communicated in these few words, he can see that a poem is a poem not only because it is short, sits a certain way on the page, or possibly fits a rhythmic structure, but because it also makes the reader see and feel something intensely.

Sometimes teachers and parents are reluctant to recognize these brief poems as complete, particularly if they are written in the first ten minutes of workshop. Because the style is telegraphic and expressive, the teacher sometimes pushes a child toward longer sentences or more new words, feeling it necessary for his development. The child may have an instinctive sense of what is complete for him but lack the polite vocabulary to tell the teacher to back off: "This is not expository prose, this is poetry."

Children will need practice with other modes of writing—full description, argumentation, and expository prose; that is what the next chapter is about. Writing in these other modes can feel more difficult to young children than writing poetry (though for most adults it is the other way around): They have to hold the pencil longer, they have to worry about punctuation, they have to remove themselves from center stage. But while they acquire other, seemingly more demanding writing skills, their awareness of poetry and skill at writing it can grow, too. We find that for many children writing poetry, or summarizing a draft into a poem, provides a welcome and relaxing change of pace, a sort of homecoming from the rigors of other writing modes.

Conclusion

Looking at children between the ages of four and eight, we have seen their progress in learning about the human art of story making. During those same years they are gaining the dexterity to hold a pencil, the strength to write a line and then a page, the confidence to share what they've written or made up, the social skill of anticipating what an audience or reader might want to hear.

A child from a talkative but not a reading family may come to school with a sharp sense of how to interest an audience, but neither the dexterity nor the motivation for putting words on paper. A child who has had many stories read to her but not much other social interaction may bring to school an ingrained feeling for story structure and a great capacity for make-believe, but no confidence in her abilities. What can a teacher go on, as she tries to get these children to share their skills and learn to write in the poetic mode?

Story making can be practiced by children in many ways other than writing. When they are hearing, telling, remembering, or inventing stories, dreams, movies, or happenings at home, children are learning to compose. When they play house they are making up a story. Only a small percentage of the stories children invent ever get down on paper, which is not surprising: A complete story requires a lot of words and considerable organization.

But most completed stories do follow certain forms. We have seen children grasping at these forms, putting on paper groups of words, a complex process that Applebee calls chaining and centering. We followed Joey and Sarah in their evolution toward story writing and looked at ways story grammar and Souriau's dramatic roles can be used to reinforce notions of form as children begin to write longer stories.

Much of the writing children do in the poetic mode is not story writing but simply an effort to create with words. This poetry writing urge needs to be recognized and encouraged as worthy.

ENDNOTES

1. Arthur Applebee, *The Child's Concept of Story: Ages 2 to 7* (Chicago: University of Chicago Press, 1978).
2. Susan Sowers, "Young Writers' Preferences for Non-Narrative Modes of Composition" (paper presented at the Fourth Annual Boston University Conference of Language Development, Boston, 1979).
3. Wendy Watson, *Lollipop* (New York: Thomas Crowell, 1976).
4. Amos Tutuola, *The Witch-Herbalist of the Remote Town* (Boston: Faber & Faber, 1981), p. 47.
5. "Taleisen," Lady Charlotte Guest, trans., in *The Mabinogion*. Quoted in Joseph Campbell, *The Hero with a Thousand Faces* (Princeton: Princeton University Press, 1972), p. 127.
6. An interesting variant of this and other familiar tales is found in Idries Shah, *World Tales* (New York: Harcourt Brace Jovanovich, 1979).
7. Robert Scholes, *Structuralism in Literature* (New Haven: Yale University Press, 1974).
8. Lucy Calkins, *The Art of Teaching Writing* (Portsmouth, NH: Heinemann, 1986).
9. Stephanie McConaughy, "Using Story Structure in the Classroom," *Language Arts*, 57 (1980): 157–165.
10. Etienne Souriau, *Les Deux Cent Mille Situations Dramatiques* (Paris: Flammarion, 1950).

CHAPTER 10

Writing in the Transactional Mode

Alex's mother gave the authors a message she found under his pillow (see Figure 10–1). It's to the Tooth Fairy ("T. fary"). He lost one tooth and now a second has come out. He is asking the Tooth Fairy please to find the first tooth, but also to recognize that "this one has silver in it."

Writing can be used for different purposes. Sometimes we use it to express whatever thoughts and feelings happen to be crossing our minds. Sometimes we use it to tell a story. And sometimes we use it to get something done, as Alex has in his note to the Tooth Fairy. Writing used in this last sense is called *transactional* writing, or writing in the *transactional mode*, because it serves as a piece of business between the writer and the person or persons he is writing for.

In this chapter we shall examine the attempts of some first-, second-, and third-grade children to write in the transactional mode. There are two distinct types of transactional writing that we will observe. Sometimes transactional writing consists of sharing information or explaining something,

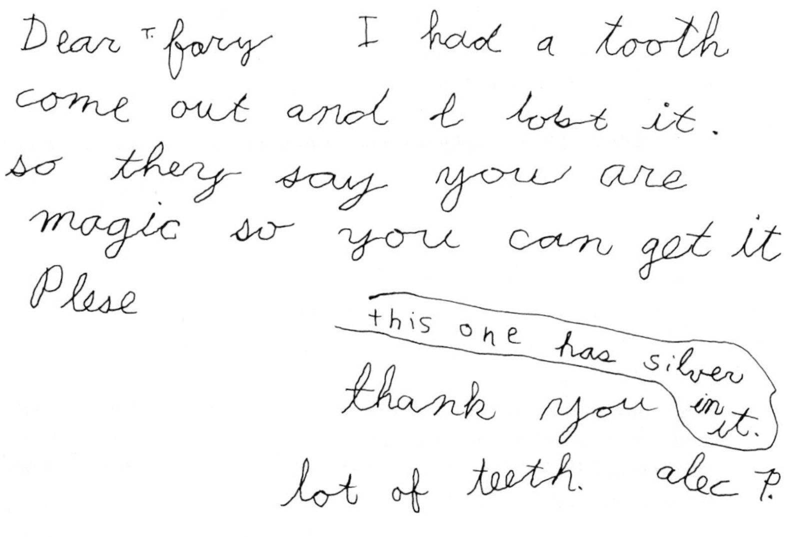

Figure 10–1
Alex
Grade 2

Dear ᵀ fary   I had a tooth come out and I lost it. so they say you are magic so you can get it Plese

this one has silver in it.
thank you
lot of teeth.   alec P.

which is called *expository writing*. In this chapter we will look at two sets of papers that contain expository writing. The second type of transactional writing consists of an attempt to persuade someone to do something or to believe something. This sort of transactional writing is called *argumentative writing*, and we will explore it as well.

Transactional writing has a definite pattern of organization. This is not to say that all transactional writing has the same pattern, or even that all writing of a certain type of transactional writing does either. Every piece of transactional writing, though, normally has *some* pattern, some structure around which the information is organized.

Readers and writers both count on some sort of organizational pattern to guide them in comprehending and presenting written information. Very young writers have begun to get a handle on patterns of organization through conversations: They have some practice in explaining and in describing things. To extend this experience into the realm of writing, children need to hear and to read expository prose as well as stories. Then they need practice at writing it.

Figure 10–2
Eric
Grade 1

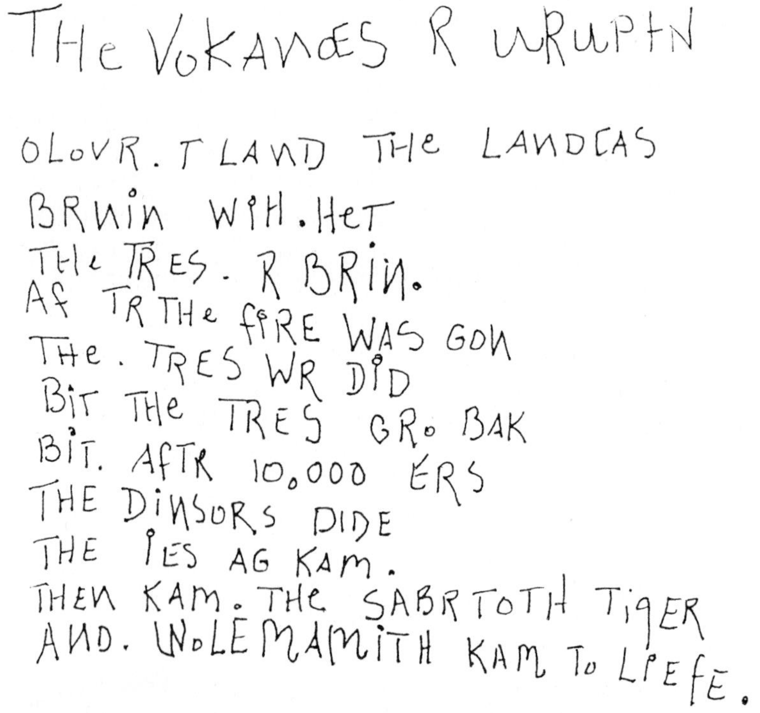

THe VoKANœS R WRWPtN

OLoVR. T LAND THe LANDEAS
BRWiN WiH . HeT
THe TRES . R BRiN.
AS TR THe fiRE WAS GOW
THe . TRES WR DiD
BiT THe TRES GRo BAK
BiT. AfTR 10,000 ERS
THE DiWSoRS DiDE
THE iES AG KAm .
THEW KAm . THe SABRTOTH TigER
AND. WoLE MAMiTH KAm To LiEfE .

(The volcanoes are erupting all over the land. The land is burning with heat. The trees are burning. After the fire was gone the trees were dead. But the trees grew back. After 10,000 years the dinosaurs died. The ice age came. Then came the saber-tooth tiger and wooly mammoth came to life.)

Many children, given their choice of writing topic, will choose subjects that require transactional prose, most often expository. Eric wrote his piece on volcanos (Figure 10–2) toward the end of his first-grade year.

Hugh wrote "Swamp Life" in the second grade.

Swamp Life

The best places to find swamps are in the rain forest. An alligator slips into the water. Frogs jump from lily pad to lily pad. A snake goes into the water. A snake uses the water as his hunting ground for frogs and toads and fish.

Hugh, Age 7

In classrooms where everyone is writing stories or poems, it is sometimes a good idea to remind children that expository writing is very interesting and acceptable too.

> *Teacher:* Could you write up what we learned about cheetahs this morning in a way that would be interesting to the kindergartners?
> *First grader:* Can I put in pictures?
> *Teacher:* Well, I would think that the kindergartners would want pictures *and* words, wouldn't you?

There are also many reasons in school for children to write transactional notes (see Figure 10–3).

Those of us who teach the same group of children all year can usually find ways to make sure each child practices various forms of transactional writing. Because we know each child's interests, we can make individualized suggestions for their topic lists, such as cooking instructions or a letter to their senator. Help can be given with these modes, as needed, during conference times in a process-writing classroom.

Other teachers give direct group assignments and notice that, occasionally at least, children seem to benefit from writing to one assignment and comparing notes. For our immediate purpose, which is to study the kinds of successes and problems young writers have with transactional writing, it is interesting to look at batches of papers written in response to the same assignment.

Figure 10–3
Emi
Grade 1

Mrs. Temple,
    Remember to tipe
Deep River Bluse !

Assignments for Expository Writing

When we give children writing assignments during instruction time, we can often influence the purpose for which they write. Thus, we can give them valuable practice in exercising the different modes of writing and also gain an opportunity to see to what extent they are able to use the different modes. But we must be careful in making judgments, even when children are writing for an assignment, because children may not interpret an assignment the same way we teachers do.

An assignment usually specifies three things:

1. A *topic*—what the writing is to be about;
2. A *purpose* or *function*—what the writer should do about the topic (e.g., explain it, give directions, describe it, tell a story about it, or argue for it);
3. An *audience*—to whom the writer should assume the work is addressed.

We should examine our assignments carefully to see how clearly they specify topic, purpose, and audience before we evaluate the writing that results from them. Sometimes children do not adequately honor one or another element of an assignment because the assignment was not sufficiently explicit. Other times they do not honor some of the elements of an assignment because they are developmentally unable to. It is important to know the difference.

As an example, let us consider an assignment that was given to groups of first and second graders.

The "Expert": An Expository Assignment

"How many of you feel you're an expert in something?" asked the teacher. All of the children raise their hands. "Let's talk about who's an expert in what." A class discussion follows. "I have a roll of adding paper tape in my lap. Johnny, you said you know all about sharks. Do you know this much?" The teacher pulls tape to about six inches in length.

"No, I know more than that," said Johnny.

The teacher, pulling tape, asks, "Do you know this much?"

Johnny says, "More."

The teacher continues pulling the tape until Johnny says "stop" and gives him the paper.

Later the teacher says, "Now all of you have your own paper. Today each of us is going to write about something that's very familiar, something we feel we know a lot about. Everyone has chosen his own topic, so every person's paper will be different from his neighbor's. As you write, remember you're the expert and we, your audience, probably know very little about your subject. Keep this in mind as you write, and try to explain exactly what you mean—exactly what you know. If you need more paper you can just tape some extra onto what you've taken. If you've asked for too much, you can just tear the extra off. Feel free to draw if you'd like."

The assignment makes the *topic* very clear: Each student is to write about something in which she or he is an "expert." The *purpose* of the writing is a bit ambiguous: Are the children to tell us *about* something, or are they to tell us *how to do* something? That is, should a child describe the excitement of participating in a particular sport, or should she tell us how to play the game? The writer will have to decide. As for the *audience*, that has been made clear: It is the teacher and other students in the class.

As you read the papers in Figures 10–4 to 10–11, ask yourself these questions:

1. Which of the writers stuck to the topic?
2. How did each writer interpret the purpose?
3. Which of the writers consistently addressed whichever purpose was chosen?
4. Which of the writers seemed to keep in mind the same audience all the way through?

The children stuck fairly well to the topic of this assignment. All of the children wrote about something they considered themselves an expert about. Nevertheless, they interpreted the "something" in different ways: Brian wrote about a sport; Rachel, Marc, and Bryan wrote about hobbies. These are

Figure 10–4
Rachel
Grade 2

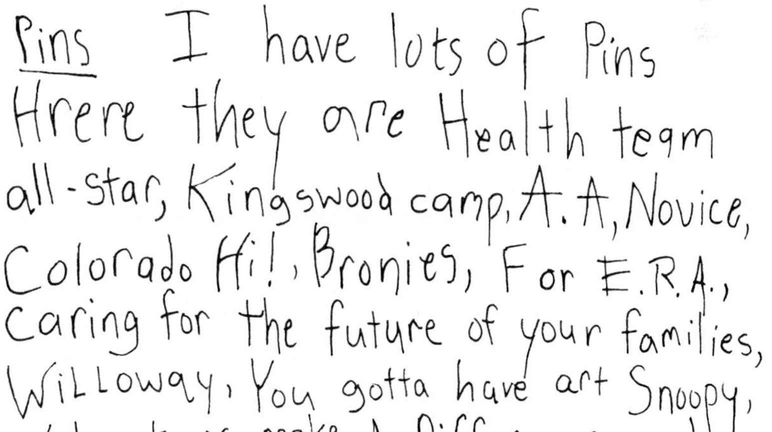

Pins   I have lots of Pins
Hrere they are Health team
all-star, Kingswood camp, A.A, Novice,
Colorado Hi!, Bronies, F or E.R.A.,
Caring for the future of your families,
Willoway, You gotta have art Snoopy,
Volunteers make A Difference and
ribons, Zionism, Doggie, One with Stones.
Old fasio gifl. I like my Pins.

Art

Art is fun. You can learn a lot of things from it. And most of all you have to have a lot of pacantes. And I like to make things in Art and one day in art we made paper masa. In school the art teacher is Mrs. Gill. She is very nice. I like it because I am very creative and That is why I like to do Art. And I'm a very, very, very good Artist. And I love makeing things with clay, and I like makeing things with paper. And I like makeing things made from paper masa, but, most of all I like makeing faces of people, cartons, Comics,

Building Models.

It's like a jig saw puzzle at first and now it is so simple I could finish it in a half an hour matering what kind it is I could finish a snap together modle in 10 minits and I could finish a hard glue together in a half an hour and let its dry and put it on my shelf and show it to my freinds I have in motle I glue together and and 7 snap togethers in and oher I get time I gaint then I have 18 cars 1 helcopter and 5 air plane and the ones tat are titeley together I play with and have Fun and with my brother with my air planes and I always win. I never lose.

Hockey.

I know how to play forword and defents and goley. I know how to shoot the pyk. I know how to play write wing and left wing. I know how to play

left defents and write defents. Hocky
is very very very fyn. I
yshyly play defense.

Mice

One thing about mice is that a cat will get Rid
of mice, mice love cheese most of all. they live in
holes in the wall. People don't like mice so they
put traps in the house. If it dosent work get
a cat. Mice are in some Books in the library.
Mice are good. Mice and cats don't get alon
to well.

Space

The sun was made by gases and dust forming a big cloud. one
day the cloud started to burn and the dust and gasses get
tighter turned in to a ball of fire. This is watt the sun is
today. in about 5,000,0000,000 years it will run out of gas to
burn. then it will burn up earth and mars then it will get
white and very smal. A teaspoon of it would way about a ton.
then it would turn in to a hole. The sun is a medeim
size star. there is no air in space so jets can't fly, but rokets can.
When people make rokets they can't make it go so far. the have only
gone to the moon.

Figure 10–10
Ian
Grade 1

Siuprman. Siuprman Ram See thrir anenthig Be Cas he has a X rai vitin ahd he is the Stnogest in the Wirild and he kan fili and he is fatr than a ScPetcy dulat and he is AbuL to Lep tuL buldeg in a Sege Ldod and

Figure 10–11
Mara
Grade 1

BaBy

thy mack in thar Pans and criy all the time they Sleip in a crip and thr up all niht and slep in the day they crey if they don have fiod whan they Want it they srem in my eras but ther is sum tigfunny Bucus When my mom picshim uP he stops and sum time When my mom pits him down he sceme he only nos tow Wrds he stac uP til midniht But Sum times hes Jes fin.

alike in that they are activities in which the children participate—activities that might lend themselves to papers that explain how to *do* the activity. Susan, Mara, Ian, and Paul wrote about things they *know* about. These approaches lend themselves to papers that provide facts about the topic. Thus, there were potential differences in the way the children approached their topic. One group could have described a procedure, and the other group could have presented facts. Nevertheless, all of the children presented facts.

How well did the children achieve the *purpose* of explaining? What sort of purpose did the children take the assignment to be requesting? All of the students addressed what would be considered an expository purpose; there were no stories and no purely expressive pieces handed in. Within the expository purpose, as we already noted, none of the children elected to give directions for a procedure, although we might have expected such results from the assignment.

How consistently did the children stick to their purposes? This varied, with strong shades of expressive writing entering into most of the papers.

Brian (Figure 10–7), for example, has interpreted the assignment in a personal way, and we see he has written an inventory of all the positions he can play and things he can do. In total, his paper explains his expertise in hockey , and indirectly the reader learns a little about the game.

But Brian, the writer, is in center stage in this piece, giving an account of his own experiences and feelings. "Hockey is very very very fun." Brian's piece is organized around all of the things he knows how to do. Harking back to Susan Sowers's term, we would call this organization a *knowledge-based inventory*—more of a list than a structure. This is a feature of expressive writing. Rachel (Figure 10–4) chose to write a paper about collecting pins. She, like Brian, has also written an inventory, in this case an inventory of the pins she has collected.

From Marc's paper (Figure 10–5), we learn something about art. But just as in Brian's paper, we also learn a great deal about Marc. the writer. The "very, very, very good artist," who feels very creative and who loves making things with clay and likes making faces of people, cartoons, and comics is full of pleasurable feelings he wants to share. He also has the beginnings of conventional expository organization emerging in his paper. He has given us a main idea—"art is fun"—and provided supporting statements for it—"You can learn a lot of things..." and "you have to have a lot of patience." He lists several important things, and then tells us the most important: "I love . . . ; I like . . . ; but most of all, I like . . . " But his focus is still personal, still expressive.

Bryan (Figure 10–6) is as wrapped up with building models as Marc is with art.

From the papers we have examined so far it might appear that what all these children need to do in order to write more informational papers is focus a little less on themselves. Limiting the topic is also a consideration.

Susan's composition (Figure 10–8) is less expressive than Bryan's, Brian's, or Marc's. She is attempting to focus on her topic and limiting her personal intrusion into the paper. Yet we sense she 's not nearly so comfortable with her theme as the previous writers were with theirs. Susan seems to be searching for things to say. Her jump from catching mice to "mice are in some books in the library" and "mice are good" is a disconcerting leap for her readers.

Her paper might have a more natural focus if she were writing about some personal interest, as did the writers whom we've discussed thus far. Although she seems to have moved beyond the focus on her own likes and dislikes, she has yet to replace it with any other strong center. Of course, Susan is only a first grader! Her piece is an inventory. Eventually, for her writing to have a concentrated punch to it, she must learn to limit her topic to one aspect of the facts and integrate the points she makes about her topic into some kind of organization.

Baby

1. they make in their pants and
2. cry all the time
3. they sleep in a crib
4. and they're up all night and sleep in the day
5. they cry if they don't have food
6. when they want it they scream in my ears
7. but there is some thing funny
8. because when my mom picks him up
9. he stops and some time when my mom
10. puts him down he screams
11. he only knows two words
12. he stays up til midnight
13. But some times he's just fine

Mara, Grade 1

Mara is writing from personal experience (Figure 10–11), while trying to keep herself in the background. Mara knows a lot about babies because her mother has recently had one. She manages to begin her paper with a detached "expert" voice. Presenting information as one who knows, she writes, "They make in their pants and cry all the time." But Mara 's voice changes in the second half of her paper (line 7); now it's more personal and expressive, " . . . when my mom picks him up he stops." Suddenly, she substitutes "he" for "they," the specific for the general. Now we leave the detached realm of factual description and enter Mara's world. Mara's composition is a good transitional piece between the expressive and transactional modes.

Sometimes a child's topic is so removed from personal experience that it's not very difficult for him to sustain an objective point of view. Ian's description of Superman (Figure 10–10) is objective, but this doesn't mean that he is a more sophisticated writer than Mara or the other children. He's learned about Superman indirectly, so he doesn't have the problem of step-ping back. Moreover, he has heard the familiar catalogue of Superman's powers again and again. Nevertheless, one can't help but be awed by his ex-traordinary invented spelling effort. He has forged through his words the way Superman slashes through steel!

Paul's paper (Figure 10-9) is the last piece we'll discuss. It could use a few adjustments, but Paul's is a fine piece of exposition. He restricts his sub-ject to the sun's evolution and change. He carries his idea through from the time it was "made by ashes and dust" until the time when it will "turn into a hole."

A few children in first and second grade will write expository papers like Paul's, but not many. Paul's paper satisfies an adult reader's expectation of what expository writing should look like. But teachers should be aware that children must move gradually away from writing that puts themselves first toward writing that succeeds in giving an organized accounting of a sub-ject and satisfies most of the reader's need to know.

What effect does the audience have on children's writing? These chil-dren wrote their pieces in school, for their peers. It seems that this audience invoked personal expression because the writer was justified in assuming that the audience was as interested in herself as in her topic.

When children are writing in school, the writer-audience relationship is known; the child's audience is Miss Jones and the class. Consequently, teachers should assume that expository papers written in school will often be more ex-pressive than transactional. They will often take the form of elementary person-al essays, where the child, not the subject, is in center stage. Let us look at anoth-er expository assignment that was given to another group of second graders.

Another Expository Assignment: How to Ride a Bicycle

This time the assignment more clearly specified the purpose the teacher was after. Here is the assignment:

> *Teacher:* I'll bet you all know how to ride a bicycle. (Most of the students said they did. Many started to describe the procedure to her.)
>
> *Teacher:* Well, some people over in Victoria [that is a city where two of the authors worked] want us to write down how to ride a bicycle for them.
>
> *Child:* Teacher?
>
> *Teacher:* Yes?
>
> *Child:* Don't they know how to ride bicycles in Victoria?

As you read the papers the children wrote (Figures 10–12 to 10–15), decide

1. Which children stuck to the topic?
2. Which children honored the purpose of giving directions?
3. Which children kept their audience consistently in mind?

bicycle
first you must take your
left leg and put it on the
pedal.and then you take
your right leg.and put on
thepedal, and push the pedal
with your right leg. and hold
on to the bars. and when
you want to turn you take
your bars and either push
the right or left, and never
ride, without holding onto your
bars .

Figure 10–12
Andy
Grade 2

first thing you do is
to pettle, than you

balance yourself so you

won't fall off your bike

than you steer so
You won't run into
Something, and thats
all you have to know.

Figure 10–13
Russell
Grade 2

Figure 10–14
John
Grade 2

Deskib abuot a bike
You got to geep your bales
and pedol and keep the wheel
stat and turn going around
a turn.

Figure 10–15
Lois
Grade 2

All you have to do is petel the
bike and the wheels will turn

around and around. And when you want

to stop pull backward on the
petels.

We can see that virtually all of the children stuck to the topic. They all focused on bicycles and how they are ridden.

As for the discourse mode, they stayed within the expository form on this assignment far better than in the previous one. All of the writers kept in the background; the focus was on the task of riding a bicycle, not on the person who could do it. There were no personal statements, such as "I like to ride my bicycle" or "Riding a bicycle is fun" or even "I'm very, very, very good at riding a bicycle."

Why did the writers keep themselves in the background of their compositions this time? We suspect it was largely because of the audience. First, they were aware that the papers were being written for strangers—for people they would never see. They may have known that the readers would have been more interested in bike riding than in the writers themselves. Or they may have been shy about sharing a lot of personal material with people they didn't know and couldn't see. However, it could also have been because the topic clearly called for them to explain how to ride a bicycle, not to talk about bicycle riding. The wording of the assignment, that is, made it clearly inappropriate for a child to list all of his experiences and feelings related to bicycles.

Note how well organized most of these papers are. The children kept closely to a sequential, step-by-step pattern for presenting their ideas. By their questions, we may gather that the children understood their task. They succeeded very well in thinking through what steps would be helpful to share, and in what order.

The contrast between these papers and the previous assignment is striking. Most of the children responding to the expert assignment put themselves prominently into their papers, but these children did not. Moreover, several of the children writing for the expert assignment chose to write about processes (building model airplanes, playing hockey, doing art, and collecting pins), but none of them explained how to perform those processes. In contrast, all of the children responding to the bicycle assignment explained how to ride a bicycle.

It is not always necessary or desirable to give children explicit assignments for the writing they do. But when the teacher does want to make assignments with the intention of having the children practice writing in a particular discourse mode, the assignment must be worded very carefully. The teacher should discuss the assignment with the children to determine what they understand the assignment to mean.

An Assignment for Argumentative Writing

In general, argumentative writing includes works that attempt to persuade a reader of a certain point of view. In children's writing, however, argumentative writing more often takes the form of an attempt to persuade someone else to do something, such as give the writer something, allow him to do something, do him a favor, or the like.

Argumentative, or persuasive, writing is an appropriate form for children to practice, because in this form the topic and the audience are inherently made clear. The topic is *what we want;* the audience is the person or persons *from whom we want it.* The mode of argumentative writing may pose difficulties, however, that have little to do with writing. Persuasion requires that a person know how to structure an argument according to his social standing vis-à-vis her audience. For example, we can say some things to our close friends by way of persuasion for which we would be sent to our room if we addressed them to our mother, or thrown in jail if we addressed them to the president of the United States. The following is an argumentative assignment that was given to a second-grade class:

> Think of something that you would like to do, but for one reason or another cannot do. Write a letter to persuade the person who is preventing you from doing what you'd like to change his or her mind.

This assignment was followed by class discussion, and then the children wrote. Several of their papers are reprinted here, but before we look at them, let us decide what to look for.

This assignment points to a definite topic, but it leaves the writer latitude to determine exactly what the topic will be. The assignment leaves it to the writer to decide who his audience is, but it does make it clear that he must decide.

The discourse mode is suggested also. The purpose, at least, is clear: The writer is to persuade someone to let him do something. But it is up to the writer to decide how the persuading is to be done and how to organize his points. It is also for the writer to note that he may wish to structure his arguments differently, to use more or less politeness, depending on his audience. Consider now Figures 10–16 to 10–22. How did the children treat each of the elements of topic, purpose, and audience?

First of all, how many of these children thought of a topic and stuck to it? All of them, really. Johnny chose to write an inventory of all the things he wanted to be allowed to do rather than pick one and arrange an argument for it. All of the others stated their request and then sought to drive it home somehow. Johnny may have found it easier to make an inventory of requests rather than to structure an argument for one request.

How many of them kept their audience constantly in mind? All but two; John and Alexis did not consistently address their compositions to their parents, the supposed audience. But in John's case that is surely because his request to be allowed to drive the family car was fanciful anyway (see Figure 10–20). His work turned into a story toward the end. The device of dialogue showed up as a method of structuring his composition. This is a manifestation of expressive writing. John's writing did not come off as a persuasive

Figure 10–16
Corey
Grade 2

Corey F.

Dear Mrs. Vargas   why   won't   you
let   us   talk in the   cafatearia? We
have   a   right to!   after all   you talk
in   the   longe.   any way.

Figure 10–17
Johnny
Grade 2

dear mom and dad,

I want to ride my bike
on the dirt road. Let me
play with frogs. I want
to run splash in the
mud.

love,

Johnny

Figure 10–18
Jeanette
Grade 2

Dear Debbie,
One day Debbie. Pow!
Write in the ciser. O.K. Why
is it allways we have to
play baby. We never ride
bikes.

piece. Perhaps if the topic had been derived from a need that was real to him rather than imagined, his paper would have shown a more definite structure.

Alexis's paper (Figure 10–22) resorted to a bit of dialogue at the end. After making his pitch about being allowed to stay up until midnight, he had his mom say, "Okay, you can only stay up to midnight for only eight weeks." This paper, too, might have stayed more faithfully in the persuasive mode

Figure 10–19
Annie
Grade 2

Dear Dad,
     Why can't I get a hourse?
I would keep my room clean.
I'd tak care of it. I'd be extra
good I never would fight.
pleas? pleas? I would let my
sisters ride it.

                    Sincerly,
                    Annie

Figure 10–20
John
Grade 2

              I want to drive a car
     Dean Mom and Dad. Would you
let me drive your car no-o-o-o! Ok
I want to no-o. I'll go drive the car
tonight. There asleep I'll go get the car.

               The End

Figure 10–21
Andy
Grade 2

Dear, Mom and dad. How come I cant ride
   into town on my bike. I'm careful enoagh
around the block. If a car rides on the right
and I'm on the right then I'll stop.
   And if a cars on the left and I'm on the
the left I'll stop. And I'll ride on the
side of the road

had the child really intended for his parents to read the letter and make a determination on the basis of it.

The children stayed within the argumentative mode of discourse, with the two exceptions we have just mentioned. Their papers generally began with the request and then listed support for it. The arguments they put forward took various forms. Annie's paper (Figure 10–19), for example, was a tit-for-tat argument. She would keep her room clean, be really good, wouldn't fight, and even let her sisters ride it, if only her parents would get her a horse. Alexis (Figure 10–22) use this line of argument too, promising to wash the dishes, cut the yard, and water the plants. Alexis also used the tack of explaining his request: because spring is here and he wants to hear the frogs sing.

Corey (Figure 10–16) use a fair-is-fair approach. If the lunchroom manager gets to talk in the lounge (her rest area away from work), then by rights the children should be allowed to talk in the lunchroom (their rest area away from work).

Jeanette (Figure 10–18) uses the get-tough approach: "One day, Debbie, Pow! Right in the kisser!"

Figure 10–22
Alexis
Grade 2

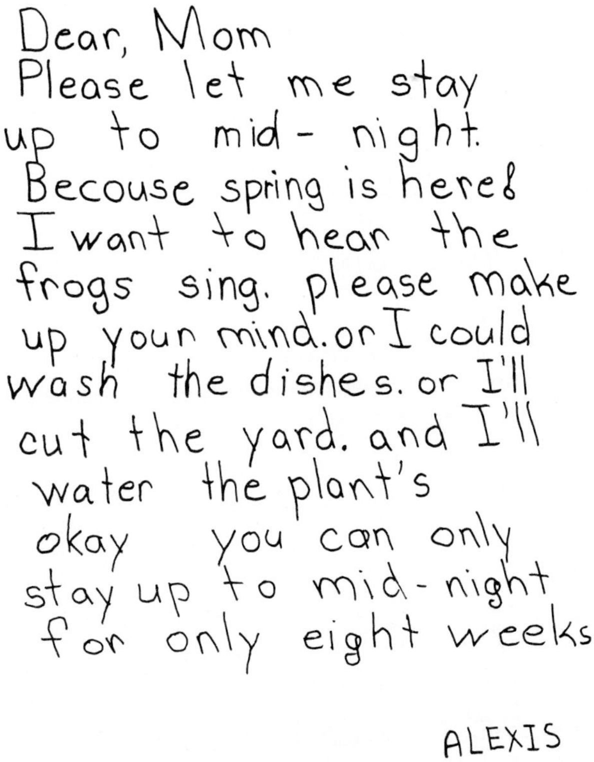

Dear, Mom
Please let me stay
up to mid - night.
Becouse spring is here&
I want to hear the
frogs sing. please make
up your mind. or I could
wash the dishes. or I'll
cut the yard. and I'll
water the plant's
okay you can only
stay up to mid - night
for only eight weeks

ALEXIS

Andy (Figure 10–21) uses perhaps the most sophisticated approach of all. In his piece about bicycle riding on the street he anticipated his parents' objections. He put himself in their place and realized that their objection to his riding his bike on the street was a concern for his safety. Then he set out to convince them that he knew how to be safe. This is a sophisticated approach, and it is also pitched at an effective level of politeness for parents.

Johnny (Figure 10-17) provides no support for his requests, but rather adds other requests to the list and makes an inventory.

The children in this group were able to rise to the challenge of writing an argumentative or persuasive piece fairly well. A couple of them could have used some encouragement when the assignment was given in order to approach it in more realistic terms. This would be easier if the assignment had arisen from a real need and the letters could actually have been mailed. For the group as a whole, the children raised a remarkable variety of persuasive tactics, from tit for tat to fair is fair to threats to anticipating and allaying objections. The teacher could capitalize on this diversity by sharing the papers and discussing the various approaches. He could ask: How could we make an argument like Alexis used to ask permission to talk in the lunchroom? How could we make an argument like Annie used to talk Debbie into riding bikes?

Another issue to which the teacher could call attention is the difference in the way arguments are couched for different audiences. Jeanette could be asked how she would have worded her argument if she had been addressing

Figure 10–23
Elizabeth
Grade 3

Tuesday 11/1/83

Dear Mr. Reagan,
please take apart

missiles to prevent
War, and make som-
thing non-explosof out
of them.
        Recpectfully
    Elizabeth Russo

Figure 10–24
Rebecca
Grade 1

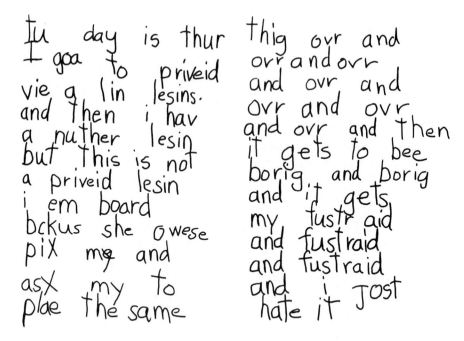

her mother. Alexis could be asked how he might have worded his argument differently if he were addressing it to his big brother or to the babysitter. These questions get at an important but often overlooked aspect of language learning. That is, we use different language forms and degrees of formality and directness with different audiences.

The idea of writing persuasive letters and the skills to do so carry over from this type of assignment into writing workshop. Figures 10–23 and 10–24 were written on the children's own initiative.

Encouraging Writing in a Variety of Modes

What are some ways to encourage writing in a variety of modes without directive assignments?

We are convinced that children learn best by being shown the process of writing and choosing their own topics on which to write. We are also aware that a major problem for many young writers is finding things to write about that seem worthy of all the thought and effort. School life and the information learned in school are a huge part of a young child's life. We want children to realize that not only their home life but everything they study, every story they read, playground, make-believe, and school politics are all grist for the writer's mill. Some teachers promote variety in children's modes of writing by giving occasional assignments like how to ride a bicycle or the argumentative assignment previously discussed, usually during a writing instruction time.

Something like a class newsletter comes in handy in creating new and definite audiences for the children's writing, which, as we have seen, helps children write in the transactional mode. The following instructions were written by a first grader for the class newsletter just after the children had learned to make cornhusk dolls (see Figure 10–25). Complete with drawings, it took Marissa five days of workshop time, or approximately four hours of concentrated effort, to produce this piece, of which she was justifiably proud. Her self-imposed task required her not only to remember every step of a long procedure, but to put herself in the reader's place and judge whether or not the reader would be able to follow the process with only her instructions as guide.

Some teachers simply model different subjects and modes of writing during workshop time. Others assign writing as part of other areas of study and let the children continue their efforts during writing workshop time if they so desire. On the following pages are some writings from second, third, and fourth graders who took their inspiration from a social studies investigation of the Roanoke colony and the nine children who were part of it.

> David's Diary:
> *April 20th, 1587*
> I got aboard the ELIZABETH, with John White as captain. The room for sleeping is three feet, up and down; my bed is a block of wood. It is nicer on the poop deck.
>
> *April 21st*
> For meals there is bread, wine, fish. I had fish and meal for lunch. I read stories from the Bible and write in my diary.
>
> *July 20th*
> Land in sight. Smoke mysteriously rises from the woods. We will probably land today, we are sailing very fast. White says we will make huts from bark and sticks tied together at the top and bark laid on them to make a bark tepee to live in and tomorrow we 'll start on the houses. All we have left to eat is ship biscuits. Sometimes we catch a few fish. I am seasick and homesick.

David, age nine, is able to slip into the shoes of one of the colonist children with no trouble. Orion, on the other hand, who is only seven, finds it easier to write from a detached point of view, in an expository voice, and yet it is clear as his story progresses that he sees himself as one of the crabbers.

> Four hundred years ago a ship came over to Roanoke to drop nine children and a hundred and seventeen women. That day they made huts out of mud and sticks and a few nails that they took over. That

Figure 10–25
Marissa
Grade 2

How To Make a Cornhusk Doll by Marissa McHale Blank
School is fun. Today we made cornhusk dolls. I made the one you see.

First you take a piece of cream-colored cornhusk and take two cotton balls and put the cotton balls inside the cornhusk, and bunch the cornhusk and tie a piece of thin cornhusk. Wrap it around the neck of the head you just made. The head should look like this:

Make one long arm by rolling a piece of cornhusk up in a scroll and tying it at both ends, and then you have made arms.

Then take a piece of blue or red cornhusk; take a piece that looks like this

and make a diamond hole in the same one and put it on the head of the body.

Then take five pieces of blue or red cornhusk that look like this, tie them around (the middle of the body) and bend them around.

night the children coughed upstairs because there was too much smoke. The smoke came from the chimney. The chimney was leaking.

The next morning five boys went to catch crabs with sticks. One boy jumped into the water with his stick and pushed a crab out of the water. The other boys put their sticks down and took rocks and shot them at the crab. The crab died and that's how they killed the crabs. The boy that was in the water got pinched by a crab that was behind him. The boy screamed. All the men and women came to see what was going on. A big Indian and a little Indian were peeking out from behind a rock. The little Indian ran away like a penguin and the big Indian ran after the little Indian. The big Indian said STOP in their language, the little Indian stopped. . . .

Orion's expository writing has turned into an action story, with the reader drawn right into the middle of it.

Elizabeth, eight years old, maintains one voice throughout; so do Micah, Orion, and Andrew.

January the 17th, 1587
Dear Grampa and Granma,
    I eat mostly deer; it is cold in the winter. I hope we see you soon. The people who were here before us which our people call savages stole the deer meat so we had to go without anything except for water for two days. Micah and I have to go almost every night to the neighbor's hut to borrow some fire. We only have one more rag for the tinderbox. Grandma please send me some of Grampa's rags. We send you two wolf skins and five fox skins when a ship comes. Our next door neighbor's house burned down. It caught on to ours so we had to build another one. Micah and I found ten nails. One Indian girl named Pomawak is my friend. I go meet her every day in the woods in a clearing. Three days we pick berries together. We taught each other our languages with our hands, so we can talk to each other a little bit.
    Love,
    Your granddaughter Elizabeth

Dear Granny,
    I made a goose trap and my friend and I caught five geese. Every thing is going fine except for the weather.
    Your grandchild Micah (Age 7)

Dear Grampa,
    I am freezing to death but I don't die. Orion (Age 7)

Dear Grampa,
    Things are getting worse. First I thought the savages were bad, but now I have to go over to chief Okracoke for medicine and food. My mother is getting scurvy but she's lucky her teeth aren't falling out. We are lucky to have the savages. They give us crab, duck, geese and mush, but now they don't have that much so we are starving. The Indians say that in forty-one more days the weather will be warmer. If it wasn't for the Indians we would be dead.
    Your Grandchild Andrew (Age 9)

Some of the children decided to write from an Indian child's point of view:

> Today white people came to this land. They are really white. They look so different from our people. They even dress differently. They have something that covers their legs and also something that covers their chest and back. It doesn't look like they know how to build a house. I was hiding up in a tree with Pakla, my sister. We saw a big canoe. I ran to my village to tell my father, the chief, that a big canoe was coming. He warned me to stay away from them.
>
> With special permission Pakla and I went down to the village that the white people have built. Pakla saw a little girl sitting outside a hut crying. Pakla showed me. I said let's go down and see what the little girl was crying for. We ran down the hill into the village the white people had built. We got to the little baby and kneeled down to see the baby better. All of a sudden a man came out of the hut and was waving his arms and shouting at us. He was shouting something Pakla and I could not understand. But we were smart enough to know we weren't welcome right then. We ran as fast as we could to father, and told him everything.
>
> *Elizabeth, 8, with Sarah, 7, and Erin, 8*

> On the fourth day Pamawak and I spied ten white people coming up the hill and we ran to tell our father the chief. The chief came down and about halfway we bumped into them making signs that meant corn for a bag of dry biscuits, so our father traded the corn for the biscuits and we had them for supper. They were not very good but they were different.
>
> *Sarah, 7, with Elizabeth and Erin*

Once again we are struck by what a boon to good writing a strong curriculum is! We often hear it said that to learn to write, children need to be shown the process of writing, that they need to be encouraged to write about things they care about for a real audience. Such statements are true but incomplete; they overlook the importance of subject matter.

The truth is, if they are to have things to write about, particularly in an expository way, children need to be immersed in interesting content. But it is not enough to trot children through disconnected bits of freeze-dried content. They need to engage their imaginations deeply in interesting curriculum, and they need to take the time to explore ideas actively and fully.

Writing is a necessary part of a sound curriculum, and when it is, the power of genuine interest in subject matter, the resonance of rich reading, and the excitement of having their ideas deeply engaged and their ideas taken seriously will go a long way toward enabling children to craft well-structured and vivid prose.

Conclusion

Young children write slowly. To write successfully in the transactional mode requires a writer to maintain in her mind her topic, purpose, and audience during repeated trips to the pencil sharpener and conversations with neighbors. It is not surprising that early attempts to write in this voice are highly personal, or that they tend to feature inventories of ideas rather than integrated arguments. It is good practice to steer children toward transactional writing, to remind them of occasions that call for this mode.

But, at least in the early years, we should not be too disappointed if children write mainly in the expressive mode, as long as what they are writing holds their interest. The goal in these formative years is fluency, with variety in writing tasks important to the extent that it helps keep the students' interest sparked.

Nonetheless, children need to be immersed in rich content if they are to write fluently in the transactional mode. Descriptive and expository writing require that children know and care about things to describe and explain them. Argumentative writing requires that children have things they care to argue about.

CHAPTER 11

Writing: The Child, the Teacher, and the Class

In the previous ten chapters we have been concerned with the *forms of writing*—the configurations that make letters, the patterns that make spelling, the organizations that make composition types—and how children learn them. But an important question remains unanswered: "What is the *activity of writing,* or, if you will, the *process of composing,* and how do children learn to do it?"

Writing as a Social Activity

As we begin to talk about teaching writing, we must broaden our focus to take in, simultaneously, the individual child and the whole class, including the teacher. Writing is a quintessentially social activity. You cannot teach a child to write without teaching her to interact with others through print. Some of the most important interaction—important because of its value for modeling helpful interaction—is between the child and the teacher. But if there is anything we have learned about writing in the last twenty years, it is that you cannot restrict growing writers to the audience they find in the teacher, anymore than you can teach a group of children to square dance if you are the only allowable partner.

What Sort of Learning Is Learning to Write?
Some friends of ours, both college professors, were recently on a long car trip with their two sons, one aged seven and the other just two. They were playing Twenty Questions:

"Are you thinking of something *made by people*?"
"No."
"Are you thinking of something *mineral*?"
"No." And so on.

After the game had gone on for some time the little one couldn't stand being left out any longer, so he suddenly chimed in with perfect intonation:

"inky umping—*doggies*?"

"inky umping—*Mommy?*"

He kept it up until the game dissolved in laughter.

William Corsaro was studying the strategies four-year-old children use to work their way into the group activity of their peers. His young subjects didn't ask "May I play?" because there was a good chance someone would say "No!" They didn't wait to be invited, because they couldn't count on being told anything, or told what to do. They simply moved in and began doing whatever it was the others were doing, and before long they were part of the group.[1]

A number of researchers have begun to look at school learning as if it were a *game* that children wanted to take part in. Instead of only describing the cognitive learning of individuals, they have begun to describe a significant part of children's learning as *learning to do school*[2]—learning to play one's own role in the ongoing activity of the classroom. Cognitive learning, in turn, is the eventual result of participation over time in school tasks. If we want children to learn to write in school, then we might start by establishing ongoing routines in the classroom that invite and require writing (and reading). We should establish what Nancie Atwell has called a *literate community.*[3]

By now, thanks to the vigorous research and observation that have been focused on the writing process over the last decade, we have a fairly clear idea what activities people must carry out in order to become writers. We will summarize these activities—what we call the *process of composing*—in this chapter. Then we will lay out in much finer detail the procedures that have helped us set up literate communities in our own and others' classrooms.

A Description of the Writing Process

Milan Kundera came of age in Czechoslovakia under a government whose policy of censorship would not allow him to publish his books. He was put in jail more than once. He and his friends dreamed of the West, where even schoolchildren could write and publish what they wanted to. They longed for the almost unimaginable power to write what one truly wished to say and share one's most important thoughts with an attentive public.

Kundera's is the strongest demonstration we know of the point that writing begins with a will to say something to someone else. Marvelously, we have found that, although many of our own adult voices have been muted by our school experiences or displaced by the canned excitement of the electronic media, children still want to write. In the following pages we will share what one professional writer and writing teacher describes as the process he and many other writers go through in order to write—the stages, step by step. But you should always keep in mind that before any set strategies will work, the will to say something to someone else must be present and encouraged. A classroom that focuses on these strategies without the communicative intention they are to serve will not keep faith with its children.

The Stages of Writing

Donald Murray has written a description of the writing process professional writers appear to use.[4] His description seems just as viable for school writing. In Murray's model, writing is a *process of continuous thinking, experimenting, and reviewing.* The activity of writing a paper develops in three stages: rehearsing, drafting, and revising.

Rehearsing is the stage in which writers discover what they have to say. Teachers can encourage rehearsing by means of brainstorming sessions, in which children think and write down as many details as they can about a person, a place, or an event that is meaningful to them. Sometimes teachers promote free writing during the rehearsal stage. Free writing is timed writing in which the writer puts down absolutely anything that occurs to him, without stopping and without making any corrections, for a specified period of time, usually five or ten minutes.[5] Both methods are intended to bring out into the open a wide range of particular ideas and details, which a writer can subsequently employ in his deliberate writing. There are other activities used during the rehearsal stage that we will describe later.

The second stage in the process of writing is *drafting.* The term is chosen because this sort of writing is a tentative activity. When we speak of a first draft or a second draft, we imply that a piece is undergoing change, that other drafts may follow. It is during the drafting stage that the writer experiences clearly what she has to say. Drafting enables the writer to put her thoughts outside of herself and to consider them as if they belonged to someone else. The writer may thus have a dialogue with herself through the drafting process. She can appraise the work with some detachment in this stage, considering it as something that can stand on its own before a reader.

Revising is the final stage, although we should remember that revision can lead to further rehearsal and further drafts. The writer examines his piece and clarifies for himself what the writing should say. When necessary, the writer prunes words or adds them, all in an effort to make the meaning that is in the piece speak more clearly. Sometimes revising is a matter of patching up phrases or sentences in order to make them smoother or clearer. Sometimes, however, the writer discovers whole new possibilities that should be developed in the work. In the latter event, revision can mean changes to larger parts of a work, and sometimes to the whole work. In Murray's words, "the writing stands apart from the writer, and the writer interacts with it, first to find out what it has to say, and then to help the writing say it more clearly and gracefully."[6]

Betty Flowers suggests a way to make the different mental forces that are at work in writing comprehensible to children. She presents students with four role models, the madman, the architect, the carpenter, and the judge.[7] Ideally, a writer takes on each of these roles, one at a time, as she works through her drafts. We have found the models very helpful to children who have begun to acquire some fluency in writing, but we remind you that writing is not usually a linear process. The roles Flowers outlines are just that, roles. While contemplating her role models we should remember, for example, that revision can lead to further rehearsal and new drafts.

The *madman* is, of course, doing what Murray calls rehearsing. He is "full of ideas, writes crazily and perhaps rather sloppily, gets carried away by enthusiasm or anger, and if really let loose, could turn out ten pages in an hour."[8]

The second worker, who might be called the next day, is the *architect*. She comes in, reads over what the madman has written, and looks for parts that are worth keeping and developing. "Her job is to select large chunks of material and to arrange them into a pattern that might form an argument. The thinking here is large, organizational, paragraph level thinking."[9] The architect might also ask if there are any basic supports missing for what we want to say.

Once the architect has gotten together the basic structure of the piece—and this might involve cutting and taping and adding to the madman's work—we are ready for the carpenter.

The *carpenter* nails the ideas together in a logical sequence, making sure each sentence is clearly written, contributes to the paragraph, and leads logically and gracefully to the next sentence. When the carpenter finishes, the piece of writing should be smooth and watertight.

Only at this point are we ready to call in the last of the workers, the *judge*. The judge reads over the whole piece as a newcomer, reflects on what he hears, and compares it with what the author wanted to say. Is the idea or argument convincing? Is the tone right? Does the whole seem polished and ready?

Madman, architect, carpenter, judge is an easy sequence for most children to remember, and it promotes the same process that we see in Murray's sequence of *rehearsal, drafting, revision,* and *possible redrafting.* An added advantage of Flowers's method for young writers is that it gives a sense of individual purpose to each draft and each rereading and keeps the judge at bay until suitably late in the process.

Before we leave Murray's stages and Flowers's roles, we should remind the reader that both of these approaches to the writing process are ideals, approximations that are not always honored in practice. Some writers find that thinking about what they are going to write before they write it fills them with dread: writer's block. Others write so slowly and thoughtfully that they rarely need to revise what they say. More to the point of this book, first-grade writers invest so much energy in the crafting of even a line of print that revising may seem like cruel punishment for them. Having said all that, the authors still believe, after years of working with both these models, that devoting some attention to generating ideas and planning writing, drafting with an experimental attitude, and being prepared to rewrite their works to satisfy an audience are worthy goals for all children.

Atmosphere, Assignment, and Response: The Teacher's Role in the Writing Process

It is now time to discuss the teacher's role in all this. In light of our previous discussion on the writing process, what classroom characteristics and activities are most helpful to children in their growth toward literacy? We will explore the issues of atmosphere, assignments, and responses in an effort to forge an answer.

An Atmosphere for Writing

Every classroom has both a physical and an intellectual atmosphere. Some basic features of the physical atmosphere are crucial to children's well-being: for example, lighting and ventilation. Provided these necessities are met, however, the intellectual atmosphere should be one with a curriculum rich in substance, where writing is received with enthusiasm and respect, where praise is judiciously bestowed, where children are helped to discover their next goal, and where a purposeful audience exists for each student's writing. In a healthy intellectual atmosphere, young authors feel they can take risks and make mistakes without fear of censure. As Eric, a first grader, told us recently, "Don't worry if you make a mistake, you can do something with it. You may be able to turn it into something good." Ideally, children come to know that trying new forms and experimenting are an important part of the writing process. Dazzling writing centers, with prepared booklets, notebooks, borrowed typewriters, paints, crayons, and paste, are fine but not essential. All too often they are more show than substance.

Intellectual constraints that take discovery out of the writing classroom and replace it with formulas for sentence patterns, rules for punctuation, and demands for correct spelling are more difficult for children to overcome. Concerns for mechanics have their place, but teachers who are sensitive to their children's writing development make sure that a preoccupation with correctness does not take the place of the intellectual "romper room" that effective composition demands.

Choosing Topics for Writing

Just as the atmosphere in a classroom affects children during every stage of the composing process, so do the topics we encourage children to choose. A person's choice of topic can either set the writing stage or destroy it. Generally, when we write about things that matter to us and that we know about, we welcome the rehearsing and drafting stages for the chance to better express how we feel and say what we know. At such times we are glad to revise because we have the opportunity to try and get closer to our thoughts, closer to what we really mean. On the other hand, if we are forced to write about issues that inspire no images or ones that strike no emotion, revision is pointless: We have nothing in mind that we're trying to capture.

Appropriate Responses to Children's Writing

An important part of the composing process is receiving some response to one's writing. Writing is, after all, an attempt to trigger some kind of mental experience in a reader. Writers, like target shooters, improve their aim as they see where their efforts go, which depends in large part on the nature of the response. In this chapter we will be concerned with who makes the response, when it is most useful, and in what forms it should be made. Responses to what has been written and the discussions that ensue provide the classroom dynamics for children's writing development. Unfortunately, in many classrooms response is limited to bright stickers and stamped smiling faces. If we see our task as encouraging writing development, this type of response must yield to a more sensitive and knowledgeable commentary from the teacher.

What follows is a discussion of two writing programs that have proven successful for us, for the teachers with whom we work, or for teachers whose programs we have read about in national journals. The first program centers upon the kindergarten year; the latter program is intended for first, second, and third graders. Both programs are sensitive to the composing process Murray describes and to the important areas of the writing teacher's responsibility: atmosphere, assignment, and response.

The Kindergarten Year

In Chapter 8 we defined composition as the act of putting together the details of a message in a form that is understandable to an audience. We went on to point out that children can compose before they can write. In fact, they do it all the time in kindergarten. Watch any five-year-old compose as she pretends to be pouring coffee for a friend in her classroom's playhouse corner. And isn't it composition at its best when a kindergarten child rescues her buddy from a "fire" that's blazing and consuming the class jungle gym? Composition doesn't always come in letters upon pages. Composition is thinking and creating. Composition is moving ideas from hidden spaces within our minds to detectable spaces in our outside world.

Marilyn Snyder, a kindergarten teacher from Walled Lake, Michigan, knows that writing has its beginnings in oral composition. From opening day her children begin writing through their talk. Marilyn schedules "writing" early in the day. She always calls this activity writing, as opposed to sharing, drawing, or coloring, because she wants her children to understand that composition entails pulling together one's thoughts for others to interpret and enjoy. The children come close to her and sit in a group. They talk of things they want to write about or topics that she has asked them to consider: melting snow, hatching chicks, growing seeds. (Note the topics defy the common assumption in literacy development that narrative, or story, is somehow primary.[10])

After the children talk, they go back to their tables to "write." They draw and chatter while she moves about the room helping individual children. She finds herself commenting on drawings, asking questions, giving suggestions, taking dictation, and occasionally helping children sound out words.

Time is set aside later in the day for sharing. The children are pulled together in a group and called one by one to the author's chair.[11] Once seated, each youngster holds up his drawing and begins to speak. The rest of the class listens and is encouraged to ask questions. Marilyn asks questions, too.

In this way Ms. Snyder is addressing three needs of a beginning writing group:

- the need to establish an approximation of a literate community, in a room where almost none of the children can read or write in the conventional sense;
- the need to draw out children's language and lead them to compose orally; and
- the need to find a connection between written representation and spoken language.

Setting Up a Literate Community

Later in this chapter we consider in detail procedures for setting up classroom environments that encourage interaction among students by means of and concerning the medium of writing. Note for now how Marilyn sets up routines for discussion, writing, and sharing that provide durable frameworks to support children's growth. Those children who can only draw, may draw. Those who are ready to experiment with letters can do so. In fact, this activity format can be used to organize writing time throughout the elementary school years. Imagine the good fortune of the teacher who gets Ms. Snyder's children next year. These children will already know how to plan and write and share.

Drawing Out Oral Language

When children ask questions of the child who is sharing his or her paper in Ms. Snyder's classroom, they are participating in a most important part of the composing process. By answering questions, children are nudged into sustaining their topics, telling more, and yet more. With encouragement and regular opportunities for asking and answering questions, children will eventually be able to ask their own as they write.

James Britton says that sustained narrative speech is likely to be a lead-in to writing.[12] James Moffett suggests why:

> The first step towards writing is made when a speaker takes over a conversation and sustains some subject alone. He has started to create a solo discourse that while intended to communicate to others is less collabora-

tive, less prompted, and less corrected by feedback than dialogue. He bears more of the responsibility for effective communication. . . . The cues for his next line are not what his interlocutor said, but what he himself just said.[13]

Connecting Writing and Speech

As we suggested in the early chapters of this book, young children need to develop an understanding of how writing represents ideas. Dyson found that children in kindergarten used letters and pictures interchangeably. One child, for example, drew a picture of a boy and wrote the letters J–I–M, then said, "These both say 'Jim.'" At this early stage, however, both pictures and letters seem to serve as tokens, as reminders of a longer discourse.[14] In Chapter 9 we described how Tyler wrote the letters OSOPNOTM, then told a story about a unicorn. Asked to read her writing a second time, Tyler produced essentially the same story, but with different words.

During the kindergarten year, we expect children to move from a point where they talk about print in the same loose way that they might talk about a picture to the realization that print represents language in an exact way. Then we expect children to acquire the alphabetic principle, the realization that print represents language by its sounds and sounds at the level of phonemes. They will also have to learn the identity of the letters of the alphabet and several concepts about print, including the conventions by which print is arranged on the page. They will have to acquire the *concept of word*, the ability to divide language mentally into units of words, and to find a match between the bound configurations on the page and the words they hear the teacher pronounce when she reads aloud.

Teachers must take care to see that children develop these concepts that orient them to print, though children's own active discovery processes, along with guidance from the teacher, are usually sufficient. However, it must be stressed that if children think about print in a way that is highly variant from the way it actually works, their early writing experiences will be more confusing than productive.

Judith Hilliker, a kindergarten teacher from Durham, New Hampshire, has developed means of working children through this transition from picture to picture-plus-print. She begins with lots of shared book experiences: reading aloud to children from enlarged versions of books, pointing to the words, and calling attention to the ways the letters signal the sounds of the words she reads. At the same time, she encourages children to make their own print predictions with paper and pencil. As soon as her children begin to recognize that letters represent sounds, she invites them to use that knowledge at the writing table.

Hilliker points out that at first the text might be just one letter, but "when a child who know that 'P says puh' prints a capital P next to a four-legged oval with a squiggle, he's communicating more fully that his picture shows a pig." Hilliker goes on to say that pretty soon he'll be asking her how to make a "guh." Then he'll want some medial consonants, and later long vowels. Writing helps the prereader understand how reading works because by this point the text has enough clues for him to read it. The young writer who prints BOT can probably read it as boat, even without the picture. "And when he does," says Hilliker, "his concept of reading suddenly tumbles out of the realm of mystery."[15]

Many kindergarten teachers prefer asking children to choose their own topics rather than choosing topics for them. In these classrooms the children draw and write as best they can while the teacher circulates around the room. Teachers help, the way Judith Hilliker does, by supplying letters and giving encouragement. When a child completes a piece, Hilliker dates it, transcribes the invented spelling (inconspicuously), then places it in her ready-to-read box for storytime. After a child's piece has been read to the class, she stores it in a writing folder. She watches the child's progress and assesses his development in three areas: "letter formation, phonics skills, and understanding of the mechanics of print."[16]

While shared book experiences are a part of both kindergarten classrooms we've described, until now the focus of our discussion has been on emergent writing and reading at the word and letter level. It would be a mistake to leave the kindergarten experience here, however, because sharing literature also provides grist for intuiting global elements of different types of text. Stories, for example, are typically organized into schemes that encompass an obligatory initiating event, sequent event, and final event.[17] Information books have obligatory global elements, too; topic presentation, description of attributes, characteristic events, and a final summary. Christine Pappas has provided kindergarten teachers with powerful data that demonstrate the necessity of our sharing stories as well as good information books. In her case study of a kindergartner, Jean, Pappas shows us that children internalize the distinctive features of stories as well as nonfiction literature; thus she has reinforced the importance of an eclectic literary diet.

> We should share and have children read good stories in the classroom, and we should encourage them and provide opportunities for them to write stories on their own. But when we promote only story, children will not learn about the functional potential of language regarding written language. The initial competence we have seen in Jean's reenactments of the information book will fade (as research on older elementary children had indicated) if a diet of only stories is provided. If good information books are not available for children to read, their writing of nonfiction will not develop; and the Great Divide, or expository gap, will persist.[18]

We agree, and fortunately there are some fine books that list high-interest nonfiction books for young readers.[19]

The Primary Years

In the remainder of this chapter we will discuss a general system for implementing a writing program for first through third grades—a system, like the kindergarten program, that is sensitive to the writing process Donald Murray describes and to classroom characteristics that support writing growth. The discussion will be divided into eight sections:

1. an overview of a process-writing classroom;
2. an outline of what to do the first day;
3. a typical day;
4. suggestions for setting up a writing classroom in general and writing folders in particular;
5. the dynamics of moving a promising draft along;
6. conferencing techniques;
7. publishing possibilities; and
8. suggestions for evaluation.

We have found this system to work well for us over the years, but we assume that our techniques will be modified by anyone who chooses to use them. We have not found it easy, by any means, to set up and sustain process-writing classrooms,[20] but the rewards continue to make the effort worthwhile. We reflect with pleasure on the honest industry we have seen each day in children who are writers, the sound of pencils scratching furiously across page after page of text, the earnest voices of children talking to one another about their evolving drafts, the pride we see in children's faces as they share their finished products, and the heightened, almost collegial curiosity our young authors show toward the adult authors who write the stories they read and love.

An Overview of a Process-Writing Classroom

In process-writing classrooms we attempt to create an atmosphere where even a professional writer would feel at home. Here children choose their own topics and write for people that matter: themselves, their classmates, their friends in the school community (pieces are shared between classrooms), their teachers, their parents and siblings, as well as the literary community at large (work is submitted for publication).

You will see boxes that hold writing folders; trays for works in progress; jars of pencils, crayons, and colored markers; shelves of published books; an author's chair; and bulletin boards, which sometimes celebrate a published author but just as often celebrate a member of the class. At least one table is available for group conferences, and small places are created (spaces under tables, for example, or room corners) where pairs of children can collaborate in peace.

Though a part of each writing period is quiet, perhaps fifteen minutes, a good portion—twenty minutes, or so—is not. Like professional writers, chil-

Figure 11–1
Peter
Grade 1

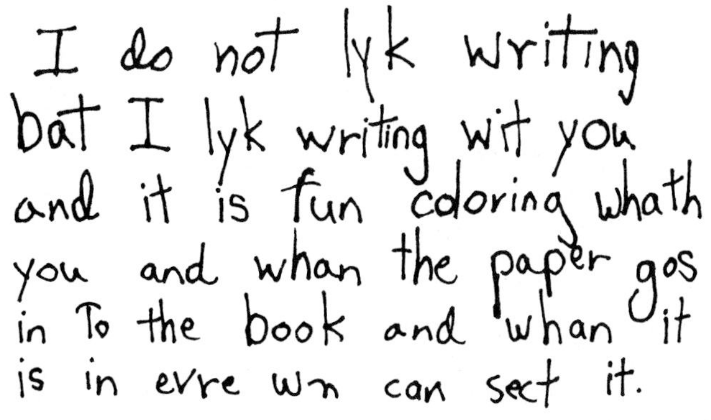

I do not lyk writing bat I lyk writing wit you and it is fun coloring whath you and whan the paper gos in To the book and whan it is in evre wn can sect it.

(I do not like writing, but I like writing with you. It is fun coloring with you and when the paper goes into the book. And when it is in, everyone can see it.)

dren are encouraged to talk to others about their drafts. They talk to their teachers and their classmates. They ask for an ear, first to attend to meaning and later to grammar and style. They ask for an eye, first to attend to spelling and later to mechanics.

Writing is a cooperative effort between teachers and children in these classrooms. It is joyful, noncompetitive, and nourishing, while at the same time highly demanding. Children write at length, they revise, and they edit, but in an atmosphere of acceptance and *respect*. This milieu is set up and maintained with several purposes in mind, but perhaps the major purpose is to prevent loathing of the whole process later on, as Peter nearly did (see Figure 11–1).

What to Do on the First Day
According to Donald Graves, the tone is set in process-writing classrooms by what the teacher *does*, not by what the teacher *says*.[21] We agree. A good way to begin is to show children how *you* go about making your own topic choices (an overhead projector is helpful here). We try to choose topics that are simple and close to home, like watching a caterpillar spin a cocoon or building with Lego® blocks. Generate at least three or four topics, choose one, and then tell the children the reasons for your choice. We tend to pick topics that conjure up lots of memories or ones that would make us feel good in the writing.

Then take time to let the children generate their own topics, encouraging them to talk about their list with a friend. Ask each child to circle just one topic. (You might want to first review the teaching suggestions from Chapter 6 for ideas for encouraging children to write when they haven't been taught the spellings of words.) Be aware that first graders often draw pictures of possible topics rather than listing their topics using invented spelling.

Figure 11–2
Sample cluster
sheet

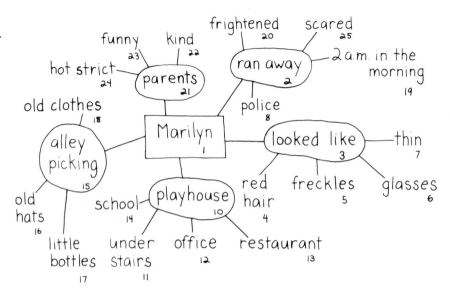

Next, still using the overhead, we write (or draw) our favorite topic in the middle of a transparency, circle it, and then begin letting words that come into our mind flow onto the sheet. When we do this, we are showing children how to prepare a *cluster sheet,* one prewriting strategy we use frequently. We write slowly but deliberately. With first graders we might only draw little figures around our topic. Figure 11–2 is a cluster sheet about a best childhood girlfriend, Marilyn. (The numbers represent the order in which the words were written.)

You will notice when looking at the numbers in the diagram that all the words related to a subtopic (i.e., "alley picking," "playhouse," "looked like," etc.) were not written before another subtopic came to mind. This is how prewriting works: One idea leads to another, then back again.

Believe it or not, even first graders can do this. However, in Matt's example (Figure 11–3) you will notice that the smaller circles are not connected in a logical way. First graders often just draw a picture for their prewriting experience.

Once you have finished this activity, let the children chat with a partner for a few minutes with their cluster sheets in hand. Then pass out some draft paper (we use either tossed-out computer paper or primer paper, the kind with a lot of wide lines) and begin writing. We encourage those who want to add to their drawing or cluster sheet to do so. Again, we write/draw on the overhead using a new transparency while the children write/draw at their desks. Everyone is quiet now and we insist on not being disturbed.

Figure 11–3
First grader

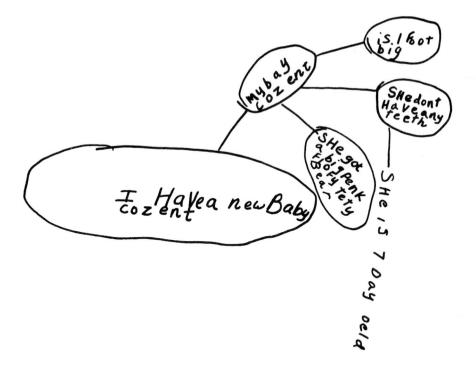

About five minutes into our own writing we leave the overhead and begin walking around the room to help any children in trouble. Usually a simple question centering on some aspect of his cluster sheet or picture is enough to get a youngster moving along.

After about fifteen or twenty minutes, ask the children to bring their drafts to a corner of the room where you have set up two chairs, a child's chair and a large one. Have a few children in mind, and one by one ask them to share what they have written or drawn. Be sure to guide your first reader to the larger chair, while you take the smaller one. This puts the child, literally, on top of her world, even if only for a few minutes. After you have told the author how you felt hearing the draft and mentioned something specific you liked, encourage the other children to tell the author how *they* felt when they heard the piece and what they liked or remembered. Then allow a few children to ask the author questions.

Continue this routine for at least a week until each child has written on several topics. Once a number of drafts have been completed (any number more than one, but perhaps just one for your reluctant writers), a single draft can be chosen for publication. Let us put off publication for just a bit, though, and describe a typical writing day later in the year, a day that will come sooner than you think.

Beyond Day One: A Typical Day

Our writing periods are usually forty-five minutes long (see Figure 11–4): fifteen minutes for writing, twenty minutes for having conferences, and ten minutes for sharing. The order of activities frequently changes.

As with the very first day, it is usually best to begin each writing period with everyone writing, including the teacher. We, as well as our children, need a chance to get in touch with our own writing processes. (Please refer to the Epilogue of this book.)What's more, children need to see us write.

After about five minutes of writing, we suggest that you walk around the room, talking briefly with a few of your students, the ones you believe may need you the most. *Hunt for youngsters having problems.* Watch for either very little writing or for drafts that look extremely scribbled up or full of holes. Consider such marks or a lack of writing as clues to children in trouble, and choose these children for your early rounds. Sometimes writers in trouble just need a few minutes of your undivided attention. Giving this needed attention early in the day helps: You will have let these youngsters know that you care and you may, incidentally, prevent unwanted interruptions later on.

After you have circulated among your students, call four to six children to the conference table. Since it helps children to know when you are going to conference with them—they have a chance to think about what they're going

Figure 11–4
Writing period

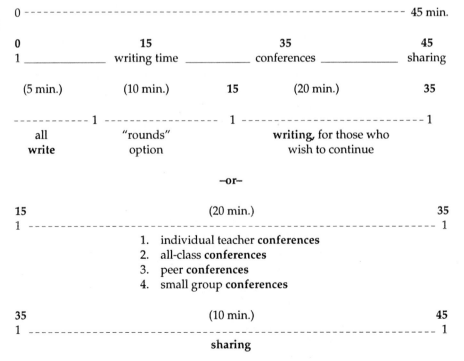

to say—consider assigning them to certain days (i.e., specific children may be assigned to Mondays, others to Tuesdays, and so on). Alternatively, you may choose to have a conference box in your room. When a child has a draft that she needs to share with you, as opposed to sharing it with a peer, the youngster may put her draft in the general conference box. We signify "general" because later, when children are publishing, we have several conference boxes, each marked for a specific purpose.

While some children are holding conferences with you, the other children should continue writing. (It might seem impossible to keep twenty or thirty children busy while you're holding conferences, but it's not. By the end of this chapter you will understand just how busy your children will be!) As the year progresses, students not in conference with you may do other things as well:

- continue writing/illustrating
- hold peer conferences
- illustrate a piece for someone else
- read to another child from the author's chair
- be part of a group conference
- publish

Conference time usually lasts about twenty minutes, although at first you may be frustrated and want more time. The thing you can do that will make the biggest difference is to *read your children's drafts the night before.* Beginning a conference unprepared will naturally result in a less efficient meeting.

Quite often it's helpful to hold all-class conferences rather than individual conferences. During these conferences, work with the entire class (or a group of children) on one skill, such as the use of commas in a series. Take a child's rough draft that needs some work (with the child's permission, of course) and transfer it to an overhead. We frequently make a ditto as well so each child can follow along easily. Then work together to locate some of the rough spots and correct them together.

Although adding commas is an editing skill easily covered in all-class conferences, such conferences can be used to demonstrate revision as well. We especially like dealing with problems of audience sensitivity this way. For example, children often use pronouns without specifying who their "he" or "she" is supposed to be; or they refer to a previously unmentioned character, assuming you, the reader, know exactly who the character is. These types of audience sensitivity problems are easy for children to detect, *when they're not reading their own writing,* which is why we like working on this troublesome issue in a group. Other easy problems to work on together are

- prying apart drafts that have more than one topic;
- hunting for dead wood (unnecessary words);

- expanding *telling* lines (e.g., "it was funny") into *showing* lines or paragraphs (i.e., lines that describe the events that were funny); and
- choosing the best words, using varied sentence patterns.

Don't worry too much if your first attempt at an all-class conference falls short of perfection; you will find experience to be your best teacher.

The last few minutes of every writing day should be spent sharing. Since you want this to be a time when children hear well-written work, choose volunteers carefully; it's probably best to choose pieces you've read recently.

Setting Up the Classroom

The Classroom.   We have never needed very much: a lot of paper; colored markers and pencils; a folder/binder for each child, complete with pockets and clips for holding papers and works in progress; a manila folder for everyone, to house already published or unwanted drafts; some colorful baskets, which we number to accommodate the steps that drafts go through on their way toward publication; an author's chair that the children use whenever they read their work, which we decorate; some bulletin board space to celebrate our authors or to depict the writing process; at least one round table for group conferences, whether teacher-led or child-led; a bookshelf to house our ever-growing classroom library; and a typewriter or computer to print out final drafts.

Most classrooms have these materials, or things similar, available to them as part of the school budget. An author's chair can be found at a garage sale, and bookshelves can be makeshift if need be. The point is, you shouldn't need too much. Two luxuries we allow ourselves, however, are pads of stick-on note paper and a rubber stamp that says DRAFT. The sticky pads allow us to record all sorts of information for authors, or let authors take their own notes, while freeing the author to place the sheet wherever he needs it on his draft. The DRAFT stamp encourages young authors to write freely, without worrying about mechanical, grammatical, or spelling errors. Drafts are just that, and the DRAFT stamp proves it!

The Writing Folder.   Works in progress have to be housed in a folder/binder, and we use ones with pockets and center clips. When open, they look like Figure 11–5. The left-hand pocket holds topics and cluster sheets, and the right-hand side holds drafts in progress. The center holds the writing manual we've compiled (discussed at length later in this chapter).

Topic Sheet.   We've tried all types, but we prefer ones similar to those shown in Figure 11-6. Children fill in their names on day one and then, as topics occur to them, they write them down on their topic sheets. When they choose

Figure 11–5
Writing folder

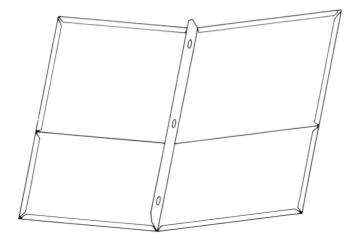

one of the topics to write on, they fill in the square under the number (see Figure 11–7).

First-grade teachers might prefer fewer spaces for topics, like the one in Figure 11–8. You will notice that this topic sheet has several triangles beneath

	TOPICS		TOPICS	
Figure 11–6 *Topic sheet* *(left)*	**Your Name**_____		**Your Name**_____	
	1. ▢	7. ▢	1. ▢ *bike rideing*	7. *Kivin*
Figure 11–7 *Second grader's* *topic sheet* *(right)*	2. ▢	8. ▢	2. ▢ *seleing*	8. ▢ *socer*
	3. ▢	9. ▢	3. ▢ *goldfish*	9. ▢ *fishing*
	4. ▢	10. ▢	4. ▢ *skoll*	10. ▢ ▰
	5. ▢	11. ▢	5. ▢ *pano*	11. ▢ *t. chess*
	6. ▢	12. ▢	6. ▢	12. ▢

Figure 11–8
First-grade
topic sheet

Topics   Name_____

_____

1.
ΔΔΔΔ

- -

2.
ΔΔΔΔ

- -

3.
ΔΔΔΔ

- -

4.
ΔΔΔΔ

each number, whereas the previous topic sheet has only one square. This is because many children like to write on the same topic several times.

Another option for first-grade teachers is simply to fold a piece of manila paper in half and have the children draw just two possibilities.

Cluster Sheets.   One way to engage children in prewriting is through the use of cluster sheets. Some children don't want to use them, preferring to draw, though many children find them helpful. Like a picture, a cluster sheet serves as a memory bank for young authors. You'll find that first graders often add to them even after a draft has been started. Figure 11–9 is one type of cluster sheet.

Figure 11–9
Cluster sheet

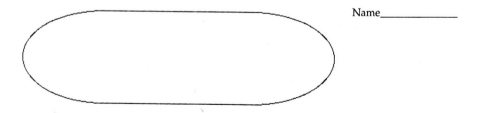

Name_____

Figure 11–10
Sample manual
sheet

Things I Can Do During Writing Time

☞1. I can add to my topic list. ✚✚

☞2. I can brainstorm a new topic. ♥♥

☞3. I can begin a new draft. ✎

☞4. I can improve or add on to a
    draft I have started. ✎✎✎

☞5. I can draw some pictures for one
    of my drafts. 🖌🖌🖌

☞6. I can underline misspelled words.
    (This is proofreading.)

☞7. I can look for words that should
    be capitalized.
    (This is also proofreading.)

☞8. I can read my drafts to myself
    and decide which one I want to
    publish.

The Manual. A writer's manual for first, second, and third graders isn't going to be very detailed. Nevertheless, there are guidelines and resource materials that we find helpful to have on hand. We don't pass the manual sheets out all at once (and a few teachers we work with don't use them at all). What follows are some suggestions of what to include in a writer's manual.

    Figure 11–10, entitled "Things I Can Do During Writing Time," allows children to review their options before they begin writing. As the year progresses, children color in the little hands by the options that have been discussed and are in use at the time. Teachers vary on how they use this sheet—some allowing children to use all the possibilities at once, others going more slowly—but it has been our experience that most teachers use the sheet in one form or another.

Figure 11–11
Sample manual
sheet

Things I Can Do During Conference Time

☞1. I can do anything from my <u>Writing</u>
     <u>Time</u> list.

☞2. I can hold a conference with a
     friend.☺ or ☺☺

☞3. I can write at a friend's desk or
     at a place we find comfortable.
     ✏☺✏☺✏

☞4. I can draw some pictures for one
     of my friend's drafts.🖌🖌🖌

☞5. I can hold a conference with my
     teacher. 👤 or 👤

The sheet in Figure 11–11, entitled "Things I Can Do During Conference Time," is also a popular one because, like its predecessor, it lets the children know what they are allowed to do. Unlike the silent nature of the writing-time activities, most of the conference-time activities involve interaction. You will note that writing is still an option during conference time, when conferences are permitted and talking is encouraged. Children especially love option number three: writing with a friend. They either pull their desks together or crawl under a nearby table with their drafts.

In addition to the writing-time and conference-time sheets, we include a sheet in the manual outlining simple conference guidelines (see Figure 11–12). Although children can meander from our formula when they need to, the guidelines provide a starting point for peer interaction.

As with everything else, we model peer conferences several times before we expect children to confer with each other. Some of us have our children use a listener's guide (see Figure 11–13) during peer conferences to keep them on task.

To bring closure to the writing period we use a writing log, which is also part of the manual. (Figure 11–14 is one example of such a log.) Children write in these eagerly, so teachers should go through the folders periodically and read them. Fundamentally, however, the logs are meant for the children, to chronicle their own writing behavior. A typical example reads, "I had a hard time getting started today, but I wrote a lot finally. Jason helped me."

Figure 11–12   **Conference Guidelines for 2nd, 3rd, and 4th Graders**

1. Listen to your partner's draft.

2. Tell your partner what you like about the draft or what you thought was interesting.

3. Listen to your partner's draft again.

4. If you have a question about your partner's topic, this is a good time to ask it. (If you have time, write your question down and give it to your partner. This will help your partner remember what you asked.)

Figure 11–13   **Listener's Guide to a Peer or Group Conference**

YOUR NAME _____ Date _____

CONFERENCE WITH _____

THEIR STORY TITLE/TOPIC_____

What I liked or thought was interesting:

_____

_____

_____

_____

_____

What I would like to know more about:

_____

_____

_____

_____

_____

Suggestions for improvement:

_____

_____

_____

_____

_____

Figure 11–14   **Writing Log**   Name_____

Date   What I did today   How today went

                                                    Great   OK   Slow Moving

_____

_____   _____

_____

_____   _____

_____

_____   _____

_____

_____   _____

_____

_____   _____

_____

_____   _____

_____

_____   _____

_____

_____   _____

_____

_____   _____

_____

_____   _____

The Dynamics of Moving a Promising Draft Along
Publishing children's work is an important part of process-writing class-rooms, but because children write so much, we find we cannot publish every-thing. This state of affairs is probably healthy. After all, professional writers don't publish every draft they produce: *everything* isn't good enough. For professionals, what does get into print is always a matter of choice, and so it should be for children.

Right from the beginning of the year the children are told that some of their work will be published and some will not. Every time they have completed a certain number of drafts on separate topics, perhaps two or three, maybe even four, they are to choose one and send it on a publishing journey. We explain that professional writers must do this too, often sending their work back and forth through the mail five or six times. Children have no problem understanding this, and they eagerly await our explanation and instructions to guide their foray into publishing. This is what we tell them.

When you have selected your best draft, we would like you to make a sandwich with it. This might sound kind of funny, but listen carefully. Your draft will be like the peanut butter or the tuna fish you would use if you were making a sandwich: it will be your filling. Your top piece of bread will be a journey sheet (see Figure 11–15) and your bottom piece of bread will be a proofreading checklist (see Figure 11–16). Use the stapler and staple your sandwich together, at the top. Then, follow the instructions on your journey sheet and send your draft on its way. (Some experts with whom we have corresponded find the term "sandwich" condescending. It has never hit us this way, but you may prefer a different term, perhaps publishing packet.)

Though we will talk about the journey sheet shown in Figure 11–15 as if it were the only one, in truth they are as varied as teachers themselves. This one was designed by Betty Morris, a second-grade teacher in Birmingham, Michigan, with Ruth Nathan, one of this book's coauthors.

Glancing through Betty and Ruth's journey sheet, you'll notice the first thing a child must do after choosing a draft is to write the date on the journey sheet (Step 1). The youngster must then read his draft to a friend (Step 2); since writing time is a quiet time, conference time is the natural sharing slot. (During writing time this child would have to work on another draft.)

After conferring with a friend, our youngster will work on revising his piece if he needs to (Step 3). We find that children ask their peers questions all the time, and many youngsters opt to add on after their conference sessions. Here are several questions a classmate asked Amy about her draft on witches (Figure 11–17).

1. How do you know all of this?
2. What do they do when the bats perch on their noses?
3. Can you describe the stubs?
4. How come they have the power of 500 strong men?

Amy kept track of these questions, which were written on sticky notepads, and worked some, but not all, of the answers into her draft.

Step 4, editing the draft, is a helpful step for two reasons: Teachers like knowing their children respect them enough to give them readable work, and children benefit from attempting to edit alone. We ask our students to use red pencils when they edit so we can celebrate their discoveries with them.

Figure 11–15   **Publishing Journey**

NAME _____ Grade _____

Date

_____   1. Choose a draft you would like to publish.

_____   2. Read your draft to a friend. Use your conference guidelines.

_____   3. Work on your draft if you need to. Add some information, or move words around.

             4. Try editing your draft by yourself.
   (a)   Underline any words you think are misspelled.
   (b)   Look for capitals, periods, or other punctuation you may need. (Use your editing pencil.)

_____   5. Put your draft in **CONFERENCE BOX 1.**
   This is when we read and share together. I will point to interesting things I remember, and I may ask you some questions in order to learn what you have to teach me. Then you will work on your draft if you need to.

_____   6. Hold another peer conference. Use your conference guidelines.

_____   7. Put your draft in **CONFERENCE BOX 2.**
   During this conference we will look at your editing and discuss at least one new skill you may need to learn to complete your piece. Then you will work on your piece.

             8. Recopy your draft if you need to.
   (You only need to recopy your draft if it is too hard to read.)

_____   9. Put your draft in our **PRE-PUBLISHING BOX.**
   During this conference, one of our aids or I will ask you how you want to finish your book. (For example: How many pages do you want? Where will each page start and stop? Where do you think you may want your pictures? What would you like on your cover? Do you want an "About the Author" page?)

_____   10. Put your draft in our **TO BE PUBLISHED BOX.**
   After I have looked at your draft one last time, you will recopy it on publishing paper, or we will send it to a typist.

_____   11. Day book was completed and read to the class.

Figure 11–16   **Proofreading Checklist**

❑   1. Did I spell all words correctly?

(Underline/circle words you are unsure of. Try looking some of them up.)

❑   2. Did I write each sentence as a complete thought?

(Here is an incomplete thought, "On the street." Here is a complete thought: "The little puppy stood all alone on the street.") Note: Sometimes writers use an incomplete sentence on purpose to create a certain effect. Here is an example: "Not me!"

❑   3. Do I have any run-on sentences?

(Here is a run-on sentence: "The little puppy stood all alone on the street and he couldn't find his mother and he was so, so frightened that he thought he would die and so he looked around to find a friend and he didn't find one so he walked on and on.") Note: Sometimes authors deliberately write run-on sentences. See Shel Silverstein's <u>Lafcadio</u> for examples.

❑   4. Did I end each sentence with the correct punctuation?

(Here is a sentence that has the wrong punctuation at the end: "Could the puppy find his mother." This sentence needs a question mark, not a period.)

❑   5. Did I begin each sentence with a capital letter?

❑   6. Did I use capital letters correctly in other places?

(Names, days of the week, months, titles, etc.)

❑   7. Did I use commas, apostrophes, and other punctuation correctly?

(Commas are used between words in lists, before a conjunction introducing an independent clause, after salutations, etc. Apostrophes are used with possessive forms [Jimmy's shoes, the boys' lockers] and in contractions [can't, it's].)

❑   8. Did I indent each paragraph?

(New ideas require new paragraphs; dialogue also.)

Once Step 4 has been completed, children put their "sandwiches" in Conference Box 1 (Step 5). Papers in this box are now ready for us to read. We read four or five of them after school in preparation for the formal teacher-child conferences we will hold the next day, or on the next writing day. (We refer to these as formal conferences because during our daily rounds we often talk with children informally about their drafts.)

The first conference we hold with a child centers on meaning. We frequently tell children how their draft makes us feel and point to interesting parts of the draft. If a piece isn't too long, we may ask the youngster to read

All witchres are Very ugly. They have long grcn Bumpy noises, and some Bats might purtch on it. Witch noiseslook like there made of paper mashy. They have Wiges with sowigly measy hair on them. They are all BalD and wair maecks, Becaus they have stubs. They have Black Cat's with Gleewing green eyes. They alse have monsters that they keep in cages chaned to walls. They feed them Banana Peals and They also eat long sticks of Butter. Witches Sleep on sement flowers. They alwes wear capes, hats and Dark Black Clower There head's a shaped like Onons, and smell like skunks, And There head's are as fragle as mash gataitos. Same witches are good But Mast are Bad. Witches have the pawe of soo strong men from the Circes. They are very strong and have the magic of 79 Migishons. They can tur into the tallest Giant To the smalest fly. Witxhes eat flys and slime. And there favret Dish is spider wibe pie, with honey on top. The good witches are very, Very, good, and very, very, nice. But witches eat childrer with a Bit of salt and a Bit of Pepaer. They have a specl masheen. It's a Bike with the Back wheel in a pot with Baling hat water. And knives stalded in to yeu, way Down, deep. you peadel and the Back whel and it migkes you the salt, pepar a your Blod. And that Tastes Better Than spider wibe pie with honey on top.

the whole draft out loud. Just hearing a child read her piece gives us information about what we should do next. (Rather than going into conferencing techniques now, we will defer this discussion to our conferencing section and move on to Step 6 of the journey sheet.) At the end of the first conference, we ask the children to look over their proofreading checklist (Figure 11–16) and mark the editing skills they think they can use by themselves. This way, before putting their drafts in Conference Box 2, they have had an opportunity to try their hand at editing once again. Several first and second graders check off numbers four and six: many have already completed number one. Again, the children are asked to use red pencils so that we can see which improvements they were able to make without our help.

Step 6 calls for another peer conference. The more interaction young authors have with an audience, the better. This is because children are egocentric: They aren't quite aware of what their audience knows and doesn't know, nor of what their audience needs to understand in order to comprehend the message. (Early drafts produced by adults writers are egocentric to some extent, as well.) Consequently, the journey sheet provides many opportunities for interaction.

Our second formal conference with a child is an editing conference. During this second editing conference (Step 7), we look at how well they have corrected what they said they could manage. If they haven't done a very good job, we help them with one of the skills they identified as being "known"; if they have found all of their errors, we celebrate this and then move on, teaching them one, and only one, new skill.

Once a child has edited as much as he can, we frequently do the rest alone, although sometimes we do this with the youngster nearby. We use a different colored pencil when editing to remind us of the skills we need to teach. Then, if the draft is readable, the piece moves on to the Pre-publishing Box (Step 9); if not, it has to be recopied (Step 8). We try to avoid Step 8 at all costs, especially with less mature children. During the pre-publishing conference we do little things like decide on page breaks. If we are fortunate enough to have an aide or a volunteer parent on hand, he or she holds this conference with the child. Sometimes our children simply do this with one another. Another helpful hint is to request that authors find a partner who will read the draft back to the author. If the child's partner can't read it, chances are the typist won't be able to either.

When the draft is ready for publication it moves on to Step 10, where it is placed in our publishing folder, or box. It either gets sent to a typist—often a parent—or the draft is recopied by hand onto special publishing paper by the child or teacher (this rarely happens in our classrooms).

The letter you see in Figure 11–18 is one a writing consultant sent to teachers who were initiating a process approach in their classrooms. Several schools we work in have a central clearinghouse for drafts that are to be published. Teams of parents collect these drafts periodically and type them, using school computers. Papers are sent to the office with a slip similar to the one in Figure 11–19, and drafts come back typed and ready to be illustrated.

Figure 11–18
Letter to
teachers about
publishing

Dear Teachers,

   We are extremely fortunate to have five parents available to type for us. Here's how the system will work.

   1. Attach a "Publishing Request" form to each draft you'd like typed. (The forms are located over your mailbox in the office.)

   2. Fill out the form exactly as you wish it typed. Circle the type size you want.

   3. Put the draft (with publishing request attached) into the metal box over your mailbox.

   4. Your typed draft will be delivered to you.

   Remember: 1. All drafts must be edited-completely

              2. page breaks must be clearly visible
                 (Sample: [_____]
                          [_____]p1t
                          [_____]p2b)

              3. State, by each page number, where you want the words typed.
                 t = top   m= middle   b= bottom
                 c = centered over entire page

Figure 11–19
Publishing
request

Publishing Request

Child's name _____

Date _____

Teacher _____

Type Size ___20___   ___40___   ___80___

Typist's Signature _____

When a child's book is completed, which means it has been printed and illustrated, the date is written on the last line of the journey sheet, Step 11. This is a big day for a youngster because she knows that soon she will be sitting in the author's chair sharing her work with the class. And the class will clap when she's done and tell her about their favorite parts. Some will say, "I love your illustrations," some will comment on the parts of the story (poem, essay, etc.) they enjoyed the most. Others will wonder, "How did you think of all that?" while still others will wish they had written the book themselves, and they will say so.

Recently we've added extra pages to every book we publish, which we title "Comments from my Readers." During the year, classmates write notes to the authors on these pages. An "About the Author" page is a new addition, as well, where authors tell their likes, dislikes, hobbies, other publications, or interesting aspects of the book at hand (e.g., "This is my first nonfiction book").

As we said earlier, the particular journey sheet we have led you through is just one example. Once teachers are aware of the journey concept, they can create their own. A first-grade teacher designed the one in Figure 11–20; a second-grade teacher, Kevin Keller of Walled Lake, Michigan, used some original graphics for his (see Figure 11–21).

Conferencing Techniques

Conferences can be arranged between the teacher and children, between two children, or among small groups of children. We'll take a look at each type in turn.

Teacher-Child Conferences.   Teacher-child conferences can be of two types: *individual*—one teacher, one child—or *group*—one teacher, a few children. Individual conferences can be *informal*, conducted during your writing-time rounds, as we've mentioned earlier; or they can be *formal*, meaning prearranged. Drafts going through publication journeys are formal encounters, one-to-one interactions with authors during conference time.

During informal encounters we find ourselves helping children troubleshoot, usually by listening to problems, asking relevant questions, or making open-ended suggestions. For example, Randy, a second grader, might tell us he doesn't know how to end his piece. We might respond by suggesting he write two endings and then pick the one that sounds the best. In this case we'd encourage a peer conference as well. If Sandy, a first grader, tells us she doesn't know how to get started, we might ask to see her drawing or cluster sheet and then start asking questions. Informal conferences are short, the purpose being to help a child move on quickly.

Formal teacher-child conferences are different: They've been arranged and frequently center on a draft pulled from one of the conference boxes. During the first, planned conference over a draft pulled from Conference Box 1,

Figure 11–20
First-grade
journey sheet

First Grade Journey Sheet

Your Name _____

Date _____

1. Read your draft to yourself. ☐

2. Read your draft to a friend. ☐

   ✎ Whom did you read it to? _____

   ✎ [Let your friend tell you what was great.
       Let your friend ask you questions.]

3. Put on your editing hat. Edit your draft for

   ☐ spelling [Underline words that need help.]

   ☐ capitals   [ꞙ means make it a capital
                  ꞙ means make it lower case]

4. Put your draft in our
   Publishing Box. ☐

Figure 11–21
Alternative
second-grade
journey sheet

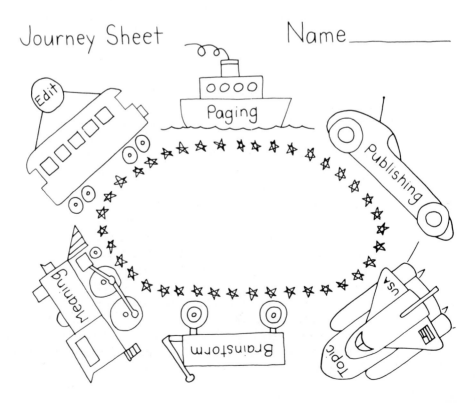

which centers upon meaning rather than mechanical or grammatical issues, we often begin by telling the youngster how we felt about his piece while reading it and by pointing to what we enjoyed the most. Then, we may attempt to help a youngster make his piece better, pointing, perhaps, to an inconsistency or unexpected turn of events. The whole process is delicate, however, and we've found intuition plays an important role. For example, consider this story by Elizabeth, a third grader, as well as Ruth Nathan's approach to the conference.

Little Witch's Friends
dedacatid to Michael

Once there was a wich that had to move. and her mommy siad that she could packe her stuf so she could tell her mom what to give away. So little wich packed her stuf And carred her pet bats. When they got ther the big wich let little wich play in the yard. Then while she was playing she notise a haunted houese. nere by so she dcided to explor the house. Then after she walked in the house she herd a scare noise and then she saw smoeke. Her mom started to call her. Little wich left the hunted house. She saw that the house was on fire. Her mom said she had walked in and the house was on fire, but she hadn't stated unpacking. So litle wich shode her mom the house and they live in the other house but, someone was living there but they let the wich's live there too. So they became friends. And then they went outside to play!

Elizabeth, Grade 3

If I were to approach this conference using the approach suggested above (what's good/what needs work), I might have told Elizabeth that I was pleased to learn about Little Witch, as well as her mother, through their *actions*: that I knew Little Witch was a caring character, for example, because she was careful to remember her pet bats. I knew that the mother was caring, too, because she allowed Little Witch to "packe her stuf so she could tell her mom what to give away." The old saw, "show don't tell," seems to be working here, and what Elizabeth chooses to show has implications for her story's end: the two witches are allowed to move into the haunted house with the ghosts—perhaps they might all get along.

I might have gone on to ask Elizabeth about the plot. As a reader, I found the scary noise followed by the fire confusing. A story that I thought would have depth seemed to be taking on a high-action profile. The lack of cohesion didn't help either. Perhaps through this discussion, *Little Witch's Friends* might get a bit clearer and more plausible.

I chose, however, not to take this approach with Elizabeth's piece. I knew I needed insight, and my conference time would be short. I also doubted that she put in the fire for the sake of sensationalism. (We need to trust children more, I've learned.) I began, instead, by asking Elizabeth how she got the idea for the story, wondering if she might help me. This is what she said:

> It was around Halloween and I heard stories about witches and stuff, and they usually live in haunted houses. And then once our house caught on fire, but it didn't burn down, but it almost did! And we had to live in an apartment for a year. And from moving, I got the idea because when my grandma moved, she was in a house, but she had to move to an apartment because my grandpa died, and she didn't have enough money to pay for all the water and stuff.

I followed this question with "You chose this piece for me to show your mother. Why?"

> Because it had witches and stuff in it. Most of my other ones have people. This is better because I like stories that are fake—that are fiction.

Then I asked, "What's your favorite part of *Little Witch's Friends*?" She said:

> The part where she finds the haunted house cause when we were at the apartment I wanted to be back in our house—but we couldn't move back. They almost took the whole ceiling apart! We didn't have anything to do! A haunted house would have been fun.

When my conference was over I was glad I had taken the conference alternative I had. Elizabeth went on to proofread her piece, deal with the few cohesion issues that presented themselves (which house was often unclear), and publish it.

As teachers we know a lot about what makes a story good. We know we need believable characters, a problem that matters, characters who change, and plausible solutions. A child's desire to play and enjoy the results is not held in high esteem. For young authors, it should be more the rule than not that writing is used to satisfy the human need for fun, for chances to be creative, for control over their own lives.[22] In addition, we as teachers don't have enough understanding of how writers develop to always be of the greatest help. Elizabeth attempted a Halloween story, replete with appropriate characters and setting, and had fun doing so: "This is better because I like stories that are fake—that are fiction." As far as she's concerned, it's her best piece yet.

Elizabeth has done what all accomplished novelists do, created a fictional world using her life for all it's worth. And we've still not mentioned the *power* of writing—of the humanities—to reduce one's own fears, to have some control over our lives, our memories, our ability to carry on. What Elizabeth has done is so extraordinarily complex for an eight year old that we stand in awe. There will be time, as Jack Wilde[23] and tens of others have so aptly shown us, when we need to do more. Determining that time is what we call intuition, and we believe teachers need to trust intuition more.

As an aid to helping your children grow as writers, we have included Donald Murray's "Qualities of Good Writing" (Figure 11–22). This list will help you to identify what you most certainly know intuitively about good writing, but for which you may not have found good labels. We refer to this list all the time as we sort out what we might say to a child during our teacher-child conferences, or what we might ask.

Following Murray's list you will find one of our own (see Figure 11–23), which has examples of conference questions that can spur children to develop their writing more fully. Nested within our list are questions that relate to Murray's qualities. A note of caution, however, is in order: Don't overdo it when trying to help a youngster improve her work. We hardly ever address more than one issue at a time, and frequently a piece is published that is short on most of these aspects but long on at least one. The story we shared about Elizabeth should provide adequate warning against any sort of heavy-handedness.

Figure 11–22

The Qualities of Good Writing
Donald Murray

1. **MEANING**
   There must be content in an effective piece of writing. It must all add up to something. This is the most important element in good writing, but although it must be listed first it is often discovered last through the process of writing.
2. **AUTHORITY**
   Good writing is filled with specific, accurate, honest information. The reader is persuaded through authoritative information that the writer knows the subject.
3. **VOICE**
   Good writing is marked by an individual voice. The writer's voice may be the most significant element in distinguishing memorable writing from good writing.
4. **DEVELOPMENT**
   The writer satisfies the reader's hunger for information. The beginning writer almost always overestimates the reader's hunger for language and under-estimates the reader's hunger for information.
5. **DESIGN**
   A good piece of writing is elegant in the mathematical sense. It has form, structure, order, focus, coherence. It gives the reader a sense of completeness.
6. **CLARITY**
   Good writing is marked by a simplicity which is appropriate to the subject. The writer has searched for and found the right word, the effective verb, the clarifying phrase. The writer has removed the writer so that the reader sees through the writer's style to the subject, which is clarified and simplified.

It is my belief that these qualities are the same for poetry and fiction as well as nonfiction.

Figure 11–23   **Conference Questions Teachers May Consider**

Introductory Questions
–Tell me about your piece of writing.
–Why did you choose this subject to write about?
–What surprises you most about this draft?
–What kinds of changes have you made from your last draft?
–What questions did your conference partner have of you?
–What problems did you have or are you having?
–Where is this piece of writing taking you?
–What questions do you have of me?

Questions That Deal With Meaning
–Do you have more than one story here?
–Underline the part that tells what this draft is about.
–What is the most important thing you are trying to say here?
–Explain how your title fits your draft.

Questions That Deal With Authority
–Can you tell me more about this?
–This part isn't clear to me. Can you tell me what you mean?
–Can you describe this for me?

Questions That Deal With Voice
–How does this draft sound when you read it out loud?
–Circle the part that is most exciting.
–Show me a place where I can tell *you* have written this piece.

Questions That Deal With Development
–Can you tell me more about it?
–Do you have enough information?
–Can you tell me where you are going in your draft?
–How did you get to this place in your draft?

Questions That Deal With Design
–Are you happy with your beginning and ending?
–How does the beginning of you piece grab your reader's attention?
–How have you tied your ending to your beginning?

Questions That Deal With Clarity
–Can you be more specific here? (e.g., How did you go into the house?)
–What are your action words? Can you add others?
–Can you think of a different way to say this?
–Is this the best word here?

Questions (when a draft is not finished) That Help a Writer Move On
–What do you intend to do now?
–What do you think you can do to make this draft better?
–What works so well you'd like to try and develop it further?

Questions That Help Children See Their Growth As Writers
–What did you learn from this piece of writing?
–How does this piece compare to others you have written? Why?
–Can you think of something new you tried in this draft that you have never
  tried before?
–How are you a better writer now than you were at the beginning of the year?

We said earlier that teacher-child conferences can be with an individual or group. Sometimes it helps to have a number of children around you and available for talking when you're holding a conference with a child. Children are usually very attentive and make good suggestions, so we hold group conferences often. Small groups provide a good opportunity to work on a particular skill that several children need help on. (Review the discussion of all-class conferences in the section labeled "Beyond Day One.")

Peer Conferences.   Children need time to talk to one another about their drafts and not just about work that is headed for publication. They get stuck. They get tired of writing. They get bored with their own ideas. They need inspiration. All good reasons, we think, for letting them talk to one another, which they do during conference time.

There are rules, for sure, and procedures as well: (1) we ask children to sign up for peer conferences so we can think about the pairs and make sure we approve; (2) we insist on not being disturbed during conference time because we're busy, too; (3) when children conference with a peer, they are to log it in their writing logs (see section entitled "The Manual") and they may be asked later on to tell us what they accomplished; and (4) we frequently ask them to write down one comment they made to their conference partner and one question they asked as well. We confess that we abhor asking them to do this (we don't ask this of first graders), but classroom control is an issue and little tactics like this help. Once the children appreciate how interesting process writing is, strategies like this become unnecessary.

During the first few months of the school year, we're not sure how much gets done during peer conferences; children simply haven't had enough time with us. We haven't modeled asking questions much or shared and discussed quality literature. As the year progresses, however, the children get better in terms of their behavior and the quality of their peer conferences.

All-Class Conferences and Small-Group Conferences.   A lot of one-to-one teaching goes on in process classrooms, but it can't all be this way! Sometimes it's advantageous (and life saving) to teach a concept to everyone or to a small group. All-class conferences can be oriented toward meaning or editing concerns; the procedure is the same for both. Identify a problem in a draft. Ask the youngster if you can reproduce it on an overhead transparency. Make a ditto of the draft, if you can, and pass out red pencils with the copies. If you'd prefer not using a child's draft, make up one highlighting the issue and use this instead.

We discuss the problem with the class first. For example, in the piece about fish (Figure 11–24), the problem we addressed was sentence order. We mixed up a paragraph from the basal reader first, then asked the children what was wrong. Later, we talked about how writers might get themselves into this fix. We noted that writing is difficult and demands attention, and

My fish have little mouths but
they eat like pigs but thats ok.   **1**

I feed them every morning just a
pinch. **2**

I started out with five fish 3
femails and 2 mails. **3**

Now I have 8 fish. **4**

And I like them a lot to. **5**

It's hard to hold the food in two
fingers but I can do it. **6**

They are gupies. **7**

We did not name them yet. **8**

The cup we put the food in is
about two inches long. **9**

I have pebbels that are colored and
plants to in it. **10**

that sometimes it is worthwhile just to get the whole draft out first, worrying about other things later. Drafts are just that, drafts.

Our next step is to put the draft on the overhead and pass out the copies. Each child works alone in an attempt to make the piece better, then pairs meet and work together. While working with the fish example, one child suggested we cut the transparency apart, by sentences. The children then took turns coming to the overhead, rearranging the sentences and explaining their improvements. A discussion of paragraphs was a natural outflow of this exercise, as was pronoun comprehension (e.g., the "it" in line 10). Correcting the spelling was also fun, but this came last (what a switch!).

Sometimes children can hold small-group conferences, which are like extended peer conferences. When a number of children would like to conference together, all sharing their drafts and getting feedback from one another, we let them do so. We ask them to follow their conference guidelines and not to leave the group until everyone has had a chance to read. To insure this, we label oaktag cards as Group A, B, C, etc. and numbered sequentially. We pass one card out to each child (e.g., A1, A2, A3, A4), and the children keep them in their folders until everyone is finished. If conference time is over before everyone has had a turn, the children keep the cards and meet with their group during the next conference period, when they finish hearing everyone's draft.

Publishing Possibilities

The list is endless. Of course, books are a favorite, and the simplest way we know of to make books is with a binding machine. Binding machines (available in all office supply stores and costing about $300) are a valuable addition to any school, and parent-teacher organizations are often eager to raise the needed funds. Once a book is typed, illustrated, and a cover is made, the binding process takes less than a minute.[24]

Classroom literary journals are another option, and they can be sophisticated or kept simple. Simple ones entail children copying their drafts onto dittos and teachers, or aides, running them off. Children love to do the collating and stapling, and should be encouraged to do so. Since literary journals can be sold, advertising proves to be yet another writing outlet. Berkshire Middle School in Birmingham, Michigan, opted for a fancy journal, so they hired a professional printer. Such journals get paid for through pledge campaigns, bake sales, or incentive grants.

Classroom newspapers are also a natural outlet for children's writing. Children often write about trips and visitors, so why not use these drafts in your paper? A literary corner might become a permanent column, along with traditional news and editorial slots. Feature articles certainly could come from your children's writing.

One classroom puts out a paper, RUMORS, every three weeks, which involves two days of writing workshop. The day before RUMORS is written, some of the children work up a list of possible topics with the teacher. Since one purpose of RUMORS is to inform the parents about what's going on in the classroom, they brainstorm what they've done or experienced recently: the new guinea pig, their current read-aloud, classroom projects, their current classroom novel(s), what's new in math, a funny incident (the clay sculptures melting on the window ledge), an up-and-coming event, a school-wide assembly, etc. The next day the whole class reviews this list and then adds to it. There is a column, Family Album, where one or two children put in a favorite photograph of themselves and tell all about it. There is also a Dear Mr. Henshaw column. Mr. Henshaw in the class guinea pig and the children write to him about their problems. He writes back, too! (Ghost writers in the room help him out on the electric typewriter.)

The children have forty-five minutes to write their articles. The next day is spent editing, proofreading, and swapping articles to insure that others can read their work. (The teacher usually writes an article, too.) The following Saturday, the teacher types RUMORS on her Macintosh computer, which has a program that scans the children's art work, so all illustrations in RUMORS are originals. By mid-January, the children will be typing RUMORS themselves on the classroom computer (they've had to learn the keyboard).

In addition to classroom publications such as RUMORS, national magazines such as *Stone Soup, Highlights,* and *Cricket* encourage children to write and to send in their work. (Check your local or school library to obtain addresses for these publications, and begin compiling your own list of innovative ideas for student publishing.)

Evaluation

It is hard writing about evaluation without getting philosophical. After reading a text written by Marjorie, a seven-year-old, you can see that giving this piece a grade would not be easy.

> I have to atmit that I wot get a sicker (sticker) on my unit. Because it was hard. And I don't whnat tu be a scardy cat. so I will tell ya that I am not a scardy cat.
>
> *Marjorie, Grade 1*

What will our grade reflect? Our ability as teachers? Marjorie's prior knowledge? Her product in light of other products written by children her age? The piece's meaning? Grammatical and mechanical correctness? Spelling correctness? Marjorie's effort? How much she has grown since her last effort?

We think evaluation is most helpful if it provides children with the type of feedback that will produce skillful writers. For us, this means we must evaluate and give feedback throughout the writing process. Carol Steele, a writing consultant from Grand Rapids, Michigan says, "Evaluation needs to happen at the point in the process when the input will be most helpful."[25] So when children stare at their empty topic sheets, we *help* them think of interesting aspects of their lives; we *read* first drafts and *point out* what has been said well; we *ask* for clarification when we feel lost as readers; we *look* for closure in pieces that lack endings; we *evaluate* and then *teach* the skills that need to be learned. The list could go on.

By providing checklists and sets of questions we teach self-evaluation too. As Steele says, "self-evaluation helps train students to turn their powers of observation and analysis toward their work."[26] Through all-class conferences, small-group conferences, teacher-child conferences, and peer conferences, children become increasingly adept at analyzing their writing. While we might consider evaluating their growing awareness of their writing needs or weaknesses, one quickly sees that the amount of teacher-child interaction is a crucial element in the equation. So we are back to square one, at least in terms of giving Marjorie's piece a grade.

If we have to give grades for writing, evaluating Marjorie on her writing performance in class seems a bit more realistic than assessing the quality of her drafts. But before evaluating Marjorie, even upon her performance instead of her products, we had better evaluate ourselves. We've compiled a list of teachers' behaviors that we routinely use to evaluate our *own* performance before evaluating that of our students. (A Student's Behavior checklist is also included.) It is our belief that if we do well in all of these areas, Marjorie will do well also.

Teacher's Behavior
1. Do I insist upon writing during writing time in order to grow as a writer?
2. Do I share my own evolving drafts with the class?
3. Do I keep track of children's progress in a systematic way?
4. Do I have a structure or system in the classroom to support the writing period?
5. Do I provide opportunities for children to publish in a variety of forms?
6. Do I see to it that children share their work with other children?
7. Do I seek out support materials to help children write?
8. Do I have a literature component in my writing program?
9. Do I share professional material with other teachers?
10. When holding teacher-child conferences, am I sensitive to the child's intention as well as his/her development level?
11. Do I periodically show students how they are growing as writers?

Student's Behavior
1. ____ writes during designated time
       always   sometimes   rarely
2. ____ uses constructive strategies for getting drafts started
       always   sometimes   rarely
3. ____ takes the conference period seriously by
    a) being willing to listen to classmates' drafts
    b) realizing other children may have meaningful suggestions
       always   sometimes   rarely
4. ____ is growing in his or her understanding of the difference between revising (e.g., adding on) and editing
       quite a bit   some   very little
5. ____ uses the support systems in the classroom (e.g., manual guidelines, spelling sheets, dictionaries, etc.)
       frequently   occasionally   infrequently
6. ____ is learning to view revision as part of a healthy writing process
       yes   no
7. ____ is an active participant during share time
       almost always   on occasion   almost never

We don't mean to be glib by avoiding product evaluation, but we simply don't know how, nor do we see any purpose in doing so. By sharing our interpretation of Marjorie's writing behavior with her, however, we may help her products indirectly. If she isn't using support systems, we can show her how; if she seems to be playing around during conference time, we can let her know *we* know and that it matters; if she doesn't write during writing time we might encourage her, via our checklist, to become more serious; if she never talks during share time, again, the checklist might help. Some children benefit by knowing their behavior is being chronicled, and therefore we encourage periodic process evaluation. But a final word of advice: Our checklist is but a prototype, meant to be altered.

Conclusion

What we have described in this chapter is a support system for the process of writing, which can be used with some variations throughout elementary school. For the sake of clarity, we have focused on the procedures that the teacher needs to initiate to set up a process-writing classroom—topic choice, expanding a topic, conferences, revisions, editing, publishing—at the risk of making the school day seem rather mechanical. Although it may take some time for both children and teacher to get used to these procedures, in our experience they do provide children with a sense of security and control, thus encouraging creative and productive work. Knowing the procedural ropes doesn't suppress the excitement children get from their writing; it channels it and keeps it alive.

What we have only touched on in these recent chapters is the essential complement to this program: the sources of inspiration with which teachers and parents surround young writers—conversations, explorations, substantive information. The process-writing classroom works best within a cultural context as rich and exciting as teachers and community members can make it. This means continually bringing the world into the classroom and the children into the world. The many ways of doing this, fascinating as they are, must be the subject of other books.

ENDNOTES

1. William Corsaro, "'We're friends, right?': Children's Use of Access Rituals in a Nursery School," *Language in Society, 8* (1979): 315–336.
2. Ann Haas Dyson, "Learning to Write/Learning to Do School," *Research in the Teaching of English, 18* (1984): 233–264.
3. Nancie Atwell, "Writing and Reading from the Inside Out," *Language Arts, 61* (1984): 240–252.
4. Donald Murray, "How Writing Finds Its Own Meaning," in *Eight Approaches to Teaching Composition,* Timothy R. Donovan and Ben W. McClelland, eds. (Urbana, IL: NCTE, 1980).
5. Atwell.
6. Murray, p. 62.
7. Betty Flowers, "Madman, Architect, Carpenter, Judge: Roles and the Writing Process," *Language Arts, 58* (1981): 834–836.
8. Flowers, p. 834.
9. Flowers, p. 834.
10. For an excellent and detailed discussion that centers on processing and writing nonfiction texts during the kindergarten years, read Christine

Pappas's article, "Fostering Full Access to Literacy by Including Information Books," *Language Arts, 68*: 449-462.

11. Donald Graves and Jane Hansen, "The Author's Chair," *Language Arts, 60* (1983): 176–183.

12. James Britton, *Language and Learning* (Harmondsworth, England: Penguin, 1970).

13. James Moffett, *Teaching the Universe of Discourse* (Boston: Houghton Mifflin, 1970), p. 85.

14. Ann Haas Dyson, "Research Currents: Young Children as Composers," *Language Arts, 60* (1982): 884–891.

15. Judith Hilliker, "Kindergartners Can Write," *Learning, 15* (1986): 74.

16. Hilliker, p. 74.

17. Ruqaiya Hasan, "The Nursery Tale as a Genre," *Nottingham Linguistic Circular, 13* (1984): 71–102.

18. Pappas, "Fostering Full Access to Literacy by Including Information Books," p. 461.

19. Two excellent booklists of quality fiction and nonfiction are Eileen Burke, *Literature for the Young Child* (Boston: Allyn & Bacon, 1990), and Mary Jett-Simpson, *Adventuring with Books: A Booklist for Pre-K–Grade 6* (Urbana, IL: NCTE, 1989).

20. See Ruth Nathan's letter to the editor, *Language Arts, 68* (1991): 400.

21. Donald Graves, *Writing: Teachers and Children at Work* (Portsmouth, NH: Heinemann, 1983).

22. For more information of how children use writing to control their lives, see William Glasser, *Control Theory* (New York: Harper & Row, 1984).

23. Jack Wilde, "Play, Power, and Plausibility: The Growth of Fiction Writers," in *Breaking Ground*, Jane Hansen, Thomas Newkirk, and Donald Graves, eds. (Portsmouth, NH: Heinemann, 1985).

24. For a fine resource on book publishing possibilities, see Paul Johnson, *A Book of One's Own* (Portsmouth, NH: Heinemann, 1990).

25. Carol Steele, "Evaluation of Writing," *Michigan Council of Teachers of English Newsletter, 38* (1986): 11.

26. Steele, p. 11.

Classroom Environments for Reading and Writing Together

They're all different, these classrooms. Kindergarten children in miniature chairs, pressed so close together their knees touch, listen intently to a classmate explaining the picture he's drawn during writing workshop.

A cluster of third-grade students in an alternative school ponder a color photo of the White House they've just received in the mail and wonder in what sense it can be considered a reply to the letter they sent to the President urging him to stop spending money on Star Wars and to start buying books for children.

A second-grade class listens intently as their teacher reads Bill Peet's autobiography. Soon they will be writing their own stories, as Peet has, so they are interested in his topics as well as his way of telling.

They're all different, these classrooms, but they share a core of similarities: They stress the *processes* of reading and writing, they seek *connections* between reading and writing, and they set up *environments* that approach reading and writing as social activities.

An Emphasis on Processes

The emphasis on process in current reading and writing instruction has become commonplace. But it is both so new and so important that it deserves comment. Not long ago, innovations in teaching were so long in coming that they inspired critics to voice this discouraging maxim: Teachers teach the way they were taught. If that were true, innovation would be impossible.

That maxim is almost miraculously *untrue* of current reading and writing instruction. Most of us were taught by methods that stressed correctness and skill development in reading and writing methods that too often assumed you could read and write or you could not.

The way we teach reading and writing now has nothing to do with the way we were taught. In the past decade or so we have learned, really for the

A different version of this chapter appeared in Timothy Shanahan (Ed.), *Reading and Writing Together* (Norwood, MA: Christopher-Gordon, 1990). Adapted with permission.

first time, to teach reading and to teach writing. We teach by actually showing children how to read and how to write. Using big books and following
the story line with our finger, sometimes covering all but a letter or two of a
word to show how we identify it from context, is an example of *teaching* reading. Writing in front of children on an overhead projector, crossing out words
and making changes as they occur to us, is an example of *teaching* writing.

This process approach has radically changed what it is to teach reading
and writing. In a wonderfully apt metaphor, Donald Graves said that writing
is a studio craft. He meant that if you are going to teach others to write, you
must write in front of them. A pottery teacher shows us how she throws a
blob of clay down on the exact center of the wheel, gouges with both thumbs
and pulls straight walls up out of the spinning muddy mass. A teacher of
reading and writing displays a list of potential topics, discusses the pros and
cons of each one, then chooses one and begins to focus in on its possibilities:
clustering, brainstorming, doodling on a transparency as he goes. The pottery
teacher doesn't just "assign" a pot and evaluate the result, leaving the students guessing how the creative work is done, and a reading-writing teacher
doesn't proceed this way either. This comparison between reading-writing
and arts and crafts points out that reading and writing are largely cognitive
and linguistic processes that can be observed, taught, and learned.

Environments That Make Reading and Writing Contagious

When we spoke of writing as a process, we quoted Donald Graves's maxim,
"Writing is a studio craft." We can extend Graves's metaphor a little further.
The pottery teachers we know are potters, and the drawing teachers are
artists. Each has identified herself with her craft, so that we can gain from her
not only a technique and skill but also a vicarious love for the craft and an appreciation of what it is to be committed to it. We are not only informed by
these people but *inspired* by them as well. The same is true of teachers who
are readers and writers themselves.

This points to a second aspect of teaching reading and writing—the *social side* of these activities. Those of us who have followed research in reading
and writing for a while will appreciate the contributions that the psycholin-
guists—especially the language acquisition researchers—made to our field.
But now we see that they misled us, too, because much of the early work on
language acquisition seemed to show that learning to talk—and, hence,
learning to read and write—were universal and unilinear processes. That is,
all people everywhere who were learning to talk, read, and write were doing
the same things. Now we see that is not so. The work of Shirley Brice Heath,
Michael Cole, and others has showed us that language use is intimately connected to one's social group, and different social groups use language differ-

ently. Heath's *Ways With Words* demonstrated that it is possible to be a successful language user in one's own cultural group and still have difficulty learning to read and write in school situations—possibly due to the interference or mismatch of language proficiencies.

To teach children to read and write is not just to teach them a set of processes and skills, but to invite them into a community of people who use spoken language in elaborate ways and who also make much use of reading and writing. This is another dramatic change from past experience. The last two decades in education have seen an emphasis on *individualized* instruction, on "meeting individual needs." Children have worked on different tasks, alone. They have been taught and tested to maximize their individual gains. Receiving the services of specialists, some have come and gone so frequently as to make their classrooms seem like bus stations. But a reading-writing classroom is not a bus station; it is a community of language users. Children who are very fluent and others who are not very fluent still write so each other can read and comment. All children, whether their reading ability is well-oiled or problematical, spend large amounts of time indulging the pleasure of reading. Language is communication, and it requires people to talk and write and to read and listen. It requires a community of people who are respectful of each other, who are in touch with their own ideas, and who are interested in each others' ideas.

To establish such an environment requires that teachers attend to at least three things: First, they should become models of what they expect their students to do; second, they should set up classroom routines that establish a literate community in the classroom; and third, they should create classrooms brimming with ideas, books, and connections to the world.

The Teacher Goes First: Establishing a Trusting Environment

Teachers often tell us their children don't want to share their writing, especially when they're approaching the upper elementary and junior high years. Even if their children do share, that share time is nebulous: not much gets done. Often these same teachers follow their statements about timidity and lack of peer-conference content with the question, "What can we do about it?" When our workshops bend in this direction, we usually look to the teachers we're working with for answers. Generally we find the collective group knows exactly what to do.

The Teacher as Writer
We ask, "How many of you write and share your writing with your children?" A few teachers nod, and so we ask them to tell us why. The answers are often long and passionate. Teachers who write tell us things we know are

true because we're writers ourselves.[1] They usually detail the effect their authorship has on how they talk to their students and thus how their students begin talking and sharing with one another.

If you are a teacher, they say, holding a conference with a young writer is not easy. The problem is twofold: Authors break easily, and teachers tend to criticize. Authors, especially authors who happen to be children, do not want advice right away. Teachers who write know this. Authors want readers to tell them they've done a good job. A fourth grader recently put it simply: "I want people to say, 'That's EXCELLENT!' "

Teachers who write also understand that advice, while necessary, must be given at the right time and by a trusted individual. They know how a writer feels when a piece is shared—the chemical twang, the wildly beating heart, the mental involvement, the "I'm out there and feeling vulnerable" sensations. We find it doesn't really matter if teachers write well; that's almost (but not totally) irrelevant. What does matter is that teachers attempt to write something well and that they share their drafts as they ask their students to do.

Another reason teachers write in order to encourage quality sharing is that only after they have seriously attempted to get an idea across on paper does the difficulty inherent in the writing process become obvious. Ideas, far too many of them, enter our minds all at once, and writers (unlike the computer on our desks) must eke them out one at a time—slowly. Furthermore, we don't have gestures to help us get our points across as we do when we're talking. Gestures, and other cues like intonation, help our audience understand us. When we write, all we have is a blank sheet of paper and our ability to handle the English language. The difficulty in matching what's in one's head with what's on the page is difficult to explain to anyone who hasn't grappled with the problem, really caring to get the ideas right.

Teachers who write are the best conference partners in the world because they respect their children's efforts. It's that simple. When it seems as though a piece is breaking down, a teacher who writes is more apt to ask herself, "What's this writer doing that's new?" instead of thinking, "This piece is impossible!"

All of this—knowing that modeling is important, feeling vulnerable, and understanding the difficulty inherent in getting your paper to say what you mean—adds up to an honest workshop environment where writing takes the shape of the craft it is meant to be.

The Teacher as Reader

Establishing a trusting reading environment is to risk monster behavior: children who chomp at the bit to read; tell their peers *what* to read, emphatically; roar for new titles; make connections between books; and demand time *in class* to talk books, write books, and *read*. Teachers who do not routinely find the time to read for pleasure or information themselves may not understand what all this means nor how to bring it about. For those who do, it comes naturally.

Fearing that many teachers don't carve out niches of reading time for themselves often enough, I routinely give an assignment to my summer graduate students at Oakland University, where I teach a masters' course, "Literature/Writing Connections." The assignment reads: "Choose a book you'd like to read but have put aside due to lack of time. Bring it to class. It will be one of your three textbooks." My graduates are both amazed and thrilled. A typical response to the syllabus is, "I haven't touched my professional literature in months, let alone le Carré!"

I tell them to take their guilt and throw it out with the trash! The notion that one shouldn't, or *that one need not,* be a reader to teach reading, or writing for that matter, needs shedding. "Say goodbye to that 'I've no time' skin, and look in the mirror," I say. "First remember yourself as a child, perhaps when you read *The Hardy Boys, The Bobbsey Twins, Mr. Popper's Penguins, The Secret Garden, The Thirteen Clocks.* Do you remember reading under your covers with a flashlight in hand?"

"Now, bring up an image of listening to your fifth-grade teacher reading to you. Do you see yourself and your class in that mirror? Recall how you felt hearing Wilbur in *Charlotte's Web* would be spared, how you roared over Toad's escapades in *The Wind in the Willows,* how you gasped when you realized Johnny Tremain was in love. Do you remember hearing the incredible story of Galileo or Leonardo da Vinci? Did your class ever get a class-size subscription to the local newspaper? Did you read about Martin Luther King in one of those issues? Or Sputnik?"

"Teachers who gave you all those opportunities to read were readers themselves, just as surely as I'm standing here." I assure them. So, in that university class each summer, I give my students time to read something they choose for themselves. I also give them time to write about their books in dialogue journals.[2] These logs, as they're often called, are places where readers write reactions, suspicions, questions, and predictions; where they digress, just as often, about the books they're reading to a trusted other—often another student but sometimes the teacher.

Here are two sample entries between one of my students, Linda, and me one summer when we were reading *Collaborators,* by Janet Kauffman.

> Dear Ruth,
>
> . . . I especially liked Chapter Two, which took place at Rehobeth Beach. It reminded me of the time I was living near Washington, D.C. and working at the National Institute of Health. On weekends, I'd take my daughter, then about two, to Rehobeth Beach for the day. We liked it best in the spring or the fall when it wasn't full of tourists. What fond memories . . .
>
> Back to the book . . .

I thought it was interesting how Kauffman used the tobacco farm surrounding the prison as her main setting. I know if I were reading this in Professor Fitzsimmons' class, he'd find all kinds of symbolism in that and know exactly what it meant, but I haven't figured it out yet. I'm just enjoying Kauffman's colorful use of language.

I haven't yet decided why she titled her book *Collaborators.* I'll have to look for more clues as I continue to read. What do you think? I'm also curious about who you think Andrea Doria's mother is referring to when she refers to her three lovers—grandfather, father, and son . . .

* * *

Dear Linda,

Reading the first few chapters, then your letter—what fun! I've never done this before.

. . .Yes, you talk of language. Kauffman is an acrobat. "Every singsong she treats as a crowd of words, and she is vigilant, gulping, ready for trouble," tells us so much about this lady, this mother. And, "If all my loved ones were drowning, she says to me—to me that is no one—and I had the strength to save one, I'd save Ruth." Kauffman hasn't used more than one adjective in those two quotes, yet we know so much about this woman. Think of that—

. . . I also loved Chapter Two, the beach chapter you mention. You know, that chapter is a short story in her collection, *Places in the World a Woman Could Walk.* . . . On page seven, "I calculate how to touch a collapsing wall . . . ," she's talking about waves—what an apt metaphor. And she uses "tag" rather than "touch"—"how to tag it, and how to rush off within my own splashes . . ."I wish I wrote like that! So fresh.

Regarding lovers, I'm not sure. I'll have to read on and let you know next letter swap. Ditto regarding the tobacco farm.

Getting serious about books with your students collapses the wall between you, as surely as Kauffman's waves collapse upon her shore. Linda could have as easily been a fourth grader as my college student; I could have been her fourth-grade peer as easily as her teacher. Teacher as reader, reader as teacher, young and old, it doesn't matter. As for needing to write in order to create a healthy writing environment, being a reader is *the issue* when it comes to creating a trusting reading environment. Your students need you to read books *you* choose, and for *you* to become famous, perhaps infamous, for "talking books" in the teacher's lounge, at your dining room table, at the parties you go to. Shed your "I've no time" skin—if you're someone who needs to—and take time, make time, to read.

Children and Teachers Sharing Writing Strategies

We begin this section with a story. Ruth Nathan walked into a fourth-grade class one day with a draft in hand called "The Last Windy Night." "Kids, come over here," I said. "I have to show you something." The children gathered around. "I went up to Torch Lake this weekend, alone. I stayed at a friend's cottage. Late in the day, I walked out the back door and headed toward the pier to watch the sun set. As I left, the door squeaked in a funny way, sort of like, 'Eee . . . eee . . . eeek . . . hmm . . . m.' I went back inside to try it again. Same sound. I tried it again and again. Same thing. I sat down on the back porch steps thinking about how I might use it in a story. It was such a sound! Forgetting the sunset, I ran inside and started to write; I had no idea what I was going to say.

"I plopped down on the floor with a paper and pencil and scratched out a beginning. Before I knew it, I had an idea. The sound would be a trapped ghost trying to tell me it wanted out! Once I tripped upon my idea, the rest was easy."

The children were astounded by my telling them I had no idea what I was going to say before I began my story. They were used to planning their stories on worksheets before they wrote. "Next time you get a feeling you have a story," I said, "you might forget your plan sheet and just start to write. While you may need it later, occasionally those things get in the way. Sometimes I just need to write lots of words before a good idea comes into my head."

The spontaneity of my sharing was catchy. Soon the other children in the class began to share things that happened to them as they wrote or before they wrote. One youngster said she needed to take a shower! ("I think so well then" she said.) These sharings become natural mini-lessons before writing workshop. A child would tell me something, and I would say, "Would you begin our writing workshop with that story tomorrow?" The children knew I was dead serious over wanting to learn all I could about their writing strategies, and they knew, absolutely, that I thought they could all learn from those stories. That's because we're all readers and writers; it's the bottom line.

Another telling story. One afternoon I received Wallace Stegner's novel *Crossing to Safety,* a beautiful, poignant story from a Pulitzer Prize-winning author about friendship. Do you remember what Holden Caulfield said in *The Catcher in the Rye* about a good book? "What really knocks me out is a book that, when you're all done reading it you wish the author that wrote it was a terrific friend of yours and you could call him up on the phone whenever you felt like it."

Oh how I wanted to call Stegner a *thousand* times as I read *Crossing to Safety.* I found myself spellbound as Aunt Emily read *Hiawatha* to the children, frightened as the novel's foursome almost perish on Lake Mendota, astonished over the author's "snake in the grass," and dazzled by Stegner's continual reference to literature across cultures, through the centuries. I went to class the next day (this time my students were in middle school) and started reading time by sharing Salinger's line. Then I read from Stegner's novel, in hopes that my students would understand my Caulfieldian response:

We have been tacking back and forth, ducking under the swinging boom. Sid is very busy, for the boat handles badly and the wind seems to come from every direction. The sun has gone under, too, and the warmth has left the afternoon. The sky to the left is full of bruise-colored clouds, and the hospital towers on the north shore are lost in gray shrags of rain. In the hostile airs we come almost to a standstill. The canvas flaps. Sid grates out, "Oh, God, don't *luff!*" The boom comes over, we veer sluggishly onto another tack.[3]

In no time we were all talking at once, my students calling out names of authors they wish they could meet—Pearl Buck, Jane Yolen, Lloyd Alexander, Roald Dahl, Katherine Paterson, Laurence Yep—me telling them others I'd like to know, and not letting on, just yet, that Buck and Dahl are dead. (I've written authors after they died, by accident, and am none the worse for it.) All this started a lively discussion about writing authors and, more important, about perusing the newspaper for writers giving readings at our local universities, colleges, and community centers. I said that while I might write Stegner some day, I had written Fielding Dawson a few years ago after reading *Tiger Lilies:An American Childhood*, my all-time favorite collection of childhood remembrances. And he had responded with a wonderful letter. "Bring the letter in!" they yelled. I did, hoping Fielding Dawson wouldn't mind (he has since given me permission to quote it here). Here is a short excerpt from his note:

> In the fall of 1984 I was invited to a college in upstate New York to give a talk to a class, and a reading to the students. There was a good turnout for both, and the kids were eager. I read from *Tiger Lilies*. Their teacher, who invited me, asked me to read the section about Popeye, in grade school, so I did, and became so moved I wept. I couldn't read. I stood up there, not knowing what to do, wiping my eyes, clearing my throat, the guy who invited me in tears, the whole room, a lecture room, upset, confused, embarrassed, some of the girls crying. I at last got hold, and went on, etc. and they sent me a copy of the school paper with a picture of me, and an article, no mention of you know what except a line that I have an emotional involvement with my work. . . .

"An emotional involvement with my work." The children were genuinely touched by that line. Me, too. Surely, it says what being a teacher should be all about. Just as we walk into writing classes as writers and share our enthusiasms, strategies, and frustrations, we walk into reading classrooms as readers, with our questions, excitements, and desires—desires to know authors we admire, how others feel about a book, how a book might affect the way we live our very lives. The day I received Dawson's letter I wept, too, from sheer relief that another human being would open his heart to me, a stranger; and, too, that I apparently hadn't made a fool of myself in sending him those few carefully chosen words. This behavior, because it's honest and natural, sets the stage for all that's to happen, or not happen, in our language arts class-rooms.

Guilty? Because we take time to read Stegner, Dawson, Kauffman, le Carré? The notion needs challenging. Guilty? Because we treat ourselves to a public reading once in a while instead of correcting papers? Guilty? Because we write an unrequired letter? I say, let happen what happened in Sendak's *Where the Wild Things Are*—let the monsters roar their terrible roars.

Teacher and Children as Readers and Writers

Karen has just finished a piece about her dog. Most of it is what you might expect from a fourth grader. But out of the ordinary comes this line:

> "My dog looks like a ghost with curls."

Karen's teacher turns to her and asks how she thought of that description. "He's white and curly," comes Karen's reply.

The children press, "But the ghost part."

Karen smiles and whispers to her teacher, "He's light as a feather, too" and laughs.

"What did you say?" the children shout. And Karen tells them, because she knows they want to know. Like her they are writers who publish their work, and Karen knows they want their work to be read and loved, too. Class opinion has it that Karen has done something extraordinary, and they'd like to write something extraordinary as well.

Karen's exchange with her classmates and her teacher took place in a matter of a minute or two, but small incidents like this are what teach in reading-writing classrooms. Teaching effective word choice, like most other reading-writing lessons, happens throughout the course of the day, as opportunities arise. The hard part for teachers who don't write or read very much is to know what to notice and, therefore, what to teach. This is why workbooks are still so inviting to so many.

Another room, another day, but same idea: effective word choice. The teacher is reading a passage from a book that's hooked her, *Reading the River*, by John Hildebrand. It's about a man who decides to canoe the length of the Yukon in order to know the people he had not become. The teacher had typed a paragraph from it the night before and later made copies for the class:

> Gathering in the brackish water of the Yukon Delta, the salmon under-go a transformation. Their coloring changes from bright silver to muddy red: their stomachs shrink as they cease feeding. Already they've begun to die from the tail up.[4]

She reads the excerpt aloud, after telling the children a little about the book's themes. Then she asks them to do something: "Read this passage again slowly to yourself. Then underline your favorite line or passage. Plan on telling us why you chose it." The children read and mark their pages. Several have chosen the same line, others the same phrase. The children like "Already they've begun to die from the tail up" because "That's a new way of saying dying " or "It's like 'bottom up,' but different." The children recognize fresh language. Several mention the phrase"stomachs shrinking"; they've not thought of that before. Like the teacher who recognized "ghost with curls," this educator knows, because she is a writer herself, that children are able to detect words that mean more. Word choice is part of what makes writing worth reading.

The kids catch on. "Can we do that with one of our paragraphs?" one youngster asks. They can and do. The students take a ditto master from the ditto box and proceed to copy their favorite paragraphs from their own hand-written books. When one finishes, he passes it on to the next youngster, who adds her paragraph, and so on. The teacher runs it off after school, and the next day, writing workshop starts with this:

> The next day we went to waltDisney world. We went on alot of rides. One of them was a haunted mansion. fack ghosts that were white and we saw spider webs that were torn up. There were loud noises that sounded spooky and like the wind.
>
> *Aaron, Grade 3*

> I jerked it up I took a step and I thought there were some more boards there but there weren't I'll tell you what was there. Yucky. smelly. dirty water. And when I took that step—Cusplash!
>
> *Dale, Grade 4*

The children underlined their favorite parts, talked about "Spooky and like the wind" and Dale's smelly, dirty water. They talked about Aaron and Dale's work just as they talked about Hildebrand's.

Modeling Writing Dialogue

While there are many answers to why talk flows in one story and not in another, Paul Darcy Boles, in his book *Storycrafting*, shows vividly that *surrounding description* and *explanatory action* help bring an exchange to life. Consider this excerpt from *Twenty and Ten*, by Claire Bishop, the story of twenty Christian children who help conceal ten Jewish children during World War II:

> We sat down in silence. We did not feel like talking. Soon we could tell by the very sound of the spoons that everybody was getting to the bottom of each bowl pretty quickly—too quickly.
>
> Henry sat across the table from me. He was counting the spoonfuls and swallowing very slowly to make it last: nine, ten . . . He sighed, and I heard him mutter to himself, "Perhaps three more." He threw a glance at his new neighbor, who had already cleaned his bowl. He was a small blond boy, doubled up on his chair, and he had large dark circles under his eyes.
>
> "What's your name?" asked Henry in a low voice.

"A-A-Arthur," said the boy.

"I'm Henry. Look, Arthur. Do me a favor. Eat the rest of my soup." Arthur shook his head vehemently.

Henry compressed his lips and said, "Please. To tell you the truth, I hate the stuff."[5]

Take a look at the action and the description surrounding Arthur and Henry's short exchange. (Sometimes we ask the children to underline description and action in different colors.) We have seen Henry counting out each precious spoonful of soup. We have heard him sigh and mutter for the sake of his own painfully hungry belly. At the same time, we have caught his furtive glance toward the small boy who's doubled up and laden with black circles. Against this background, the beautiful gesture offered through the words "To tell you the truth, I hate the stuff" takes on the profound meaning it's supposed to. Children, everywhere, understand the importance of that line. Boles helps us understand how it's done: How dialogue rings true depends on how it's dressed.

When I took Boles's lesson to the children I teach, I had my own rough draft in hand. I purposefully left my dialogue as it was and worked in front of them by adding surrounding description and explanatory action to make it better. The children reminded me that characters' thoughts also surround talk, so I considered that, too. Here's my piece before I worked with it, followed by my revision based on Boles's suggestions, as well as the children's. The story is the same one we mentioned earlier, "The Last Windy Night," a ghostly tale for second, third, and fourth graders. Suzanna, the main character, has just run from her bedroom after hearing a scary noise coming off the lake and through her window.

First Draft

Suzanna was not to get far, however, for just beyond the bedroom entryway stood a real, live ghost blocking her way. "Ahhhhh! Ahhhhhh" And "Ahhhhh!" again Suzanna cried. "What do you want?" she said, as she tried to make her way out of the door.

"Eeeeeee, irrrrrrk, irr, ir, ki, ki, ir, eeeeeeeee."

"What did you say—you thing, you!"

The children said, "Let's see the ghost! You're telling, not showing. (Out of the mouths of babes, I thought.)

Second Draft

Suzanna was not to get far, however, for just beyond the bedroom entryway stood a real, live ghost, blocking her way. The white mist of the thing towered over her, its arms moving slowly in strange circular strokes, its legs doing a moonish walk. "Ahhhhhhhhhhhhhhhhh!" Suzanna screamed. "What do you want?" she bellowed as she tried to make her way past it.

Suzanna was not to go far, however, for the ghost blocked her way. At first it tried to speak, but nothing came out. Its two lips moved in its face, disconnected somehow. But slowly its cheeks began to fill; its lips tightened; bigger and bigger they grew until Suzanna heard something coming from between them in a raspy, whispery voice, "Eeeeeeeee, irrrrrk, irr, ir, ki, ki, ir, eeeeeee."

"What did you say, you thing!" she snapped.

My second draft spurred some action in the classroom, enough to have warranted my doing it. Children began to look for dialogue in famous authors' books and to point out Boles's lesson. Chris Van Allsburg's *The Polar Express* was seized upon early, especially the part where the boy first sees the train outside his window:

> . . . I looked through my window and saw a train standing perfectly still in front of my house.
>
> It was wrapped in an apron of steam. Snowflakes fell lightly around it. A conductor stood at the open door of one of the cars. He took a large pocket watch from his vest, then looked up at my window. I put on my slippers and robe. I tiptoed downstairs and out the door.
>
> "All aboard," the conductor cried out. I ran up to him.
>
> "Well," he said, "are you coming?"
>
> "Where?" I asked.
>
> "Why, to the North Pole, of course," was his answer. "This is the Polar Express." I took his outstretched hand and he pulled me aboard.

After noticing the well-written dialogue, the children became more critical of their own. The children most affected in this class were those whose stories were all dialogue or those whose stories had none. Everyone, however, was eager to play with whatever they had done. That's the spirit we want to cultivate.

Publishing Children's Work

Nothing has changed us more as writers (other than computers!) than seeing our work published. Teachers who write tell us this is the same for them. A writing consultant friend of ours, Kathy Juntunen, had a small vignette (a few paragraphs) published in *The Reading Teacher*, and while Kathy has written a book on writing, this first "juried" piece making it into print was a boon. She was overjoyed and called to tell us about it—she even turned our search for it into a riddle!

Children bubble over being published, too, but even more over being read. A second grader stopped a teacher in the hall, grabbed an arm, and pulled to get an ear close to her lips. "You'll never guess what I just saw," she said.

"What?"

"Somebody reading *my* book." Karen had passed by the library, where her class's books were on display, on her way in from recess. "It was a *sixth grader*," she added. We understand just how Karen felt, primarily because we're writers. But her teacher understood, too, because she had recently published *her* first book, which is right in the library along with her children's, on display.

There are many publishing alternatives that can be found in several books already in print,[6] but there are a few principles that need sharing:

1. *Teachers need not be involved with publishing final products beyond second grade.* Too many simple publishing alternatives exist that children can use by themselves or with the help of a friend or a parent.
2. *Publishing does not always have to occur in book form.* Getting the word out can take many forms: all-school loudspeaker radio shows once a week (Friday afternoon, for five minutes), school newspaper entries, classroom anthologies (literary as well as content-oriented work), news flashes that go home, all-class sharing, bulletin board displays, school hall displays, stories turned into play form and acted out, letters to editors, letters to published authors (famous, but don't forget local school authors), etc.
3. *Published work often contains errors and teachers need to accept this fact.* Try as we might, things slip our attention. When parents detect an error, and they will, this is what we say: "It is a statistical impossibility that you will see fewer errors in my children's work than in the work of children who do not publish on a regular basis. In my room *millions* of words get into print. In rooms where only a *few thousand* words get published, you are bound to find fewer errors. Which do you want? A room where children write occasionally, and often for their teacher's eyes only, or a room where writing is prolific, authentic, and read by tens of eyes, not just two?" This response has never let us down!

Modeling Proofreading Techniques

Children in reading-writing classrooms are encouraged to write freely all the time, relegating proofreading to its proper place in the writing cycle. Many texts aren't proofread at all, such as content-area journals or log entries; prewriting cluster sheets, free writes, or lists; and literature dialogue journals. But when a piece needs proofreading—it's going to be published in book form, on the bulletin board, in a home news flash, or in the school paper—it helps to know what to do. Modeling this procedure for children fosters a spirited attitude. Children learn to do one thing at a time (and a few other tricks of the trade), as well as make the important discovery that a piece can be punctuated several different ways. Figure 1 is a page from one third grader's draft that we use frequently in class demonstrations.

Figure 1

The next ride I rod on
Was the corkshrew . When
I got on it started. It went
fast. It went up and down it
went upside down twice.
Then my cosun was
babiling about a ride
it was called the tilta
wirl. It went in circl
s.

We begin by listing what the children think they can do themselves. Most third and fourth graders tell me they think they can look for misspelled words, capitals, and periods. Some say they can tell a run-on. All the children get a copy of the draft and we make one transparency of it for us. We ask them to underline word spellings they are unsure of and invite them to work in pairs if they'd like. Then someone comes to the overhead and underlines the words that he thinks need to be looked up. Sometimes a child underlines a word that's actually spelled correctly, but that doesn't matter—the point is to make the children feel comfortable taking risks. Then we ask the children to try to read the draft backwards by sentences and listen for complete thoughts. It's amazing how much going backwards helps. (Having

them circle the periods first makes this a little easier.) The children soon discover the run-on: "Then my cousin was babilinig about a ride it was called
the tilt 'a' wirl." When they do, we ask them to fix it. They come up with several options:

1. Then my cousin was babilinig about a ride called the tilt 'a' wirl. (We
   might comment, "You've done what some writers call sentence combin-
   ing.)
2. Then my cousin was babilinig about a ride. It was called the tilt 'a' wirl.
   ("You found the problem.")
3. Then my cousin was babilinig about a ride—the tilt 'a' wirl. ("Have any
   of you used a dash before? Let's look it up in the Write Source." [7])

While we could go on and share other writing techniques, we hope our
discussion has led you to conclude that language arts teachers who read and
write lend a credibility to their work that invites mutual respect and nurtures
children's growth as writers and readers. Reading and writing classrooms
are not places of anarchy. They're highly structured environments framed by
teachers and constantly modified to meet students' needs and developmental
levels. They are benevolent places, and they are remarkably effective places
for children to learn.

Making Connections across the Curriculum:
The Real Use of Reading and Writing

In *Writing to Learn*, William Zinsser, a man with a great deal to say to teachers,
writes, "Over the years I've written or edited hundreds of articles on subjects I
had never previously thought about."[8] Think about that. How is it possible
that a man of Zinsser's stature could do such a thing? How irresponsible. But
Zinsser knows what all writers know, that writing leads to clearer and deeper
thinking. In this confession, Zinsser is not alone. Carl Sagan expresses the
same eagerness to use inquiry in his book *The Dragons of Eden*. In the introduction, Sagan tells his readers that the book gave him the opportunity to revise
and expand his earlier thinking about the origins of intelligence. He says:

> The subject is a difficult one. . . . I proffer the following ideas with a sub-
> stantial degree of trepidation. . . . At the very least, this inquiry has pro-
> vided me with an opportunity to look into an entrancing subject.[9]

In this country, no one has expressed this concept more succinctly than
Toby Fulwiler, editor of *The Journal Book*. In his introductory remarks to that
text, Fulwiler lists several cognitive activities people engage in when they
take the time to write freely with the intent to learn. While there is no suggestion the list is complete, he shares these activities: observing, questioning,
speculating, becoming aware of oneself, digressing, synthesizing, revising,
and informing.[10] Consider this entry by a fifth-grade child, Courtney Baker,

who was asked to write about how she felt dissecting a pig's lungs in class that day. Her journal entry reads:

> When I came to school today I was so excited because today my class was going to dissect pig lungs. I introduced my Dad and he called everyone up to the table and showed us how to dissect the pig lungs. I felt my heart pounding so hard, it almost came out of my chest. When it was my turn to cut, I took one deep breath and started cutting down one of the tubes. A bronchial tube is like a little pipe that the air goes in and out of. I kept cutting and cutting, the bronchial tubes getting smaller and smaller until finally you could barely see them. Afterwards I felt like I had saved a life for some reason, like looking for a little boy in a dark tunnel and finding him and feeling so glad you did. That's how I felt about cutting the bronchial tubes.

We gasped when we read Courtney's entry because of the digression at the end, the poetry and the human response that one could almost taste. Look at the entry yourself and reflect on Fulwiler's list. Share the entry and list with a colleague and decide if Fulwiler might be on to something. Into how many kinds of thinking has Courtney been invited by writing this journal entry?

Classroom Routines That Encourage Reading and Writing

The first thing that needs to be said is that the lion's share of instructional time should be devoted to real reading and real writing. As a rule of thumb, from second grade on, three quarters of each language arts block should be thus devoted, with the remainder being set aside for focused lessons on some aspect of reading or writing.

Research is beginning to show that being a reader is the best way to learn to read. Reading instruction should focus on cultivating in students the habit of reading and giving them time to read. There should be classroom libraries with at least three to five titles per child. Teachers should get to know the books and take opportunities to match books with children's interests. It is possible to get help building a book collection from several fine annotated book lists (see Bibliography) and from the regular book reviews in *Language Arts, The Reading Teacher,* and *The New Advocate.* But when it comes to telling children about a book in order to arouse their interest, book reviews are not a substitute for the teacher's having read hundreds of children's books and reading more all the time.

Teachers in reading-writing classrooms see to it that every child is reading a book for pleasure, and then they see to it that they have time set aside to read them. Lyman Hunt's idea of Uninterrupted Sustained Silent Reading

(U.S.S.R.) is still a good one: setting aside twenty minutes or more each day in which everything else stops and everybody reads.

In order to make sure that every child does read, and also to encourage the children to think about what they read, many teachers use response journals. In these, the students make notes about what they are reading. In Midge Burns's third-grade class, these notes take the form of letters to Mrs. Burns, in which the child tells her what she is reading and what she thinks about it. Mrs. Burns is careful to answer each child's letter with a letter of her own— and to do this, of course, she has to have read the same books the children have read.

Diane Barone often has students respond to a book using a Dual Entry Diary or DED.[11] In these, they draw a vertical line down the middle of a journal page. On the left-hand side, they describe something they read in the book, and on the right-hand side, they say what they thought about it. Dr. Barone is careful to write comments in the students' Dual Entry Diaries, too.

In a similar vein, time should be set aside daily for children to write. Lucy Calkins has argued eloquently for the need to fix this writing time regularly in the schedule. She notes that while the act of creating can require us to be flexible in our thinking, it helps if the setting of our creativity be stable and predictable. In a moment of inspiration, the sculptor shouldn't have to hunt for a chisel. Likewise, a child who feels a story coming on shouldn't have to wonder whether or not she'll get time today to write it down.

Many reading-writing classrooms, then, have a period of up to forty-five minutes each day set aside for writing. (See Chapter 11, "Beyond Day One," for a detailed discussion of the writing period.) A schedule of this sort is easily adaptable for reading as well. The period can begin with Uninterrupted Sustained Silent Reading (5 minutes), in which everyone including the teacher participates. Then the teacher can move around the room to visit individuals who are having problems or need encouragement (10 minutes). Then she can invite five or six students who are reading the same book to come to the circle and discuss it (20 minutes). Finally, she can invite one student to come forward and share with the whole class a book he is reading (10 minutes). Alternatively, the teacher might use this final interval to call attention to one strong feature in an author's work that the students may wish to try in their own writing, or to teach a mini-lesson on reading. Another alternative would be to begin the period with a mini-lesson on reading (for example, noting how authors use the context to suggest the meanings of words), and end the period with a checkup to see how the students were able to employ the lesson in their reading that day.

In the writing and reading workshops we just described, the lion's share of the time is spent in real reading and real writing. While some time is set aside for direct instruction, there is a delicate relationship between this instructional time and the sustained reading and writing. During instructional time, information is shared and skills are taught. During sustained activity time, information and skills may (or may not) be put to use; and during the sharing period that often comes at the end of the sustained activity time, the use of this information and these skills are commented upon.

Conclusion

The original focus of this book, as the title clearly signals, was the development of children's writing. But even before we were aware of it, children's reading slipped quietly into the picture (recall, for example, the way literature influenced Sarah's story writing; see Chapter 9). Now the necessary connection between reading and writing is much clearer to teachers—the term *emergent literacy* captures the inseparable nature of reading and writing. This book has been about emergent literacy, though we've focused more on the writing side. This epilogue is an attempt to balance the emphasis somewhat.

A teacher contemplating setting up a reading-writing classroom wants to know how to do it, and we have tried to provide some specifics. Lately, however, we have heard more than one author of popular books for teachers voice the wish that they hadn't been quite so specific in telling others how to set up reading-writing classrooms. Too often, they found that others were following the letter of their advice, but missing the spirit—and the results were disappointing. What was missing was the teacher who was a reader and a writer; or as Nancie Atwell puts it, a person to whom learners of literacy would want to apprentice themselves. Such a person, of course, could make a success of any number of approaches. And no approach is likely to be really successful without such a teacher.

ENDNOTES

1. Ruth Nathan, "Effective Teacher-Child Conferences," in Ruth Hubbard, Brenda Miller, and James Whitney, *The Writing and Reading Process: A Closer Look* (Portsmouth, NH: Heinemann, 1988).
2. For more information on dialogue journals, see Nancie Atwell, *In the Middle* (Portsmouth, NH: Boynton/Cook, 1987).
3. Wallace Stegner, *Crossing to Safety* (New York: Random House, 1987), p. 116.
4. John Hildebrand, *Reading the River* (Boston: Houghton Mifflin, 1988), p. 79.
5. Claire Bishop, *Twenty and Ten* (New York: Viking Press, 1952), p. 25.
6. For example, see Ruth Nathan, Frances Temple, Kathleen Juntunen, and Charles Temple, *Classroom Strategies that Work* (Portsmouth, NH: Heinemann, 1989); Regie Routman, *Transitions: From Literature to Literacy* (Portsmouth, NH: Heinemann, 1988); and Jan Turnbill, *Now We Want to Write!* (Rozelle, N.S.W.: Primary English Teaching Association, 1988).
7. Patrick Sebranek, Dave Kemper, and Verne Meyer, *The Write Source* (Burlington, WI: Write Source Educational Publishing, 1987).
8. William Zinsser, *Writing to Learn* (New York: Harper & Row, 1988), p. 11.
9. Carl Sagan, *The Dragons of Eden* (New York: Randon House, 1977), p. 5.

10. Toby Fulwiler, ed., *The Journal Book* (Portsmouth, NH: Heineman, 1987), p. 3.
11. Diane Barone, "The Written Responses of Young Children," *The New Advocate*, 3, 1, 49-56.

BIBLIOGRAPHY

[*Authors' note:* We have selected a *limited* number of the books, magazines, and journals we simply could not live without. While our bookshelves burst with other titles, we gritted our teeth as we asked, "Absolutely?" It was tough.]

Books That Make Reading/Writing Connections:

Atwell, Nancie. (1987). *In the Middle: Writing, Reading, and Learning with Adolescents.* Portsmouth, NH: Boynton/Cook/Heinemann.

> Specific, inspired advice for upper elementary and middle school teachers about setting up a reading/writing environment and curriculum.

Nathan, Ruth. (Ed.). (1991). *Writers in the Classroom.* Norwood, MA: Christopher-Gordon.

> Master teachers who write well explain how they teach. Chapters are divided in two, with an uninterrupted example of teacher's writing appearing first, followed by a mole's eye view of that teacher in the classroom. Chapter topics include editorials, plays, personal narrative, poetry, fairy tales, short stories, songs, historical fiction, report writing, and so forth.

Rhodes, Lynn & Dudley-Marling, Curt. (1988). *Readers and Writers with a Difference: A Holistic Approach to Teaching Learning Disabled and Remedial Students.* Portsmouth, NH: Heinemann.

> Teachers who work with disabled or remedial students will find specific strategies in this holistic perspective on reading and writing instruction. Teachers of typical children will find the details instructive, too. The book lacks only in detailed attention to the graphophonic cueing system.

Routman, Regie. (1988). *Transitions: From Literature to Literacy.* Portsmouth, NH: Heinemann/Rigby.

> Teachers of kindergarten through grade three will find *Transitions* helpful for two reasons: the specific advice on how to get started, and the marvelous lists of teacher resources, recommended literature, and appendixes with lesson plans, schedules, and so forth.

Books about Reading and Writing Poetry:

Heard, Georgia. (1989). *For the Good of the Earth and Sun: Teaching Poetry.* Portsmouth, NH: Heinemann.

> Lucy Calkins says this book is "big." No doubt that Heard's passion for poetry and her ability to transfer her knowledge to teachers gives us one of the best examples of outstanding pedagogy on the market today. A gem.

Denman, Gregory. (1988). *When You've Made It Your Own . . . Teaching Poetry to Young People.* Portsmouth, NH: Heinemann.

> Teachers who know little about poetry will find Denman's opening chapters insightful and moving. Accessible strategies, such as the use of poetry journals, make this a book teachers tend to lend.

Writing across the Curriculum:

Atwell, Nancie. (Ed.). (1990). *Coming to Know: Writing to Learn in the Intermediate Grades*. Portsmouth, NH: Heinemann.

> Written by teachers, *Coming to Know* shows children learning to take topics of interest and turning them into authentic, meaningful papers. Reports vary in form, which makes the book exciting reading. *Coming to Know* also explores the uses of academic journals. Teachers just beginning to use writing as a way of learning find the appendix of prompts at the book's end helpful.

Fulwiler, Toby. (Ed.). (1987). *The Journal Book*. Portsmouth, NH: Boynton/Cook.

> Teachers from every discipline, first grade through college, explain how they use writing to learn in their classrooms. Pat Belanoff's chapter, "The Role of Journals in the Interpretive Community," is one of the finest expositions on reader response theory/practice we have ever read.

Nathan, Ruth, Temple, Frances, Juntunen, Kathleen, & Temple, Charles. (1989). *Classroom Strategies that Work: An Elementary Teacher's Guide to Process Writing*. Portsmouth, NH: Heinemann.

> Sections on writing to explore history, literature, and science break the walls between the writing program and the rest of the curriculum. Readers will see writing, reading, talking, singing, acting, observing, performing, reporting all developed in units that prove intensely interesting to the children who participate in them.

Books That Will Improve Your Own Writing:

Boles, Paul Darcy. (1984). *Storycrafting*. Cincinnati, OH: Writer's Digest Books.

> A master storyteller teaches the art and craft of writing fine short stories. *Storycrafting* is a book we often read directly to our students as the need arises.

Goldberg, Natalie. (1986). *Writing Down the Bones: Freeing the Writer Within*. Boston: Shambhala.

> This book includes focused writing lessons that stretch writing skills. Chapters explaining the use of active verbs, the incorporation of meaningful detail, and the use of alternative syntactic forms exemplify the range of topics.

Jerome, Justin. (1980). *The Poet's Handbook*. Cincinnati, OH: Writer's Digest Books.

> Gives detailed instruction in the mechanics and art of writing poetry. An important book for beginning poets.

Zinsser, William. (1985). *On Writing Well: An Informal Guide to Writing Nonfiction*. 3rd ed. New York: Harper & Row.

> A widely published writer tells how to write clearly. The book grew out of a course in writing nonfiction the author originated and taught at Yale. New sections/chapters on writers' attitudes make the third edition even more valuable than earlier versions.

Other Basic Resources for Teachers:

Bryant, Peter & Bradley, Lynn. (1985). *Children's Reading Problems: Psychology and Education*. New York: Basil Blackwell Ltd.

> This is a very specific book on how to help disabled readers decode. We list *Children's Reading Problems* under "Basic Resources" because it is not a book to use every day with every child. We have found, however, the strategies

for decoding *very helpful* to children who have decoding problems, despite their exposure to and involvement with holistic teaching strategies.

Committee on the Elementary School Booklist. (1990). *Adventuring with Books.* Urbana, IL: National Council of Teachers of English.

An invaluable list of books children might read. This annotated bibliography helps teachers match children to books because titles are grouped by topic and reading level. (There is a junior high and high school list as well.)

Johnson, Paul. (1990). *A Book of One's Own.* Portsmouth, NH: Heinemann.

A comprehensive guide to book art with step-by-step instructions.

Muth, K. Denise. (Ed.). (1989). *Children's Comprehension of Text: Research into Practice.* Newark, DE: International Reading Association.

A fabulous collection of strategies for teaching children how to read both narrative and expository text. Invaluable.

Stoll, Donald. (Ed.). (1990). *Magazines for Children.* Newark, DE: Educational Press Association of America and International Reading Association.

An annotated list of magazines for children with a provocative introduction by Bernice Cullinan, which details the importance of magazine availability.

Strunk, William & White, E. B. (1979). *The Elements of Style.* 3rd ed. New York: Macmillan.

The *Boston Globe* says, "No book in shorter space, with fewer words, will help any writer more than this persistent little volume." We agree.

Williams, Miller. (1986). *Patterns of Poetry: An Encyclopedia of Forms.* Baton Rouge, LA: Louisiana State University Press.

Each form is introduced with a brief discussion of its origin and other relevant history. Concise instructive, and easy to understand.

Magazines We Routinely Read:

English Journal. 1111 Kenyon Rd., Urbana, IL 61801 (217/328-3870)

Articles on the language arts for middle school and high school teachers.

Language Arts. 1111 Kenyon Rd., Urbana, IL 61801 (217/328-3870)

Articles on the language arts for elementary and middle school teachers.

Learning '90, '91: Creative ideas and insights for teachers. P.O. Box 2580, Boulder, CO 80322

Articles on all areas of the curriculum, usually well-written and helpful.

The New Advocate. 480 Washington Street, Norwood, MA 02062 (617/762-5577)

Writers and illustrators of children's books, scholars in the education field, and teachers explore all areas of the language arts with an eye toward literature and its use in the classroom. The review of new books by M. Jean Greenlaw attracts wide attention. It's a "cover-to-cover" read.

The Reading Teacher. 800 Barksdale Rd., P.O. Box 8139, Newark, DE 19714-8139

Since November of 1988, this magazine has provided us with many useful language arts articles.

The Writing Notebook: Creative Word Processing in the Classroom. P.O. Box 1268, Eugene, OR 97440-1268 (503/344-7125)

There's nothing out about computer use in the classroom that's better than this small journal.

Basic Resources for Children:

Asher, Sandy. (1989). *Wild Words! How to Train Them to Tell Stories.* New York: Walker & Company.

> For grades five and up, a wonderful collection of lessons on how to make your words do what you want them to do. Asher, a playwright and well-known novelist, is writer-in-residence at Drury College.

Sebranek, Patrick, Kemper, Dave, & Meyer, Verne. (1987). *The Write Source.* Burlington, WI: Write Source Educational Publishing House.

> The best English handbook for grades 4–9 we've seen. The large section on report writing is especially helpful. A volume for high school students called *Writers Inc,* from the same company, is also excellent.

Wittels, Harriet, & Greisman, Joan. (1971). *The Clear and Simple Thesaurus Dictionary.* New York: Grosset & Dunlap.

> A young people's thesaurus that will help them choose the word that seems just right and introduce them to words they may not already know. We like it because it's not overwhelming.

Our Favorite Word Processing Programs:

The Children's Writing and Publishing Center. The Learning Company, 6493 Kaiser Drive, Fremont, CA 94555 (1/800/852-2255)

> The simplest desktop publishing program available. (A person can learn it in under fifteen minutes!) Combines words and pictures effortlessly, features easy-to-follow on-line instructions, includes varying type styles and sizes, and provides versatility as a tool for creating classroom newsletters (one column or two), reports, student certificates, awards, and more (IBM and Apple).

Magic Slate II. Sunburst Communications, 39 Washington Avenue, Pleasantville, NY 10570-2829 (1/800/628-8897)

> Appropriate for grades 2 through adult, this word processing program is easy to use, comes in 20-, 40-, or 80-column versions, allows special type styles, has cut-and-paste capabilities, and includes a feature that allows teachers to enter comments on students' papers without writing on them. Interactive programs that can be used with *Magic Slate II* include Spanish type styles and a school speller (Apple).

INDEX